HAYEK'S SOCIAL AND POLITICAL THOUGHT

Hayek's Social and Political Thought

ROLAND KLEY

CLARENDON PRESS · OXFORD

1994

Oxford University Press, Walton Street, Oxford OX2 6DP
Oxford New York
Athens Auckland Bangkok Bombay
Calcutta Cape Town Dar es Salaam Delhi
Florence Hong Kong Istanbul Karachi
Kuala Lumpur Madras Madrid Melbourne
Mexico City Nairobi Paris Singapore
Taipei Tokyo Toronto
and associated companies in
Berlin Ibadan

Oxford is a trade mark of Oxford University Press

Published in the United States
by Oxford University Press Inc., New York

British Library Cataloguing in Publication Data
Data available

Library of Congress Cataloging in Publication Data
Kley, Roland.
Hayek's social and political thought / Roland Kley.
Revision of thesis (D. Phil.)—Oxford University.
Includes bibliographical references (p.   ) and index.
1. Hayek, Friedrich A. von (Friedrich August), 1899–
—Contributions in political science. 2. Hayek, Friedrich A. von
(Friedrich August), 1899–   —Contributions in sociology.
I. Title.
JC273.H382K54 1994 320.5'12'092—dc20 94–14931
ISBN 0–19–827916–7

1 3 5 7 9 10 8 6 4 2

Typeset by Graphicraft Typesetters Ltd., Hong Kong

Printed in Great Britain
on acid-free paper by
Bookcraft (Bath) Ltd.
Midsomer Norton, Avon

ACKNOWLEDGEMENTS

In writing this book I have been helped by a number of persons and institutions. An earlier version of this study was submitted as a D.Phil. thesis at Oxford University. John Gray, who acted as my supervisor, devoted a great deal of time to discussing with me the themes developed in this book. His guidance was invaluable, and if in spite of my profound reservations about much of Hayek's social and political thought I may still have succeeded in presenting a balanced view of my subject, much of the credit must go to him. Peter Sandøe provided encouragement when it was needed most. My examiners, Norman Barry and Nevil Johnson, enabled me to grasp the historical and intellectual background of Hayek's project more firmly. Later, Ralf Dahrendorf, Peter Häberle, and Alois Riklin kindly allowed me to see their reports commissioned by the University of St Gallen in the course of my *Habilitation*. I also benefited from suggestions made by two anonymous readers for Oxford University Press. The manuscript gained further from the scrutiny of the copy-editor, and Tim Barton and Dominic Byatt saw it through the Press. To all these persons I am deeply grateful.

Work on this book would not have been possible without the generous financial assistance of various institutions. The Swiss National Science Foundation supported my years in Oxford with a Research Fellowship, the British Foreign and Commonwealth Office with an FCO Award, and in 1988 Corpus Christi College elected me to a Senior Scholarship. A grant from the Research Committee of the University of St Gallen allowed me to revise the manuscript for publication. To these institutions I wish to express my gratitude.

Finally, I owe a debt of a different kind to Heidy Stücheli. Her encouragement, understanding, and generosity were crucial to the completion of my project, and she reminded me (what occasionally I seemed to forget) that writing books is not all there is to life.

CONTENTS

Introduction
Friedrich A. Hayek's Instrumental Liberalism

HAYEK'S LIBERAL PROJECT

This is a critical essay about the liberal political philosophy and social theory of Friedrich A. Hayek (1899–1992). Liberalism, Hayek writes,

> derives from the discovery of a self-generating or spontaneous order in social affairs (. . .), an order which made it possible to utilize the knowledge and skill of all members of society to a much greater extent than would be possible in any order created by central direction . . . (1967: 162)[1]

Liberalism and the system of institutions it favours are not the product of bold social imagination and deliberate theoretical construction, he explains,

> but arose from the desire to extend and generalize the beneficial effects which unexpectedly had followed on the limitations placed on the powers of government out of sheer distrust of the rulers. Only after it was found that the unquestioned greater personal liberty which the Englishman enjoyed in the eighteenth century had produced an unprecedented material prosperity were attempts made to develop a systematic theory of liberalism . . . (1967: 161–2)

While appearing in these passages to give a sketch of its historical origins Hayek actually points to the intellectual resources on which liberal political philosophy, rightly understood, should draw. He believes the defence of liberal institutions must ultimately be grounded not in moral philosophical argument but in social theory, that is, in an understanding of the nature and causal regularities of social life. The case for liberalism crucially depends, he thinks, on a sure grasp of the two basic methods available of co-ordinating

---

[1] Parenthetical references in the text, giving year of publication and page number(s), are always to Hayek's writings. For full details, see the Bibliography.

social and economic action, and on a clear recognition of their implications.

There is, on the one side, co-ordination by central direction. This is the co-ordination principle of the prehistoric group and the tribal society, the formations in which, for the most part of human history, social life has taken place. Also, this principle appeals to the deep-seated general belief that only tight collective control over the means guarantees the successful realization of social ends. Socialism is for Hayek the most influential among the various collectivist political doctrines subscribing to central planning and direction in the economy. Yet, Hayek claims, planned economies invariably fail. They are inefficient, and their collapse can be prevented only at the cost of massive coercion. In this way, socialism inevitably degenerates into political totalitarianism.

But, Hayek says, there is a second method of ordering social and economic life. This is the self-co-ordination at work in markets and market societies. Social theoretic expression it finds in the idea of a 'spontaneous order'. Our knowledge of spontaneous orders, he thinks, we owe to a genuine 'discovery'. Nobody could have anticipated that such a seemingly chaotic method would work. Yet only spontaneous order can secure efficient co-ordination and production and at the same time preserve liberty because only the self-co-ordination in the market fully utilizes people's knowledge and skills and still leaves them free to pursue their own projects and plans. Thus, only a socio-economic system based on spontaneous order achieves what an acceptable system must achieve: human survival, general prosperity, and social peace. That is why for Hayek the idea of a spontaneous order is central for any defence of a liberal institutional framework. Indeed, the very possibility of liberalism 'derives' from the recognition that there can be unplanned order.

Though the idea of a spontaneous order is its principal concept, liberalism is, according to Hayek, founded also in a theory of cultural evolution and in the appreciation of the restricted scope of our intelligence. True liberalism, he explains, is also 'based on an evolutionary interpretation of all phenomena of culture and mind and on an insight into the limits of the powers of the human reason' (1967: 161). Against what he regards as the pretensions of institutional constructivism and the rationalistic overestimation of the human intellect Hayek maintains that our mastery of the world depends on traditional rules, practices, and institutions which we do not fully understand but to which we must hold fast because they contain a measure of wisdom and experience that individual reason is incapable of. Without going here into Hayek's more specific claims we can already see that he wants liberalism above all to be the political doctrine that, unlike its rivals, does take account of the social world and of the limits of our intellectual powers as they factually are. So at the core of Hayek's liberalism is not a political philosophy spelling out the moral requirements liberal institutions must meet but a distinct body of descriptive and explanatory theory. Yet how could such positive theory be at the centre of a normative defence of a liberal vision? To find out we must look to what are in Hayek's political thought four fixed points.

First, there are for Hayek basically only two rival political doctrines, liberalism and socialism. This dichotomic view goes back to the beginning of his career when as an economist he found himself increasingly preoccupied with political matters. Two events, it seems, had a major influence.[2]

In the socialist calculation debate of the 1920s and 1930s, together with Ludwig Mises, Hayek was the main protagonist on the Austrian side. Against socialist economists such as F. M. Taylor, O. Lange, A. P. Lerner, and H. D. Dickinson they argued that under socialism economic calculation was impossible.[3] This debate was on all sides conducted as an argument about two alternative ideal-types of economic co-ordination, market versus central direction, even though Hayek was aware that the actual picture might be blurred as not every variant of socialism subscribes to total planning (1949: 131–3).

Then there was the rise of totalitarianism in the 1930s. In *The Road to Serfdom* (1944) Hayek offered a diagnosis of the time that was singular in so far as it saw liberal Western democracies threatened not only from without but also by certain internal developments which to most people appeared entirely innocuous. His fears were that the same ideas that had engendered National Socialism and Communism were slowly gaining currency also in

---

[2] This is not to deny that Hayek's political outlook also owes something to the intellectual impulses he received in Austria in the 1920s. For more on this, see Francis (1985); Shearmur (1986); Furth (1989).

[3] For an account of this debate, see Lavoie (1985). Compare also Kirzner (1987) and (1988), Keizer (1989), and Shapiro (1989). For Hayek's contribution, see his three articles on 'Socialist Calculation' (the first two originally published in 1935, the third in 1940; all three repr. in Hayek 1949).

Western democracies. The gradual abandonment of the principles of 'individualism', the increasing tendency to entrust the state with the direction of the economy, would lead, he believed, to a totalitarianism no different from that of Nazi Germany and Communist Russia. In his analysis, fascism, communism, and 'democratic' planning each sprang from the same erroneous social philosophy, 'collectivism', that aims to subject all social and economic life to central control and, against the best intentions, inevitably terminates in unfreedom. His diagnosis Hayek combined with a passionate call for a return to the social philosophy of individualism.

Though the terminology underwent a change, the dichotomic distinction between individualist and collectivist social philosophies virtually dominated Hayek's political thought ever after. In order to bring out as sharply as possible their political implications he later tended to discuss them in the form in which they manifest themselves as political doctrines. In the case of individualism the attendant political doctrine could, for Hayek, only be that of classical *liberalism*. Among the various collectivist ideologies he chose to concentrate on *socialism*. Socialism he regarded as 'by far the most important species of collectivism' because its noble aspirations permit it to command the attention and allegiance also of 'liberal-minded people' (1944: 25). Such concentration was not meant to spare other collectivist doctrines. Criticisms of socialism, he insisted, would apply with equal force to any form of collectivism (1944: 25). Mediating positions attempting to bridge individualism and collectivism, such as limited market interventionism, he ruled out. According to the thesis advanced in *The Road to Serfdom* and largely reaffirmed later (e.g. 1973: ch. 3; 1944: preface to 1976 edn. repr. in 1986: vii–ix), a 'middle way' does not exist for, he argued, once government has embarked on economic planning it is forced further and further to extend its interventions in order to avoid the failure of its policies, being driven ultimately to assume the powers of a totalitarian state.

It is not difficult to discern how Hayek's Manichean assumption bears on his approach to the justification of liberalism. If there really exist only two major doctrines, the justification of liberalism consists in its defence against socialism. Liberalism will be established as the public philosophy that is to guide political practice if it can be shown to be superior to its rival. This is a view to which Hayek consistently adhered throughout.

A second element crucial for an adequate understanding of Hayek's political perspective and his defence of liberalism is his ethical non-cognitivism. Influenced, perhaps, by the logical positivism of the Vienna Circle,[4] he did not believe that moral values can be grounded rationally. Values and ends are 'in the last resort . . . non-rational', and 'no rational argument can produce agreement if it is not already present at the outset' (1973: 34). As early as 1935 he wrote: 'On the validity of the ultimate ends science has nothing to say. They may be accepted or rejected, but they cannot be proved or disproved. All that we can rationally argue about is whether and to what extent given measures will lead to the desired results' (1949: 130).

Though practical reason is for Hayek no more than instrumental rationality, it does not render rational discourse in moral and political philosophy impossible. There is scope for reasoned argument within already existing moral and institutional systems. Such systems are composed, he thinks, of a few ultimate values and numerous behavioural rules. These rules, though values themselves, primarily serve the realization of those supreme values. Now reason can, Hayek claims, identify and resolve conflict among those rules but it must accept as given, and cannot question, those highest-order values (1967: 87). Practical reason understood as deliberation of means to given ends can also compare whole moral and institutional systems. It can assess the instrumental adequacy of alternative bodies of rules *if* there is general agreement on the ultimate values the rules are meant to promote (1973: 80). To improve the consistency within an existing system of rules and to judge how far alternative systems are conducive to shared ends Hayek regards as genuinely scientific tasks not violating Max Weber's principle of value-freedom (e.g. 1973: 111–12; 1978: 20–2). That in moral and political philosophy discourse can be rational as long as it does not go beyond questions of instrumental rationality is a constant position of Hayek's.

Reason appears powerless to settle the rivalry between liberalism and socialism. Capable only of judging the instrumental adequacy of alternative means to given ends it seems unable to adjudicate between the competing values which, one might think, the two rival political doctrines embody. Thus, the rational defence Hayek seeks for liberalism appears to be beyond reach, and the adoption

[4] Barry (1986: 98).

and endorsement of a particular doctrine simply the result of arbitrary choice.

Hayek claims this conclusion is unwarranted because liberalism and socialism do not differ to a great extent in their basic values. He sees both as committed to the survival of mankind, general prosperity, and social peace (for more on this, see Chapter 8). But, he says, they differ in so far as they pursue fundamentally dissimilar methods to realize those values. That liberalism and socialism are broadly in agreement on the basic values is a third important tenet of Hayek's political outlook. This assumption has, for Hayek, the following implication. Since the political belief systems differ radically only in their practical approaches but not in their basic values, they can be assessed scientifically. Social theory can examine liberalism and socialism and tell how far their respective methods of social and economic co-ordination are fit to achieve those ultimate values. Such examination does not overstretch the resources of practical reason, Hayek believes, since it requires the exercise only of instrumental rationality.

Hayek concedes that in one respect the ends of liberalism and socialism do diverge: only socialism, but not liberalism, aims at an ideal of distributive justice. Hence, the strife is also about values. Yet Hayek trusts this particular difference can be addressed in an argument about the impossibility for socialism simultaneously to realize distributive justice *and* the other ends to which it subscribes too. Such an argument would, in his view, still be of a scientific nature and would not involve value-judgements (e.g. 1944: 24). So a fourth element characteristic of Hayek's conception of political philosophy is the idea that the contest between liberalism and socialism can once for all be decided on scientific rather than moral grounds. As he declares, 'the differences between socialists and non-socialists ultimately rest on purely intellectual issues capable of scientific resolution and not on different judgments of value' (1973: 6). Hayek leaves no doubt about the eventual verdict. The socialists, as he once put it, 'are wrong *about the facts*' (1988: 6). That the rivalry between liberalism and socialism can be settled scientifically is a persistent theme in Hayek's writings, introduced in *The Road to Serfdom* (1944: 24), resumed time after time (1976: 136; 1978: 296–7; 1983: 29, 53), and again being echoed in the contents (1988: 6–10) and title also of his last book, *The Fatal Conceit: The Errors of Socialism*.

Having identified four fixed points of Hayek's political outlook, we are now able to recognize the kind of justification he seeks for liberalism and to understand how he can maintain that considerations of positive rather than normative theory decide the argument against socialism. Given the dichotomy between liberalism and socialism; the conception of practical reason as instrumental rationality; the claim about the largely shared ends of liberalism and socialism; and his insistence on the scientific nature of the argument, Hayek's defence of liberalism can, I claim, be plausibly interpreted only as an *instrumental* justification of a liberal system of rules and institutions. The overall strategy this justification pursues may be summarized as follows.

In Hayek's perspective, liberalism and socialism are seen primarily as political *methodologies* largely in agreement on the fundamental ends of politics but profoundly split over the type of social and economic co-ordination that should be employed to achieve them. Differing mainly in their practical approaches but not their basic ends, liberalism and socialism are accessible to scientific assessment. Instrumental analysis can establish how far their respective co-ordination mechanisms are capable of realizing those ultimate ends. Such analysis falls in the province of positive (largely social and economic) theory. And the final judgement about which mechanism to favour does not demand more than reason can deliver since it requires the exercise only of means–ends rationality.

Hayek's strategy implies an uncommon view of what liberalism is about. On his account, liberalism is not primarily a normative political philosophy, not a set of moral arguments about the legitimacy of the state and of state action. Rather, Hayekian liberalism is a social and economic methodology, and is based on a cluster of economic, evolutionist, and other social theoretic arguments about the unique instrumental significance of a particular mode of ordering interaction in society. Hayekian liberalism regards the ends of politics as given and uncontested, and depicts political conflict largely as a disagreement about the suitability of alternative mechanisms of social and economic co-ordination.[5] Consequently, it aims to offer scientific argument showing why certain institutional

[5] Thomas Sowell (1987) pursues a similar strategy, very much along Hayekian lines, in his *A Conflict of Visions*. Sowell, writing from what he thinks is a classical liberal viewpoint, takes aim at contemporary American liberals such as John Rawls, Ronald Dworkin, John K. Galbraith, and Laurence Tribe and attacks their 'unconstrained vision', arguing that their normative political ideals fail to take into account the limitations imposed by the human condition and the way the social world works. For incisive criticism, see Scanlon (1988).

arrangements are much more conducive than others to the ends given. There is nothing characteristically liberal inhering in these ends. What is, in Hayek's perspective, distinctive about liberalism is less a particular set of moral and political concerns deriving from a powerful ideal of individual liberty than its unqualified espousal of the market and its system of rules. To be a liberal is, for Hayek, a question not primarily of having the right political morality but of possessing the correct social and economic theory and, therefore, endorsing the only effective co-ordination mechanism. Liberalism is an instrumental doctrine.

RIVAL INTERPRETATIONS OF HAYEK'S PROJECT

The downright instrumentalist reading of Hayek, as it is advanced in this book, by no means reflects a wider consensus in the secondary literature. While the instrumental side of his liberalism has not gone unnoticed,[6] he has mostly been taken for a utilitarian and, at least by one author, a Kantian deontological liberal. In view of such diversity more must now be said to defend this reading although the full argument will be presented in Chapter 8.

Most commentators seem inclined to regard Hayek as a sort of *utilitarian*.[7] An instrumentalist interpretation is clearly at variance with this view. The differences, however, must not be exaggerated. Utilitarian and instrumental justifications share a consequentialist outlook. They see alternative actions (or rules, or systems of rules) only as means and do not consider them intrinsically important, assessing alternative options entirely in terms of outcomes. They differ in so far as utilitarianism judges the alternatives available by the overall goodness of the states of affairs each of them would produce, such goodness being measured by a single general standard of evaluation, utility. An instrumental justification, on the other hand, concentrates on certain more or less distinct ends and compares how far the various options do or do not realize them. If achieving one end impairs the realization of another and vice versa, recourse is had to a principle of conflict resolution such as a rule specifying which end enjoys priority. Unlike utilitarianism, an

---

[6] See e.g. Raz (1986: 7).
[7] See e.g. Barry (1984: 278–9); Yeager (1984: 73); Gray (1986: 59–61); Hardin (1988: 14–15, 91).

instrumental justification does not dissolve conflict by calculating the overall sum of goodness, expressed in a single currency, which a course of action would bring about. Now a decisive reason for not regarding Hayek as a utilitarian is precisely his explicit rejection of any comprehensive common denominator such as 'ends-utility' (1976: 17–23).

The repudiation of any utilitarian standard appears to be one of the features of Hayek's political theory that have led Brian L. Crowley to interpret him as a *Kantian* deontological liberal arguing for rules of justice which arbitrate among people's conflicting conceptions of the good life without themselves presupposing the validity of any such conception.[8] The same deontological perspective Hayek seems to follow when he insists that liberty as defined by the rules of just conduct must 'be accepted as a value in itself, as a principle that must be respected without our asking whether the consequences in the particular instance will be beneficial' (1960: 68). For John Gray, Hayek's political philosophy exhibits its Kantian inspiration most perspicuously in its reliance on Kant's universalization test and its rejection of any natural law doctrine.[9] There are further themes reminiscent of Kant's political thought: that freedom means the absence or, at least, the minimization of coercion (1960: 11–12, 19); that freedom thus conceived is possible only under the law (1960: 153); that state coercion is legitimate if it serves to prevent coercion on the part of private persons (1960: 21); and, importantly, that the chief rationale underlying the demands of freedom is the protection of individual autonomy (1960: 20–1).

While it is true that in his political philosophy Hayek adopts various moral notions and arguments originally developed by Kant, we must be careful not to overlook the highly unKantian context in which he uses them. As I shall endeavour to show, the seemingly deontological primacy of the rules of just conduct over consequentialist considerations of expediency is contingent on the empirical assumption that the rules actually in force are the ones most conducive to the generation and maintenance of spontaneous economic order. Should other rules turn out to be functionally more appropriate, Hayek has no argument prohibiting a change of rules even if this entails the violation of entitlements guaranteed

---

[8] Crowley (1987: 16–19, 29).   [9] Gray (1986: 7–8).

by the old rules. To the same functional logic Hayek subjects the idea of universalization so that Kant's famous test comes down to examining the consistency of the rules of the market and improving the smoothness of the market's co-ordinating function. In short: much of Hayek's Kantianism must, I believe, be seen as part of an overall perspective in which consequentialist considerations are paramount.

However, there is one Kantian notion in Hayek's political philosophy which no instrumental interpretation can possibly accommodate. This is the idea of individual autonomy. Though Hayek does not mention 'autonomy' explicitly, the idea is obvious enough in his account of coercion. A person is coerced if 'he is forced to act not according to a coherent plan of his own but to serve the ends of another'. Again the idea of autonomy underlies Hayek's explanation of why coercion is bad: 'Coercion is evil precisely because it thus eliminates an individual as a thinking and valuing person and makes him a bare tool in the achievement of the ends of another' (1960: 21). Clearly, the Kantian concern for individual autonomy Hayek expresses in these passages fits neither with a utilitarian nor an instrumentalist reading of Hayek.[10] This raises the question of how homogeneous Hayek's moral theory is.

In his *Hayek and Modern Liberalism* (1989), the best analysis existing of Hayek's moral philosophy, Chandran Kukathas is forced to conclude that the normative arguments Hayek puts forward cannot possibly issue from a single coherent and consistent moral theory and, thus, that he fails to ground liberalism on a safe ethical basis.[11] This verdict, while correct, gives Hayek the unfavourable and, in my view, undeserved appearance of someone who never really made up his mind about what the thrust of his liberal project should be. Now the finding that Hayek has no coherent moral theory can rightly form the gist of an overall assessment of his enterprise only if he really thought that the most powerful justification of liberalism was of a *moral philosophical*

---

[10] It should be added, perhaps, that Hayek's idea of autonomy, in spite of its Kantian flavour, only resembles, but is not identical with, Kant's own notion of 'moral autonomy'. Autonomy, as circumscribed by Hayek, means the freedom to choose one's own life. For Kant, ' "autonomy" denotes our ability and responsibility to know what *morality* requires of us and our determination not to act immorally. . . . [T]he autonomous person is one who, by enacting objective principles of conduct, is not only self-legislative but also universally legislative' (Sullivan 1989: 47). See also Raz (1986: 370 n. 2).   [11] Kukathas (1989: 201–4).

nature and that therefore what was needed above all, and what should be given most weight, was a normative theory of liberty and liberal order.[12]

The assumption that Hayek wanted to defend liberalism primarily based on moral philosophical argument is difficult to sustain. Of course, it must be admitted that occasionally, especially in the opening pages of *The Constitution of Liberty* (1960), he does say various things one may interpret as a programme for a normative theory of liberty and liberalism (although even there instrumental considerations are never far away). It is equally true that throughout his writings we find him resorting to other genuinely moral arguments. Moreover, it would not be unnatural to approach Hayek's liberalism as yet another endeavour to justify on moral grounds the guiding principles and basic institutions a society ought to adopt. For, after the publication in 1971 of John Rawls's *A Theory of Justice* such moral justification has quickly become the dominant paradigm of what political philosophy is all about.

However, there is strong evidence against the view that Hayek pursues the project of a *normative* liberal theory. To begin with, his moral arguments are irremediably inconsistent, as Kukathas's analysis impressively demonstrates. They are inconsistent, it must be added, to a degree that makes it hard to believe they should be the fruit of Hayek's best efforts to work out a secure foundation for liberalism. Then there are his persistent claims that reason is unable to justify ultimate values and that liberalism's defence against socialism is a matter of scientific argument. Finally, an unmistakably

---

[12] This assumption must be made even more directly by those who unequivocally interpret Hayek as a utilitarian or a Kantian. Kukathas (1989: 3–4) at least acknowledges that moral justification was not Hayek's chief aim (though in the end his critique focuses on Hayek's moral philosophy rather than his social theory). He recognizes in Hayek's liberalism two concerns. The first is to show that the defence of liberalism should and can be based on a proper understanding of the spontaneous ordering processes at work in the social world, that 'liberalism . . . has its justification in the very nature of social life' (Kukathas 1989: 2). Such analysis, broadly in accordance with the instrumentalist reading advanced here, discerns in Hayek's political thought a preponderance of social theoretic considerations. Kukathas's Hayek has a second concern, which is to elaborate a 'normative political philosophy' articulating the principles that 'underlie the liberal ideal of a free society' (Kukathas 1989: 13). Kukathas's book, while touching on Hayek's theory of spontaneous social processes and his claims about the limits of reason, is largely devoted to a (very careful) examination of his moral arguments and, in particular, to an exploration of the tensions surfacing in Hayek's thought between the Humean and Kantian approaches to the justification of normative principles.

instrumental perspective pervades Hayek's work right from his inaugural lecture at the London School of Economics in 1933[13] to *The Fatal Conceit* (1988).

Obviously, no single account can accommodate all these diverse elements. In the light of such palpable contradiction one might resign oneself simply to register the failure of Hayek's liberal project. Yet such a conclusion leaves one wondering whether he really was no more than a frantic scribbler lacking any overall vision of how best to defend liberalism. It is against this background that I suggest we read him as offering an instrumental justification of liberalism. Such an interpretation can make sense of his views about the limits to rational debate in ethics and about the scientific nature of the argument. Also, it is able to grant his own social theory the central role he wants it to play. I believe only an instrumentalist reading can give his project a measure of unity and coherence or, at least, a guiding idea, and save it from the damning verdict of sheer inconsistency. Undeniably, Hayek does rely also on properly moral arguments. Yet, as I hope to show, he does so only as a last resort, because his instrumental reasoning runs out of steam and is unable on its own to settle important questions a liberal theory must answer.

Hayek's instrumental approach is unique in contemporary liberal political philosophy. Among the main protagonists of recent liberal thought none follows a similar strategy. Liberal theorists such as John Rawls,[14] Ronald Dworkin,[15] Joseph Raz,[16] and David Gauthier[17] seek primarily to work out the foundations of liberal political morality and try to justify on moral grounds what they regard as liberalism's overriding concerns. Though agreeing that liberal political philosophy must take cognizance of the insights provided by social and economic theory[18] or by the theory of institutions,[19] they are far from giving such considerations the kind of primacy accorded by Hayek. The emphasis these theorists put on moral rather than instrumental justification results from a different diagnosis of the nature of modern political conflict. The source of such conflict they do not locate in a disagreement merely

---

[13] The lecture was published under the title 'The Trend of Economic Thinking' in *Economica* (1993*b*). Caldwell (1987) gives a brief exposition and discusses it in the context of Hayek's later development as an economist.

[14] Rawls (1971; 1993).   [15] Dworkin (1978).   [16] Raz (1986).

[17] Gauthier (1986).   [18] e.g. Rawls (1971: 137–8).

[19] e.g. Raz (1986: 3).

about the institutional means to universally shared ends but in the very ends and values themselves to which legitimate government must be committed. Hence, they see it as the premier task of political philosophy to provide a justification of those ends and values.

Still, while Hayek's instrumental approach is, in political philosophy, undoubtedly singular, it should not be considered outlandish. There has been at least one recent attempt, by the noted American philosopher Nicolas Rescher, to explore the scope in ethics for instrumental reasoning.[20] Rescher examines how far an ethical code could be justified on instrumental grounds and outlines the strategy such a justification would have to adopt. This strategy comprises three stages. First, empirical enquiry must determine the values and ends actually operative in the social group. Secondly, the internal structure of these values and ends must be worked out; their relative weight *vis-à-vis* each other must be established and, crucially, the dominant values and ends have to be identified. Thirdly and finally, an instrumental analysis must be carried out of the ethical code the group observes; the code must be assessed in terms of its capacity to realize the dominant values and ends identified at stage two.[21] Such an analysis, Rescher says, leads to a conclusion of the form that 'such-and-such an ethical code affords a method for guiding the conduct of human affairs that is effective in conducing to the realization' of the objectives given.[22] We need not follow his discussion further here to recognize the parallels with Hayek. It clearly illustrates that the idea of an instrumental approach to the justification of behavioural rules and norms is not as exotic as at first it might appear.

Hayek is of special interest not only because his approach departs from the mainstream of contemporary liberal political philosophy. His instrumental perspective, with its emphasis on social rather than moral theory, brings into focus a problem perhaps neglected by present political thought. This is the problem of how much plasticity there is in the social world. Clearly, not everything goes. Not every blueprint for the ideal society is practicable. Or so one would think. Yet what are the constraints? What can social theory tell us about them? How far can it assist us in the choice of viable political principles? Therefore, when Hayek's instrumental

[20] Rescher (1973: 133–52).   [21] Ibid. 134.
[22] Ibid. 143, emphasis omitted.

justification of liberalism is examined below, the enquiry may at the same time also be read as a case-study exploring the division of labour in liberal thought between normative political philosophy and positive social theory. However, far-reaching and final insights into how one should properly conceive of this interdisciplinary co-operation are not to be expected. Hayek's own social theory is one among several and, like any of them, not beyond dispute. This heavily qualifies whatever conclusions we may reach.

A CRITIQUE OF HAYEK'S PROJECT: APPROACH AND METHOD

It is the aim of this book critically to examine Hayek's liberalism. More must be said now about the research interest guiding the enquiry and, consequently, about the approach to be taken and the method adopted.

Reading Hayek in an instrumentalist light brings into focus, above all, his *social theory*. If, as he claims, liberalism is the right political doctrine because it is based on a correct understanding of the nature and causal structure of the social world and on a recognition of people's limited rational and epistemic capacities, then one of the chief questions naturally to be asked is how far such understanding and recognition can really be said to re-flect our best knowledge about these things. To explain: Hayek's justification of liberalism hinges on an instrumental analysis of the alternative institutional arrangements available, that is, on a theoretical explanation of why, in the social world as it is, liberal rather than other rules and institutions are most conducive to the given ends of politics. To assess the force of Hayek's argument means, therefore, to examine the soundness of that analysis and of the theoretical resources on which it draws. Only after appraising the explanatory power of Hayek's social theory are we in a po-sition to evaluate his political philosophy and can we judge how cogent his instrumental reasoning in support of a liberal order is.

It may be noted that a critical examination of Hayek's social theory is a worthwhile undertaking irrespective of whether or not one accepts the instrumentalist interpretation advanced here. Whatever criticisms Hayek's commentators have made, they have usually regarded his social theory and especially its central notion,

the idea of a spontaneous order, as the most insightful and rewarding part of his thought. 'The most important of . . . his enduring
contributions to modern political theory' lies, for Crowley, 'undoubtedly in his clear and forceful restatement of the existence
and value of spontaneous social processes'.[23] Charles Larmore
recommends the idea of a spontaneous order as one of 'the models
of society upon which political theorists should learn to rely'.[24]
G. R. Pullen hopes that this idea 'shall serve as a point of departure
for the political theory of the twenty-first century'.[25] According to
E. Frankel Paul, the idea of a spontaneous order is 'a powerful
explanatory tool' and in 'its normative dimension . . . presents an
image of a good society to be striven for'.[26] For Norman Barry,
Hayek has done more than anyone to revive, and to show the
lasting relevance of, a venerable 'tradition of spontaneous order',
a strand of social thought reaching back at least to the scholastic
economics of sixteenth-century Spain.[27] James S. Coleman, in his
massive *Foundations of Social Theory*, approvingly refers to the
idea of a spontaneous order in his classification of social orders,[28]
and Walter B. Weimer even identifies it as the theoretical notion
that gives the social sciences their unity.[29] In business studies, Hayek
is seen as a guiding light inspiring the research into the management
of firms and similar 'self-organizing social systems',[30] and Ernst-
Joachim Mestmäcker relies on the idea of spontaneous order in
jurisprudence.[31] In view of such unreserved approbation, a critical
assessment of Hayek's social theory and idea of a spontaneous
order is exigent all the more.

Choosing to approach Hayek as a social and political *theorist*
means to disregard other possible avenues. This is not a study in
intellectual history. Tracing the influences on Hayek and of Hayek
would be an endeavour attractive enough. But this is not what
political theory is about. It is true that Hayek described his project
largely as a *restatement* (e.g. 1960: 1; 1973: iii) of the classical
liberalism of David Hume, Adam Smith, Immanuel Kant, and
others. Still, the thrust of his project was not merely reconstructive
but political and practical. Above all, Hayek wanted to be taken
seriously as a thinker in his own right who makes systematic

---

[23] Crowley (1987: 287).   [24] Larmore (1987: 107).
[25] Pullen (1989: 156).   [26] Paul (1988: 261).   [27] Barry (1982).
[28] J. S. Coleman (1990).   [29] Weimer (1987).
[30] Ulrich and Probst (1984).   [31] Mestmäcker (1985).

positive and normative claims about how the social world works and what the institutions of a free society should be. Even if in politics incontrovertible truth may be unattainable, the plausibility of these claims can be examined, and they must stand up to scrutiny irrespective of their historical and intellectual origins.[32] Also, this is not a study of Hayek's economics. Economic arguments, especially about the informational role of the market, are crucial to Hayek's defence of liberalism, and various aspects of his social theory have a distinctly economic inspiration to which due attention must be paid. Nevertheless, a comprehensive treatment of his economics would go far beyond what is required and offered here, and must be left to others.[33]

This study restricts its scope in a further way. The collapse of the Stalinist regimes in Eastern Europe is a historical event that it would be difficult completely to dissociate from the political thought of F. A. Hayek. Still, as closely linked to Hayek's concerns as the upheavals of 1989 may have been, this book will not discuss them. In particular, it will not consider how far they do, or do not, 'prove' his case for a liberal market order. A proper analysis of those revolutions would involve empirical research far exceeding the ambit and aspirations of the present enquiry. Moreover, it is doubtful whether Hayek's thought contains the theoretical tools

[32] The influences on Hayek's intellectual outlook are many. Gray (1986: 1–26) characterizes Hayek's general philosophical perspective as a 'sceptical Kantianism' informed, especially, by the thought of Ernst Mach, Karl Popper, Ludwig Wittgenstein, and Michael Polanyi. Reservations about this Kantian interpretation are expressed by Anna Galeotti (1987: 180 nn. 18–19). Plainly, Hayek is also influenced by the thinkers of the Scottish Enlightenment, particularly David Hume and Adam Smith (see Gray 1988b). Much of the answer to the question of Hayek's intellectual debts depends on which aspects of his thought one has in mind. Even if taking this into account, I myself think (but shall not argue) that his many references to others notwithstanding he lacks a clear awareness of the thinkers and traditions that had a formative influence on him. In spite of Gray's (1986: 4) assertion to the contrary, I believe that Hayek's thought *is* essentially eclectic. This need not in itself impair the plausibility of his theoretical claims, but it casts doubts on the fertility of any systematic attempt to identify his intellectual roots unambiguously and, in this way, to shed light on the general nature of his thought.

[33] Shackle (1981) gives a helpful general survey of Hayek's economics, and Hicks (1967) explains why in the 1930s Hayek's views on money and the business cycle, though for a time attracting considerable attention, were soon superseded by Keynes's theory. Further accounts of the controversy between Hayek and Keynes are to be found in Nentjes (1988) and Dostaler (1991). Recent work on Hayek's economics includes O'Driscoll (1977; 1978); Barry (1979); O'Driscoll/Rizzo (1985); Butos (1985/86); Caldwell (1988); Böhm (1989); Haberler (1989); Schmidtchen/Utzig (1989); Shapiro (1989).

necessary for an adequate explanatory account. To be sure, he always held that socialist planning could not work. Yet, obviously, factors other than economic failure contributed to the downfall of these regimes. One of them, it appears, was the utter loss of moral credibility. Eastern European socialism with its notorious discrepancies between official rhetoric and actual achievement had created a moral wasteland of cynicism and distrust. The success of the democratic movements, and of the revolutions to which they led, arose, at least in part, from their moral strength, that is, from their successful appeal to citizenship, public discourse, individual rights, and procedural fairness, and their insistence that these notions are not empty bourgeois slogans but substantive principles to which a decent society must give institutional expression.[34] About this political morality Hayek has not much to say. This clearly limits the explanatory relevance of his political thought for those Eastern European events.

Hayek was a controversial thinker. Revered by some as the most important twentieth-century theorist of the free society, he has been reviled by others as a mere reactionary. These vastly different assessments also show in the, by now enormous, secondary literature, where work sympathetic to, and even uncritical of, Hayek has tended to dominate. Apparently those who find his general political outlook uncongenial simply refuse to discuss in any detail the social theory and philosophy underpinning it, regarding them as unworthy of further consideration.[35] Given Hayek's actual influence, this is hardly a satisfactory state of affairs. What is called for in this situation is a rigorous yet dispassionate analysis of Hayek's social and political thought based on what he really said and wrote.

Though Hayek's case for liberalism manifestly depends on his social and economic theory, it is by no means obvious how exactly the key concepts of spontaneous order, cultural evolution, and rule-following are to be understood and how they ground his defence of liberal order. Even though Hayek is commonly regarded as a fairly straightforward writer, not much given to obscurantism, anyone probing deeper will experience considerable uncertainty

---

[34] For more on this, see e.g. Lukes (1991).
[35] However, things may be changing now. Tomlinson (1990) and Ioannides (1992) are two recent book-length studies on Hayek, written by authors expressly committed to 'democratic socialism'.

as to what precisely he has in mind when speaking of such notions as 'order, 'adaptation', and 'rules'. Therefore what is required is, first of all, a careful reconstruction of his argument.

Reconstruction, in each chapter, is followed by critical assessment. In view of the fact that most readers find Hayek either profound and powerful, or shallow and repugnant, the most appropriate method seems to be one of *internal criticism*. Such criticism largely accepts the terms of reference set by Hayek and examines his argument from within, the severest conclusion possible being that his project already fails on grounds of its own making. This method, it is hoped, should be capable of meeting the concerns of both sympathizers with and opponents of Hayek. For it engages in a detailed discussion of his social theory and political philosophy and, thus, does take him seriously. At the same time it does not content itself merely with once more paraphrasing his views but endeavours to identify what must be seen as significant shortcomings and flaws.

Unquestionably this method, like any, has its drawbacks. One of them is its neglect of historical and political context. Disregarding the context of Hayek's thought limits the scope of the enquiry in two respects. It may make Hayek's project look rather strange, and it does not address the ideological uses to which his ideas may have been, and indeed have been, put. The first of the two points requires further comment.

Against the background of current political thought with its emphasis on moral philosophical reflection, Hayek's insistence on the 'scientific' nature of his defence does seem curious, and one may wonder how he could ever have fashioned the argument in that way. Not least it invites the ironic analogy with Marxism and its claim to scientific status. Still, Hayek's 'scientific' attempt to expose the falsity of socialism and other collectivist doctrines does make some sense once the era and the political climate are recalled that prompted him to turn from technical economics to the fundamental questions of social and economic order. Hayek formed his political philosophy in the 1930s, at a time when many thoughtful people, confronted with the poverty and social destitution caused by a world economy in disarray, came to regard capitalism as morally bankrupt, and concluded that the only acceptable alternative was the planned economy. The defence of a liberalism whose economic prescriptions were increasingly considered baleful called for an exceptional argumentative strategy if its political message was to be heard at all.

Taking account of the moral outrage at capitalism's failures and injustices, voiced especially by intellectuals, Hayek must have thought it imperative himself to avoid similar moral language and to vindicate liberalism in a different vocabulary, one whose appeal did not depend on a moral perspective. This could only be the idiom of science. If anything, it was 'scientific' evidence and reasoning, he must have believed, that would be capable of furnishing the kind of unassailable argument required. In addition, many of those who most forcefully rejected capitalism and the liberal order did so from a professedly Marxist point of view, that is, in the firm conviction of themselves having 'science' on their side. Given these circumstances, Hayek's attempt to cast the defence of liberalism in scientific terms loses much of its strangeness. A similar situation persisted after the Second World War. The rivalry between East and West could be interpreted as the confrontation of two ideological camps with seemingly irreconcilable political moralities. Again, it was not entirely far-fetched to try to evade the moral questions and to prove the socialist side wrong on 'scientific' grounds.

Finally, two methodological remarks of a different sort. The first concerns a particular assumption governing the interpretation of Hayek. Throughout, Hayek's social and political writings shall be treated as if he had always intended them to form one coherent body of theory. To assume so is of course eminently problematic. Those writings span more than half a century. It would not therefore be implausible to think that over the years his outlook may have changed sufficiently to warrant a diachronically sensitive approach, discerning different stages in his intellectual development. However, as far as I am aware, nowhere did he himself distinguish such stages nor did he ever explicitly retract from, or substantially modify, important theoretical positions once he had taken them.[36]

To be sure, an author's views may undergo shifts which he does not himself realize or wishes to downplay. Yet from Hayek's inaugural lecture at the London School of Economics (1933b)

---

[36] I am talking here of Hayek's social and political thought. Things may be different with his economics. For more on this, see Caldwell (1988). Hayek's political flirtations, in his student days, with a 'mild Fabian socialism' (1983: 17) are of biographical interest but irrelevant to the purposes of this study.

and from *The Road to Serfdom* (1944) to *The Fatal Conceit* (1988) there is in his work on political philosophy and social theory an astonishing constancy of themes and of theoretical perspective. Terence W. Hutchison has suggested that with regard to Hayek's views about the methods of the social sciences his work should be divided into an early Austrian praxeological and a later Popperian period,[37] yet I am inclined to follow Gray who argues that there are not enough grounds justifying such a periodization.[38] But I do not mean also to endorse Gray's claim that Hayek's system of ideas exhibits an overall unity.[39] Mine is only an interpretative assumption about how to approach Hayek. As we shall see later, his thought is marred by fundamental inconsistencies—yet inconsistencies which no periodization, however sophisticated, could explain away. The most one can say about the development of Hayek's thought is that the sweeping subjectivism advocated in his early social theoretic writings (1949; 1952*a*) gradually gave way to a naturalistic perspective, and that increasingly he came to stress the significance of cultural evolution.

The second methodological remark is about how to deal with Hayek's own vocabulary. While striving to expound Hayek's social and political theory as faithfully as possible, I shall not always adopt his terminology. Hayek believed the language of political and intellectual discourse is still dominated by an anthropomorphic and animistic vocabulary that reflects an earlier, tribal mode of thought and exhibits a built-in socialist bias. Anxious to get his liberal message across as precisely as possible, he developed a whole arsenal of (usually) twin concepts such as catallaxy and economy, cosmos and taxis, nomos and thesis, nomocracy and teleocracy, and demarchy and democracy (e.g. 1978: 71–97; 1988: 106–19).[40] Yet this terminology does not really deliver what Hayek hoped it would, and he can be discussed equitably without it. Trying to keep the text as free from jargon as possible, I shall largely avoid it. Finally, there is the problem of gender and

---

[37] Hutchison (1981: 210–19). Hutchison's thesis is challenged by J. Pheby (1988: 108–13) and B. Caldwell. See, in particular, the heated exchange between Caldwell (1992*a*, 1992*b*) and Hutchison (1992).   [38] Gray (1986: 17–20).

[39] Ibid. 1–4. Gray (1988*b*) has retracted this claim.

[40] In his endeavour to purify the language of political thought Hayek resembles, as Gray (1988*a*: 250) perceptively notes, Karl Kraus, the Viennese critic of the 1920s and 1930s, who saw the struggle against the moral decay of public life as above all a battle against the corruption of language.

language. Hayek, when referring to human beings as otherwise unspecified individuals, uses the pronoun 'he'. In this practice, I shall follow him—with the proviso, however, that I do mean 'he' to be a shorthand for 'he or she'. Hayek himself may have had certain hesitations about unreserved gender equality, as is suggested, for instance, by remarks of his about women's suffrage (1960: 443 n. 4).

OUTLINE OF THE ARGUMENT

The argument presented in this book will proceed as follows. Chapters 1 to 5 discuss under various aspects Hayek's idea of a spontaneous order, the centre-piece of his social theory. Chapters 6 and 7 consider two further social theoretic notions relevant to Hayek's political philosophy: his thesis about the tacit observance of certain rules guiding individual conduct; and his theory of cultural evolution. Thus prepared, Chapter 8 and the Conclusion examine the force of Hayek's instrumental defence of the liberal market society.

Chapter 1 gives an introduction into the broader theoretical context in which Hayek wants the idea of a spontaneous order to be placed. It presents his basic claim that such order emerges as the result of general rule-following and individual adjustment to local circumstances. It clarifies his concept of order in society and argues that he fails to distinguish two fundamentally different types of spontaneous order, orderly patterns of co-operation forming within a given system of rules on the one side, and systems of rules developing in a process of cultural evolution by natural selection on the other. The chapter ends with a rejection of Hayek's wider theoretical ambitions as they show in his theory of complex phenomena, a theory seeking to apply the same explanatory logic to social as well as natural spontaneous orders.

Chapters 2 to 4 narrow the focus, concentrating on spontaneous economic order. Chapter 2 looks at individual adjustment as the first of the two elements constituting the mechanism of spontaneous order. The idea that spontaneous economic order is, partly, the result of the individuals adapting to their local situation derives from what Hayek regards as the epistemic role of the market. The chapter shows how the market's epistemic role connects with, and presupposes, individual adjustment. It argues that by describing such adjustment merely in informational terms as responsiveness to price signals Hayek tends to overlook the sometimes dramatic impact it can have on individual welfare.

Chapter 3 deals with the rules of the market, the second element of the mechanism producing spontaneous economic order. The rules necessary for such order to form, Hayek says, are those of private property, contract, and tort. The chapter describes what their contribution to generating order consists in. It explains the ideas prompting Hayek to call them 'the rules of just conduct' and examines whether the negativity, end-independence, and abstractness which he ascribes to them really help their characterization. Further, it discusses his distinction between rule-guided conduct and purposive action and points out his wholly instrumental perspective on rules. In his assertion that economic order is the result of rule-following (and individual adjustment) Hayek depicts markets as self-regulating systems entirely independent of external organization structures. The chapter demonstrates that in this claim the social theorist Hayek denies what the political economist Hayek takes for granted: that the state must in various ways assist the market if instability and collapse are to be precluded. Finally, attention is drawn to an uncertainty in Hayek's account of the rules necessary for the spontaneous formation of order. Sometimes he postulates that in addition to the rules of property, contract, and tort a whole bundle of other rules, attitudes, beliefs, and orientations is also required should order unfold in the market. Such a move would force Hayek to abandon the universalist explanatory aspirations of his social theory.

The significance Hayek attaches to spontaneous economic order lies, ultimately, in his belief that such order is uniquely beneficial. Chapter 4 identifies and examines two arguments designed to redeem this claim. The first is the argument from the mutually advantageous nature of uncoerced exchange, the second the argument from the market's efficiency. It will be argued that the first argument fails altogether while the second comes down to average income-maximization.

Having examined the idea of a spontaneous economic order, I want in Chapter 5 to find out what further spontaneous social orders exist. Hayek takes it to be indubitable that in the social world there are many such orders other than that of the market.

For he defines social theory as the study of spontaneous orders, and more than once he implies that it is exactly the fact of its wide applicability that corroborates the theoretical power of the idea of a spontaneous order and, in turn, confirms the soundness of his explanation of the market process in terms of such order. The chapter offers various reflections exploring the concepts of 'social order' and its 'spontaneity'. Also, it distinguishes five claims representing the substance of the notion of a spontaneous economic order and examines how far they may hold for a number of other phenomena loosely qualifying as spontaneous social orders too. The conclusion will be that on close inspection the general idea of a spontaneous social order disintegrates and that it is unable to furnish the focal point of a social theory.

Hayek's social theory does not end with the idea of a spontaneous order. He makes important further claims of a social theoretic nature. Two of these are relevant to the purposes of this study. Chapter 6 looks at Hayek's thesis of tacit rule-following and detects two different claims. The first is a historical thesis about how man's previously unconscious behavioural orientations became increasingly articulated and legally formalized, finding expression in the rules of the market. The second is the theoretical claim that the interpretation and application of the rules of law are governed by higher-order rules which we do not and cannot know. In the form presented by Hayek both claims appear implausible. Chapter 7 considers Hayek's theory of cultural evolution, in essence the thesis that the rules of the market embody a social wisdom of which individual reason is unaware and incapable. The analysis will uncover a fundamental ambiguity in Hayek's account of the scope of cultural evolution and reject as unsustainable the holist functionalism and adaptationism underlying his evolutionist thought. The discussion will again highlight Hayek's entirely instrumental view of the rules of morality.

The comprehensive examination, in Chapters 1 to 7, of Hayek's social theory prepares the ground for the critical assessment, in Chapter 8, of his instrumental justification of the liberal market society. The chapter identifies the two main arguments destined to carry out this project. The first, the traditionalist argument, is inspired by the theory of cultural evolution and seeks to establish the presumption that as long-standing traditions the rules of the market are an indispensable condition of the survival of mankind.

Since reasonable persons must accept this end, Hayek argues, they must also endorse the only means able to achieve it: the liberal market society. It will be shown that this argument lends itself at best to a defence of the status quo—whatever it is—but that it cannot justify distinctly liberal institutions. Ultimately, Hayek's traditionalist argument collapses into a crude naturalism regarding all normative political principles, like all orientations and all institutions, as no more than temporary adaptations to changing environmental constellations.

The second, the proceduralist argument portrays the market as the only co-ordination mechanism capable of coping with three circumstances constitutive of modern society, and hence, as the only method securing the universally accepted ends of general prosperity and social peace. I shall grant Hayek the argument that markets are indispensable if a society is to deal with the fragmentation of economic knowledge (this being the first circumstance), yet shall maintain that this is only an argument for the market but not for a liberal market society. With regard to the two remaining modern circumstances, Hayek's argument fails. When he presents the market as a purely procedural method dispensing with any substantive distributive principle and, therefore, capable of evading the potential strife over the demands of social justice (the permanent danger of such strife being the second circumstance), he is putting forward merely his own, no less contentious conception of justice, which assigns benefits to each according to his market value. And when he recommends the market again as a purely procedural co-ordination mechanism not committed to any conception of what is worth pursing in life and, thus, able to reconcile people's conflicting individual ends (the third circumstance), he overlooks that this mechanism does not harmonize ends but decides among rival claims on scarce resources, and that the question of which ends are admissible is not settled in the 'means-connected' order of the market but by the rules of just conduct that form part of its institutional framework. The final section of Chapter 8 explains how the moral philosophical reasoning in which Hayek occasionally seems to be engaged relates to the instrumental perspective informing the traditionalist and proceduralist arguments.

The Conclusion asks what conditions would have to obtain if a justification on purely instrumental grounds of a society's system of political, legal, and economic institutions were ever to work. It identifies four requirements and argues that, since they do not and—given the modern human predicament—cannot hold, moral philosophical reflection must in political justification play the main part. This means the defence of liberalism and liberal institutions consists primarily not in scientific but in normative argument and is largely the task of political philosophy.

I

Spontaneous Order, Social Theory, and the Theory of Complex Phenomena

For Hayek, the idea of a spontaneous order is not only liberalism's 'central concept' (1967: 162) and therefore vital to its defence but, at the same time, also the notion on which all social theory converges. 'The whole task of social theory', Hayek writes, 'consists in little else but an effort to reconstruct' the various spontaneous orders existing in the social world (1967: 71). Still, while a ubiquitous theme, the idea of a spontaneous order does not receive a sufficiently systematic treatment in his writings. This shows in the secondary literature, where the views about its substance, its scope, and its significance as an analytical concept differ widely.

Gerald P. O'Driscoll identifies a 'principle of spontaneous order' as 'a cornerstone of modern economics', indeed as its 'first principle', and equates it with the empirical claim that markets possess an inherent 'tendency to overall equilibrium'.[1] In similar fashion, James Buchanan considers 'the principle of the spontaneous order of the market' to be the only one 'in economics . . . worth stressing'. Buchanan links spontaneous order to the pursuit of individual self-interest yet recognizes that in the wider field of social life there is scope for 'spontaneous disorders' too.[2] For Norman Barry, 'The simplest way of expressing the major thesis of the theory of spontaneous order is to say that it is concerned with those regularities in society, . . . those institutions and practices which are the result of human action but not the result of some specific human intention.'[3] According to W. B. Weimer, spontaneous orders—which he believes to be at the core of all social science—arise from the tension among the three 'abstract regulative principles . . . of creativity or productivity, . . . of rhythm, . . . [and] of regulation by opponent processes'.[4] John Gray observes that 'the exact contours of the idea of spontaneous order, as it is used by Hayek and other

---

[1] O'Driscoll (1978: 116–17, 133).   [2] Buchanan (1977: 25, 27–30).
[3] Barry (1982: 8, footnote omitted).   [4] Weimer (1987: 258).

theorists, are far from clear, and its content and scope of application remain profoundly controversial.'[5] Implicitly he expresses doubts about its nature as a widely applicable theoretical concept when himself calling the idea merely an explanatory 'cipher' or 'schema'.[6] Regarding it as 'value-free',[7] he thinks the idea encompasses three claims—an invisible-hand thesis, a thesis about the primacy of tacit knowledge, and a thesis about the cultural evolution by natural selection of traditions and practices[8]—which together 'add up to a conception of society as a self-regulating system, whose elements or components contribute (in ways often unknown to their practitioners) to the stability and integration of the society as a whole'.[9] The most serious reservations about whether the idea of a spontaneous social order has any definitive content are voiced by Richard Vernon who discusses it in the context of several attempts theoretically to come to terms with the unintended consequences of human action. Examining various of the clues given by Hayek as to what 'order' might mean and judging them inconclusive, Vernon ends with the conjecture that it represents a 'value-term' denoting 'a kind of orderliness or integration' in society.[10]

Such diversity of opinions attests pointedly to the elusiveness of Hayek's idea of a spontaneous order and documents the need for careful analysis. The present chapter attempts to discover what he really intends spontaneous order to mean, and seeks to understand the wider theory of which he wants that idea to be the centrepiece. Beyond mere exposition, it draws attention to various problems and, in passing, comments on the prospects for success of Hayek's huge theoretical ambitions.

SPONTANEOUS SOCIAL ORDERS AND ORGANIZATIONS

The original problem that set Hayek on the path to developing the idea of a spontaneous order

was to explain how an overall order of economic activity was achieved which utilized a large amount of knowledge which was not concentrated

---

[5] Gray (1987: 237).   [6] Ibid. 244; (1986: 119–21).
[7] Gray (1986: 118–25; 1987: 244).   [8] Gray (1986: 33–4).
[9] Gray (1987: 244, emphasis omitted).   [10] Vernon (1979: 63–7).

in any one mind but existed only as the separate knowledge of thousands
or millions of different individuals. (1967: 92)

The problem, in other words, was to show how a market society
could altogether function, given the fact that co-operation and exchange were not co-ordinated by a central authority but were left
to what appeared to be economic anarchy. The answer, arrived
at after 'a long way', lies for Hayek in

an adequate insight into the relations between the abstract rules which the
individual follows in his actions, and the abstract overall order which is
formed as a result of his responding, within the limits imposed upon him
by those abstract rules, to the concrete particular circumstances which he
encounters. (1967: 92)

What, in this rather convoluted passage, Hayek describes is nothing less than the *mechanism* on which spontaneous order rests.
This mechanism has two components. Spontaneous order, he claims,
arises out of the general observance of certain behavioural rules
and the individual adjustment to local circumstances. As he puts
it elsewhere: 'the formation of spontaneous orders is the result of
their elements following certain rules in their responses to their
immediate environment' (1973: 43). And:

the individual responses to particular circumstances will result in an overall order only if the individuals obey such rules as will produce an order.
Even a very limited similarity in their behaviour may be sufficient if the
rules which they all obey are such as to produce an order. (1973: 44)

Though developed to solve a specific economic puzzle, the idea of
a spontaneous order has, for Hayek, a far wider range of application and is even the focal point of all social theory. Among
other things, it serves him as one of the two basic analytical concepts in a comprehensive taxonomy of 'social orders'. A look at
this classificatory framework will give us a better grasp of the
contours of the idea and at the same time an impression of his
theoretical aspirations.

According to Hayek, all associations, institutions, and other
social formations can be classified either as 'spontaneous orders'
or as 'organizations'. Spontaneous orders and organizations, he
asserts, systematically differ in various respects, chief among
them the way in which the orderliness they exhibit came about.
Spontaneous orders develop unprompted among individuals who

pursue their own ends, whereas organizations are the result of concerted action.

The distinction between 'spontaneous orders' and 'organizations', Hayek declares, goes against widely held beliefs. Man's 'anthropomorphic habits of thought' (1973: 36) incline him to think that all social orders are created by deliberate human effort to serve some specific purpose. But to view them all in this way as artefacts, as 'organizations' based upon hierarchical relations of command and obedience, he regards as a grave error. It is true, he says, that many social formations such as '[t]he family, the farm, the plant, the firm, the corporation and the various associations, and all the public institutions including government, are organizations' (1973: 46) but, he emphasizes, they are integrated into an all-encompassing social order that is not itself hierarchically structured and must not be mistaken for an organization. This is the 'overall order' (1973: 47) of society itself, the most comprehensive spontaneous order he finds in social life but by no means the only one. Other spontaneous social orders are '[m]orals, religion and law, language and writing, money and the market' (1973: 10). It is this distinction between spontaneous orders and organizations which provides the basis for Hayek's social theoretic taxonomy. The main aspects of this taxonomy may be summarized as follows.

1. Spontaneous orders and organizations differ in how their orderly structures came about. A spontaneous order is 'the result of human action but not of human design' (1967: 96),[11] the outcome of *self-co-ordination* among participants pursuing their own ends but having no intention and making no deliberate effort, either individually or collectively, to produce it. Co-operation in an organization is the result of *co-ordination by central direction*.

2. The two categories of social orders each rely on a different co-ordinating medium. Co-ordination leading to spontaneous orders involves rules. The members co-ordinate their activities by 'following certain rules in their responses to their immediate environment'. Order emerges as the result of their observing specific *rules of conduct* and their adjusting to the individual situation in which they find themselves. Hayek insists that for self-co-ordination to work the parties must share certain rules. In contrast, the social structure co-ordinating the division of labour in an organization

---

[11] This is a phrase Hayek borrowed from Adam Ferguson. See 1967: 96 n. 1.

is one of hierarchical relations. *Commands* determine in detail every member's activities.

3. A spontaneous order offers conditions beneficial to the simultaneous realization of *many different individual ends*. '[N]ot having been made it cannot legitimately be said to have a particular purpose, although our awareness of its existence may be extremely important for our successful pursuit of a great variety of different purposes' (1973: 38, emphasis omitted). An organization, on the other hand, is a collective instrument implemented to serve some *specific purpose* defined in advance. This difference is reflected in the co-ordinating devices on which spontaneous orders and organizations rely. The rules of conduct characteristic of spontaneous order are 'negative', merely delimiting a sphere of legitimate individual action but leaving the participants otherwise free to choose their activities according to their own plans (1976: 36–7). The commands securing co-ordination in an organization fully specify the members' activities so as to further the collective goal as effectively as possible.

4. The two categories of social orders usually differ in the *complexity* they may acquire. There are no inherent limits to the internal differentiation spontaneous orders may attain while organizations are 'confined to such moderate degrees of complexity as the maker can still survey' (1973: 38).

5. Finally, only spontaneous orders raise genuine *explanatory problems* and, thus, call for *social theory*. The complexity and fluctuating nature of such orders, Hayek concedes, seem to belie his claim that they possess orderliness and rest on a distinctive type of co-ordination. These orders, he says, 'do not obtrude themselves on our senses but have to be traced by our intellect. We cannot see, or otherwise intuitively perceive, this order of meaningful actions, but are only able mentally to reconstruct it by tracing the relations that exist between the elements' (1973: 38). Such reconstruction is the task of social theory. '[S]ocial theory begins with—and has an object only because of—the discovery that there exist orderly structures which are the product of the action[s] of many men but are not the result of human design' (1973: 37). More specifically, its task is that of uncovering the rules observance of which has led to spontaneous order. In accordance with this conception of social theory, Hayek defines 'science' as 'knowledge of general rules' (1949: 80). In his view,

organizations do not pose similar social theoretic problems. The co-ordination of activities taking place in an organization is to be explained by reference to the intentions of those who established, and direct, it.

Hayek's classificatory scheme harbours various problems. The fundamental distinction he draws between 'spontaneous' and 'made' (e.g. 1973: 37) orders becomes rather blurred when he admits that by changing the rules one may be able to influence the internal structure of a spontaneous order (1973: 41) and when he even talks of the possibility of inducing a spontaneous order by designing and introducing appropriate rules (1973: 46). Another problem concerns Hayek's latent functionalism. His claim that spontaneous orders emerge from self-co-ordination among numerous individuals fits ill with the functionalist language in which repeatedly he describes the self-stabilizing tendency of such orders (1973: 39; 1967: 77; 1952a: 80–6). Further, it must be doubted whether 'organizations' can really be said to have a single purpose. Such a view leads either again to a functionalist perspective, for instance, when he characterizes the family as the institution that fosters, and transmits from generation to generation, the psychological attitudes required for the spontaneous order of society to be maintained (1960: 90–1). Or, if 'purposes' is meant to signify the personal ends of individuals, it is plainly implausible since the family, the firm, and other 'organizations' can be, and are, the focal point of many different such ends.

Yet by far the most serious problem lies in Hayek's ambiguity about the nature of the distinction between spontaneous orders and organizations. Often he implies that any type of association is *either* a spontaneous order *or* an organization, for example, when he categorizes the farm and the firm as organizations and the overall order of society as a spontaneous one. But what he presents here as a strictly dichotomic classification appears elsewhere to be merely the characterization of two ideal-types of social co-ordination which, though they cannot be combined 'in any manner we like' (1973: 46), do complement each other. Thus, he declares that 'every organization must rely also on rules and not only on specific commands' (1973: 48) because only rules give its members the discretion needed if they are to carry out effectively the organizational tasks assigned to them.

The same ambiguity extends to the 'overall order' of society. On the one side, Hayek states that it 'relies solely on rules and is entirely spontaneous in character' (1973: 50). At the same time, he concedes that it may not be fully self-maintaining and may depend, for its continuous existence, on organizational structures which keep in check destabilizing tendencies (1973: 47). Now if 'spontaneous order' and 'organization' merely denote two ideal-types of co-ordination (which in reality never exist in pure form), then Hayek's taxonomy can provide much less than he appears to believe the framework for an ambitious theoretical edifice. It is not to be denied that the distinction between self-co-ordination and central direction may be a helpful analytical tool. Yet if no type of social order can be said exclusively to rest on either of these two modes of co-ordination, then theoretical claims, derived from those mechanisms in their pure forms, may not contribute much to illuminating the nature of actual social orders. In actual orders the interplay of the two mechanisms may produce mixed effects unknown to a theory that isolates, and concentrates on, hypothetical ideal-types of co-ordination. It must be assumed that in different types of social orders the two co-ordination mechanisms are of different importance, hence interact differently, and bear differently on the characteristics of a particular type of order. This suggests that social theory has to be sensitive to the peculiarities of the types of order it investigates and cannot expect to draw many substantive conclusions about their nature from the mere fact that they largely rely on self-co-ordination, or on central direction.

Hayek never really makes clear whether the two mechanisms are merely two ideal-types of co-ordination or how far either of them is actually constitutive, and exclusively so, of certain types of social order. As we shall see later, the almost dogmatic, and implausible, claims he advances about the self-stabilizing and self-organizing capacities of the 'overall order' of society root in a tendency of his to understand the distinction between the two mechanisms in a rigidly dichotomic way.

Though Hayek's social scientific taxonomy conveys a first impression of the theoretical ambit in which he situates the idea of a spontaneous social order, it is still far from obvious what social *pattern* he has in mind when talking of such order. It is to this question that we must now turn.

ORDER IN SOCIAL LIFE

A spontaneous order forms, Hayek says, when the members observe certain rules of conduct and adjust individually to the particular circumstances of their situation. Yet what arrangement or fabric does he mean when speaking of society's spontaneous order? The answer given here is briefly this: order in society, or social order, is for Hayek identical with the web of economic relations characteristic of a well-functioning market society.

Offering something of a definition, Hayek describes 'social order' as 'the structure of the actions of all the members of a group' (1967: 66 n. 1). 'Order in society' reveals itself as a 'matching' or 'correspondence' (1973: 36) or 'coincidence' (1973: 38) of expectations and intentions. Such correspondence he takes to be constitutive of order in society.

Living as members of society and dependent for the satisfaction of most of our needs on various forms of co-operation with others, we depend for the effective pursuit of our aims clearly on the correspondence of the expectations concerning the actions of others on which our plans are based with what they will really do. This matching of the intentions and expectations that determine the actions of different individuals is the form in which order manifests itself in social life... (1973: 36)

Elsewhere, Hayek talks of accurate foresight rather than the correspondence of expectations. Yet his notion of social order is still the same.

The orderliness of social activity shows itself in the fact that the individual can carry out a consistent plan of action that, at almost every stage, rests on the expectation of certain contributions from his fellows. ... Order with reference to society thus means essentially that individual action is guided by successful foresight, that people not only make effective use of their knowledge but can also foresee with a high degree of confidence what collaboration they can expect from others. (1960: 159–60, footnote omitted)

Hayek's idea, advanced in these and other passages, to make the correspondence of expectations the element defining order in society may be developed further as follows.

Under the conditions of modern society, the members usually pursue ends which for their realization require goods and services they are unable to produce individually but which may be provided if everybody specializes in certain productive activities. A social division of labour, co-operation, and exchange immensely improve everybody's prospects, enabling all to benefit from the diversity found in society of persons, their talents, their goals, their skills and knowledge. The part someone plays in the division of labour is instrumental for him as well as for his fellow members, or at least for some of them.

Economic activity provides the material means for all our ends. At the same time, most of our individual efforts are directed to providing means for the ends of others in order that they, in turn, may provide us with the means for our ends. (1967: 229)

Through his productive activities an individual supplies others with the means they deem necessary to achieve their ends while, simultaneously, his contribution to the realization of their aspirations secures him access to those things produced by others which he needs for his ends. Prepared to provide others with what they look for, the individual can count on their willingness to provide him with the means he wishes to command.

It is such responsiveness and reciprocity that lead Hayek to define order in society as a correspondence of intentions and expectations. There is order if the division of labour is co-ordinated, and the individuals' productive activities interlock, in a way that secures the supply of the goods they regard as essential for their own individual ends. This notion of order can be expressed in terms of 'expectations' and 'foresight' as follows. Order exists if the members can largely foresee what co-operation they may expect from others and if their expectations correspond to what these others will actually do. Or, to repeat Hayek's own words: 'This matching of the intentions and expectations ... is the form in which order manifests itself in social life' (1973: 36).[12]

---

[12] Occasionally, Hayek seems to recognize a 'correspondence of expectations', and hence social order, also in the general observance of rules. The underlying idea may be this. In society, conflict can be prevented if rules exist which delimit for each person a sphere of individual autonomy. General compliance with these rules creates orderly conditions enabling everybody to have a good chance of seeing his plans come to fruition. Now, a sort of order indeed obtains if everybody expects everybody else to conform to the rules, and if these expectations are borne out by, and 'correspond' to, everybody's factual adherence to the rules. In this sense, Hayek sometimes describes the rules of just conduct as defining everybody's 'legitimate' expectations (1976: 37; likewise in 1973: 86–7, 96–7, 99, 108–9). Still, on Hayek's own account such a correspondence of expectations does *not* already

This notion of 'order in society' inevitably recalls the picture of a market, and there is strong evidence that for Hayek such order *is* order in the market. To begin with, Hayek's definition of order in society is largely identical with his conception of 'economic equilibrium' developed in a different theoretical context several decades earlier. In his essay 'Economics and Knowledge' (1949: 33–56), he discusses the problem of what role the assumption of individual foresight (and knowledge) should play in equilibrium analysis. He observes that traditionally theorists often took it simply for granted that the foresight required for equilibrium to be attained is 'equally given to all individuals and that their acting on the same premises will somehow lead to their plans becoming adapted to each other' (1949: 38). Rejecting this empirical assumption as unrealistic, Hayek makes 'correct foresight' part of the definition of 'equilibrium'. Equilibrium obtains if the plans of the different individuals are compatible in the sense that they can all be carried out at the same time. Now this means, Hayek says, that a state of equilibrium exists as long as the participants possess accurate foresight. Foresight thus ceases to be a factual precondition of equilibrium and becomes an analytical implication of its definition. As Hayek elaborates:

It appears that the concept of equilibrium merely means that the foresight of the different members of the society is in a special sense correct. It must be correct in the sense that every person's plan is based on the expectation of just those actions of other people which those other people intend to perform and that all these plans are based on the expectation of the same set of external facts, so that under certain conditions nobody will have any reason to change his plans. (1949: 42)

Therefore, when Hayek links 'order in society' to the individuals' ability to anticipate how others will respond—'[o]rder with reference to society . . . means essentially that individual action is guided by successful foresight' (1960: 160)—he merely repeats the earlier idea that foresight is an ingredient of economic equilibrium.[13] That

represent order in society. For (as we have learned) he sees social order only as the *result of* general rule-following and individual adjustment. In Hayek's perspective, therefore, general conformity to rules is a precondition at best of order in society.

[13] In an aside, Hayek, though at the time of writing 'Economics and Knowledge' still engaged primarily in technical economics, already hints at the idea of generalizing the concept of a 'correspondence of expectations' in order to employ it also in social theory: 'It has long been a subject of wonder to me why there should, to

for him 'order' and 'equilibrium' are synonymous he confirms by occasionally using the two terms side by side (1973: 36; 1978: 184).

A few more points may be mentioned, further bearing out the claim that Hayek's conception of 'order in society' is coextensive with 'order in a market'. The adjustment of prices, of salaries, of occupation, and so on, required of the participants in a market (1976: 115–22) re-emerges in his account of spontaneous social order as the individual elements' adapting 'to circumstances which directly affect only some of them' (1973: 41). The diversity of individual goals pursued in a market returns in the spontaneous order of the 'Great Society' as the absence of any 'common hierarchy of particular ends' (1976: 109). Finally, Hayek expressly declares social relations essentially to be of an economic nature: 'the Great Society is still held together mainly by what vulgarly are called economic relations.' As he explains:

> It is of course true that within the overall framework of the Great Society there exist numerous networks of other relations that are in no sense economic. But this does not alter the fact that it is the market order which makes peaceful reconciliation of the divergent purposes possible . . .
> . . . Even the degree to which we can participate in the aesthetic or moral strivings of men in other parts of the world we owe to the economic nexus. (1976: 112–13)

These points give additional weight to the thesis that, for Hayek, order in social life is identical with the pattern of interactions arising from a market in operation.

Having clarified Hayek's conception of social order, we must now take up his view that the idea of a spontaneous order is social theory's pivotal notion. He believes the spontaneous order of the market society is only one instance, albeit a vitally important one, of a general principle of spontaneous order effective in the social world, and he seems to assume that such wide applicability is proof of its soundness and explanatory force. Yet Hayek's indiscriminate talk of spontaneous social orders obscures a fundamental difference between two distinct types of unprompted social structures.

my knowledge, have been no systematic attempts in sociology to analyze social relations in terms of correspondence and noncorrespondence, or compatibility and noncompatibility, of individual aims and desires.' (1949: 38 n. 4)

TWO TYPES OF UNPROMPTED SOCIAL ORDERS

According to Hayek, morals, religion, law, language, writing, money, the market (1973: 10), and, not to forget, the overall order of society (1973: 46–7, 50) are all spontaneous social orders. What makes them belong to one and the same basic category of social formations is, he implies, their unplanned emergence. Spontaneous social orders are 'the results of human action but not of human design' (1967: 96–7; 1978: 4), the unintended consequences of the independent decisions and actions of many.

The contrast with 'organizations', social orders set up to accomplish some specific task, serves Hayek to define the subject-matter of social theory. He thinks organizations pose no theoretical problems because their existence and particular role can readily be explained from the intentions of those who introduced them. In his view, made orders do not therefore give rise to a specific theoretical discipline. Things are different with spontaneous orders. Their unplanned emergence must arouse curiosity and warrants the establishment of 'a distinct body of theory' (1973: 20). It must be the aim of such theory 'to explain the unintended or undesigned results of the actions of many men' (1952a: 25). In its endeavour to analyse the formation of spontaneous orders, it can build, Hayek says, on a distinguished tradition of social thought founded by Bernard de Mandeville and further worked out by the eighteenth-century Scottish thinkers David Hume, Adam Smith, and Adam Ferguson, and by Carl Menger in the nineteenth century.[14] They already developed the basic conceptual tools required for a social theory showing

how, in the relations among men, complex and orderly and, in a very definite sense, purposive institutions might grow up which owed little to design, which were not invented but arose from the separate actions of many men who did not know what they were doing. (1960: 58–9)

In the account Hayek gives here and elsewhere of the subject-matter of social theory he presupposes (explicitly so, for example, in 1952a: 41) that the process of their formation is sufficiently similar to make all 'spontaneous' social orders belong to the same category and to be explained in the same way.

---

[14] For Hayek's account of the rise, in the history of social thought, of the idea of a spontaneous order, see 1967: chs. 5–7; 1973: ch. 1; 1978: chs. 1 and 15.

Yet this assumption does not hold, and Hayek's undifferentiated talk of 'spontaneous orders' and his conception of social theory as the study of the unintended consequences of human action confound two types of unprompted orders that must be kept apart. More specifically, he runs together orderly patterns of co-operation emerging within a given system of behavioural rules on the one side, and systems of rules that have developed from a selective process of cultural evolution on the other.

Hayek circumscribes 'social order' as 'the structure of the actions of all the members of a group' (1967: 66 n. 1). Also, there is his claim 'that the formation of spontaneous orders is the result of their elements following certain rules' (1973: 43). In passages such as these he unmistakably expresses the view that spontaneous order is something that unfolds when the members observe certain behavioural rules, rules already existing and in force for some time. 'Order' is not intended here to mean the system of rules itself. The economic order arising in the market, Hayek's paradigmatic case of a spontaneous order, neatly illustrates this. Spontaneous economic order emerges, he explains, from 'the operation of the market system' (1976: 115), 'produced by the market through people acting within the rules of the law of property, tort and contract' (1976: 109).

To define, as Hayek does, spontaneous orders as the result of rule-following (and individual adjustment) invites the question of how he can plausibly place spontaneous orders thus conceived in the same category as the kind of unplanned order he finds in morals, law, religion, and money. Like the market system itself each of these orders is an institution or, in Hayek's terminology, a system of rules but not a 'structure of actions' and not the product of rule-following and individual adjustment.[15] None of these institutions is, on his own account, in any strict sense a spontaneous order.

[15] Hayek recognizes that there is a difference: 'That the systems of rules of individual conduct and the order of actions which results from the individuals acting in accordance with them are not the same thing should be obvious as soon as it is stated, although the two are in fact frequently confused' (1967: 67). Unfortunately, he is far from consistent in his terminology, repeatedly (e.g. 1973: 35) muddling his own distinction between 'order' (arising from rule-following etc.) and 'system' (of rules of conduct). Similarly, in the secondary literature the discussion of spontaneous order and of the process of its formation is often hampered by an insufficient awareness of the crucial importance of this distinction.

To dissociate morals, law, and other systems of rules from the idea of a spontaneous order is not to declare them the product of design. They are unplanned in a different sense. They arise, Hayek says, from a process of cultural evolution by natural selection. Rules such as those of morals and law, he claims, emerged from a process in which 'practices which had first been adopted for other reasons, or even purely accidentally, were preserved because they enabled the group in which they had arisen to prevail over others' (1973: 9). No group or individual foresaw what the beneficial effects of the new rules would be. Certain groups began to prosper and grow simply because they 'happened to fall' (1983: 46) on them. This theory of cultural evolution will be the subject of a separate chapter. But we can see already in which sense, for Hayek, systems of rules such as morals and law are 'spontaneous', and how he is led to put the spontaneous formation of order *within* given rules and the evolutionary development *of* rules in the same category. Both the orderly structures of actions and those systems of rules are, in his view, the product of unintended consequences, 'the result of human action but not of human design'. Yet this formula conceals two different invisible-hand processes. While the formation of spontaneous economic order takes place under clearly identifiable rule-based constraints and is a permanent circular process allowing a great deal of theorizing, the evolutionary development (if it is one) of morals, law, and other institutions does not follow any 'law of evolution' (1967: 42) or any similar regularity.

There is another term coined by Hayek alleging that spontaneous order and cultural evolution are linked closely. Repeatedly, Hayek talks of 'the twin ideas of evolution and the spontaneous formation of an order' (1978: 250; likewise in 1967: 77; 1973: 23; 1979: 158; 1988: 146). But he never explains satisfactorily what renders the idea of a spontaneous order and the theory of cultural evolution 'twin conceptions'. Sometimes this notion seems designed to mean a similarity in their explanatory logic in the sense that the ideas of a spontaneous order and of cultural evolution both deal with social phenomena that are the unintended though meaningful consequences of human action, the results of invisible-hand processes.[16] Yet, as we have noted, those similarities cannot extend

---

[16] This explanatory similarity is stressed, for example, by Vanberg (1986: 80–1).

very far as the formation of spontaneous orders is based on rules, which cultural evolution is not. Sometimes, however, 'twin conceptions' appears to denote an empirical link, the claim that the rules conducive to spontaneous order must themselves have developed in the course of a cultural evolution. Now this is a claim Hayek does make with regard to the rules of the market, as we shall see later. Still, it does not hold across all spontaneous social orders (assuming, for the moment, that there are other such orders), for he admits it to be 'conceivable that the formation of a spontaneous order relies entirely on rules that were deliberately made' (1973: 45). So the notion of spontaneous order and cultural evolution being 'twin conceptions' lacks definite contours and, moreover, adds nothing to what in different form Hayek tells us anyway.

Throughout the discussion so far, we can hardly have failed to notice the huge expectations Hayek places on the idea of a spontaneous social order, its explanatory scope and fertility. Attempting to found (as he does) all social theory on this idea alone would already be a bold enough endeavour. Yet his theoretical aspirations reach much further, for he believes the notion of spontaneous order also has illuminating and important applications in the natural sciences. However, close inspection will reveal an underlying naturalism hardly compatible with any project of a social theory.

FURTHER AMBITIONS: A THEORY OF COMPLEX PHENOMENA

For Hayek, the spontaneous order of the market society is only one instance of a whole range of spontaneous orders in the social as well as the natural world. Not only market equilibria but also crystals, organisms, animal societies, and galaxies (1960: 160; 1967: 69, 74; 1973: 39) are, he believes, spontaneous orders. To address, on a high level of abstraction, the general aspects common to all these diverse orders, he postulates a 'theory of complex phenomena'.

The theory of complex phenomena is a theory about the explanation and prediction of, and control over, spontaneous orders.[17]

[17] Hayek's major texts on the theory of complex phenomena are 1967: chs. 1 and 2; 1973: ch. 2; 1978: ch. 2. However, various terminological ambiguities

To bring out the features characteristic of complex phenomena Hayek contrasts them with 'simple phenomena'. The number of elements constituting the order of a simple phenomenon is small. The orderly structure of its elements is the effect of a few one-way causal relations, and these relations are captured by the basic laws of physics. Finally, its environment does not influence the formation of a simple order. A complex phenomenon, on the other hand, consists of a large number of elements and is the result of manifold exchange processes among the elements and between them and their surroundings (1967: 70–1). These ordering processes can, Hayek says, be described only by very elaborate laws because, to model adequately the high interdependence among the elements and their sensitivity to outside forces, those laws must make extensive use of intricate loops and feed-backs. Their sophistication makes the laws describing a complex phenomenon quite unlike the familiar laws of physics, which merely presuppose causal relations between only two classes of events. In the case of complex phenomena, Hayek is therefore reluctant to apply the concept of natural 'law' at all (1967: 26, 40–2). Instead, he prefers to speak of 'rules of conduct' which the elements follow when arranging themselves in an orderly fashion.

The core content of Hayek's theory of complex phenomena is, unsurprisingly, the same as that of his social theory. Spontaneous orders, as we recall, are the result of rule-following and individual adjustment. Analogously, the elements of a complex phenomenon exhibit certain regularities of behaviour that determine the general character of the eventual order. It is these behavioural regularities that prompt Hayek to use the notion of rule-following. In addition, the elements find themselves always in a particular situation. The specific circumstances of that situation determine how they, while following the basic rules, behave in detail. Those circumstances do not influence the general nature of the order, only its concrete shape (1973: 40, 43).

render it difficult not only to establish what in detail the claims of this theory are but also to grasp its general character. For example, without further elaboration Hayek speaks liberally of the 'elements', 'variables', 'particular facts', and 'particular events' that constitute a spontaneous order and, again interchangeably, of the 'factors', 'forces', 'mechanisms', 'laws', and 'rules' that determine how the elements will 'behave' and 'arrange themselves' within the overall order. In this way, the theory of complex phenomena oscillates between animistic and naturalistic tendencies.

Hayek sees far-reaching consequences for the range of, and the limits to, our ability to explain, predict, and control complex phenomena. There is, to begin with, only restricted scope for explanation. Hayek takes it to be the most frequent case that when confronted with a complex phenomenon we will know the elements involved and may from such knowledge gather what the basic regularities of their behaviour are. This will not enable us to spell out a full explanation of how all the details of the complex order came about, but we will be in a position at least to give an 'explanation of the principle' (1967: 11). Such an explanation offers an account of how the general behavioural regularities we ascribe to the elements could have brought about the kind of order we find in a complex phenomenon. An explanation of the principle can, according to Hayek, be tested at least partly (1967: 11). Yet even if it succeeds in identifying all the behavioural regularities involved in bringing about a particular phenomenon, it will always remain incomplete as it cannot trace all the specific circumstances to which the elements adjusted individually and which determine the details of that order.

The limits to explaining complex phenomena bear also on prediction. This is hardly astonishing. Knowing how the elements of a complex phenomenon will in general arrange themselves but ignorant of all the specific initial conditions and the circumstances determining the particulars of the eventual order, scientists can at best make a 'pattern prediction' (1967: 27). At most, their knowledge of the behavioural regularities governing the elements will enable them 'to derive . . . the sort of pattern that will appear [but] not its particular manifestation' (1967: 28).

A few examples may give us a better idea of what pattern predictions are about. Since our interest is ultimately in Hayek's social theory we should look for cases from social life.[18] As far as I can see, he gives only two and they are both economic. The first is about price-control, the second about the impossibility of curbing inflation given rigid foreign exchange rates.

[I]f all commodity prices are fixed by law and demand afterwards increases, people will not be able to buy as much of every commodity as they would wish to buy at these prices. (1967: 15)

***

[18] For an example from physics, see 1973: 40.

[W]e cannot at the same time maintain fixed rates of foreign exchange and at will control the internal price level of a country by changing the quantity of money. (1967: 17)

If these examples are really meant to be representative of the concept of pattern predictions, then they illustrate more its doubtful nature than its practical value. Unquestionably Hayek thinks the theory of complex phenomena is not an a priori discipline. Yet one suspects the two examples are merely analytical statements not empirically but necessarily true. Being analytical, pattern predictions would not forecast anything and would not reflect an empirical knowledge of how the social and economic world works. In addition, it is difficult to see what the orderly structure whose emergence is to be predicted consists in. As we saw earlier, the pattern characteristic of the spontaneous order in the market society is its web of exchange relations. Such a pattern seems to be absent, especially in the second example. Finally, it is at least unclear whether the two examples, stating certain macroeconomic interdependences, are compatible with Hayek's Austrian economics and its commitment to a completely microeconomic, methodologically individualist foundation of economic theory. Now it might be argued that these doubts arise because the two examples are ill-chosen. However, from the context in which they are found (1967: 17) one must assume that Hayek regards them as fairly typical of what economics (understood as part of a theory of complex phenomena) is about. Therefore, the questions raised may be taken as an indication of the troubles inhering in the concept of pattern predictions.[19]

Limitations analogous to those of explanation and prediction pertain to the control of spontaneous orders. We may be able, Hayek says, to determine the main features of a complex phenomenon but we can never arrange all its details. All we can do in the case of natural phenomena is to create the initial conditions 'triggering' their emergence (1973: 39–40). Things are somewhat different with spontaneous social orders. We may be able to shape such orders by altering existing rules of conduct or introducing

[19] Further reservations about Hayek's concept of pattern predictions are expressed by Paqué (1990). For an attempt to make sense of a Hayekian research programme that builds on explanations of the principle, pattern predictions, and the theory of complex phenomena, see Graf (1978).

new ones but, again, 'we shall thereby be able to influence only the general character and not the detail of the resulting order' (1973: 41). With regard to the complex order of the market society, this means that one may be in a position to make the system of rules on which it is based more consistent and, thereby, improve co-ordination but that 'nobody's will can determine the relative incomes of the different people, or prevent that they be partly dependent on accident' (1976: 69).

Now what should we think of Hayek's theory of complex phenomena? The answer, in brief, is that it undermines the consistency of his philosophy of science and renders his social theory implausible.

The theory of complex phenomena makes it doubtful whether Hayek has a consistent philosophy of (social) science. In particular, his early advocacy of subjectivism seems in conflict with his later endorsement of the philosophy of science of his friend Karl Popper. In *The Counter-Revolution of Science* (1952a), Hayek had maintained that there is a fundamental difference between the approaches of the social and the natural sciences, defending especially a principle of methodological subjectivism. According to this principle, social theory, in its endeavour to elucidate the formation of social orders, must start from, and take as basic explanatory elements, the everyday concepts, categories, and beliefs on which those participating in an order rely in their actions. And it must use these beliefs as explanatory building-blocks 'irrespective of whether they are true or false' (1952a: 28). Yet in his (later) writings on the theory of complex phenomena he accepts (1967: viii), though not without qualifications (1967: 3–21), Popper's philosophy of science. Popper[20] regards falsifiability as the criterion distinguishing science from non-science and, concomitantly, emphasizes the unity of method in all sciences and the objectivity of scientific knowledge. Hayek has nowhere addressed these tensions satisfactorily.

For holding his most ambitious theory of complex phenomena Hayek has to pay a still higher price. This theory is ambitious because it pretends it can explain social as well as natural orders. Yet, as we shall now see, he can only have such a theory at the cost of sheer implausibility. Hayek locates the parallels between social and natural spontaneous orders primarily in the

[20] Popper (1945; 1957; and 1963).

mechanisms of their formation. These parallels must therefore show also in his account of the behavioural regularities which, he says, lead to spontaneous order and which he describes as the 'elements following certain rules' (1973: 43). It does not require much effort to realize that there are fundamental differences between the regularities of human conduct on the one hand and of molecular behaviour on the other. How far does Hayek's theory of complex phenomena take cognizance of those differences? What we want to know is whether, when talking of the behavioural regularities conducive to spontaneous social and economic order, he offers a plausible conception of rule-following. In our discussion, we shall focus on the rules Hayek considers absolutely vital for such order. They are the 'rules of just conduct', largely the rules of private property, contract, and tort (1976: 109; 1978: 62, 140).

Hayek's account of rules and of their observance is inadequate in a number of ways. First of all, Hayek flatly equates rule-following with behavioural regularity:

we have occasionally spoken of 'regularity' rather than of rules, but regularity, of course, means simply that the elements behave according to rules. (1973: 43)

Throughout it should be clearly understood that the term 'rule' is used for a statement by which a regularity of the conduct of individuals can be described, irrespective of whether such a rule is 'known' to the individuals in any other sense than that they normally act in accordance with it. (1967: 66–7)

Such a conception of rule-following is far too broad. It commits Hayek, for example, to regard all regular bodily functions as resulting from the observance of rules. But obviously the pulsation of the heart or regular eyelid movements are not instances of rule-following. Even in the field of human conduct proper Hayek's conception is not sufficiently precise, as can be seen with just conduct and its rules. The rules of just conduct, he says, are negative, delineating a vast range of admissible individual behaviour but not prescribing any specific course of action (e.g. 1976: 36). Yet if those rules are negative in the sense given, an individual observing them does not exhibit any discernible behavioural regularity. The fact that somebody avoids certain actions need not give his conduct the appearance of a positive regularity.

Another weakness in Hayek's conception of rule-following is far more serious. This is its naturalism. To be sure, Hayek explicitly repudiates the view that behavioural rules, particularly the rules of just conduct, are

natural in the sense that they are part of an external and eternal order of things, or permanently implanted in an unalterable nature of man, or even in the sense that man's mind is so fashioned once and for all that he must adopt those particular rules of conduct . . . (1976: 60)

This rejection notwithstanding, in numerous passages Hayek comes perilously close to a naturalist conception of rules. Of course, Hayek reveals a naturalist tendency right from the beginning, when in his theory of complex phenomena he declares that in the social as well as the natural world there exist various spontaneous orders resting on the same mechanism of rule-following and individual adjustment. If, as he pretends, iron filings on a sheet of paper ordered by magnetic forces (1973: 40) are, at bottom, no different from the members of the market society arranging themselves in a network of exchange relations, it is hard to see how the members' behaviour could be accounted for other than by causal regularities as natural laws describe them.

Hayek underlines the close proximity of rule-governed behaviour and naturally caused regularities when he adduces the fact that the elements of a natural spontaneous order do not 'know' the rules they follow as demonstrating the soundness of the idea that the members need not be consciously aware of all the rules required for a spontaneous social order to emerge.

[T]he instances of spontaneous orders which we have given from physics are instructive because they clearly show that the rules which govern the actions of the elements of such spontaneous orders need not be rules which are 'known' to these elements; it is sufficient that the elements actually behave in a manner which can be described by such rules. . . .

That rules in this sense exist and operate without being explicitly known to those who obey them applies also to many of the rules which govern the actions of men and thereby determine a spontaneous social order. (1973: 43)

Hayek betrays the same naturalist inspiration when he compares the rules of just conduct—which, being negative, exclude as inadmissible certain types of action—to Popper's view of natural laws as consisting 'essentially of prohibitions, that is, of assertions that something cannot happen' (1973: 146 n. 1); '[l]ike scientific laws, the rules which guide an individual's action are better seen as determining what he will not do rather than what he will do' (1967: 56–7, footnote omitted). The most conspicuous aspect, finally, of Hayek's social theoretic naturalism we find in his account of how the rules of conduct relate to individual action. For Hayek, action is the result of internal drives, specific external circumstances, and the constraints exerted by the rules of conduct:

> The concrete individual action will always be the joint effect of internal impulses, such as hunger, the particular external events acting upon the individual (. . .), and the rules applicable to the situation thus determined. . . .
>
> . . . It is important always to remember that a rule of conduct will never by itself be a sufficient cause of action but that the impulse for actions of a certain kind will always come either from a particular external stimulus or from an internal drive (and usually from a combination of both), and that the rules of conduct will always act only as a restraint on actions induced by other causes. (1967: 68–9; similarly in 1967: 77)

Elsewhere, Hayek describes a rule of conduct not as a built-in constraint, but as

> a propensity or disposition to act or not to act in a certain manner, which will manifest itself in what we call a practice or custom. As such it will be one of the determinants of action which, however, need not show itself in every single action but may only prevail in most instances. Any such rule will always operate in combination and often in competition with other rules or dispositions and with particular impulses; and whether a rule will prevail in a particular case will depend on the strength of the propensity it describes and of the other dispositions or impulses operating at the same time. (1973: 75–6, emphasis and footnote omitted)

These passages provide ample evidence that, irrespective of his disclaimer (1976: 59–60), Hayek is actually committed to a naturalist account of rule-following, regarding rule-governed conduct as having natural causes. Sometimes he even talks as if the rules were causally effective themselves and would determine human behaviour.

Hayek's conception of rule-following is untenable. First, rules of (just) conduct do not cause the occurrence of rule-governed behaviour. If the behavioural regularities he regards as just conduct had natural causes at all, those causes would have to be located elsewhere, in man's genetic endowment, for example, or in the neural

structure of his mind. Secondly, a naturalist account is incompatible with the idea of cultural evolution. It is one of Hayek's major
claims that the regularities of human conduct leading to the spontaneous formation of social order are the outcome of a cultural
evolution by natural selection. If those regularities are subject to
historical change, they cannot at the same time possess the immutability we ascribe to the causal regularities expressed in natural
laws. Thirdly, and most importantly, there is in Hayek's naturalist
conception of rule-following no room for genuine human agency.
According to this conception, human beings are indeed iron filings
put in their places by some anonymous social magnet. But people
are able to suspend acting and to look at their own conduct from
outside, as it were. They are not subject to an invisible hand ir-
resistibly pushing them around on the chessboard of social life.
Hayek's conception of rule-following and his theory of complex
phenomena give a thoroughly mechanistic picture of social life, in
which there is no place for individual autonomy, for persons
pursuing their own ends, and for a critical evaluation of existing
institutional arrangements and systems of rules.

To abandon this naturalist conception of rule-following is to
reject as untenable the claim that there exists a general theory of
complex phenomena applicable to social as well as natural orders.
This means the idea of a spontaneous social order must stand on
its own feet and cannot draw additional support from a more
comprehensive theoretical framework. Hayek's own account of
rule-following, though indefensible, need not be fatal for that idea,
since an alternative account allowing for individual agency and
judgement is not entirely unthinkable. For the further investiga-
tion into the social theoretic idea of a spontaneous order the insights
gained so far are suggestive in two respects. First, if we are to
acquire a better understanding of this idea, we must leave Hayek's
high theory and get down to a careful examination of the specific claims he makes about spontaneous social and economic
order. We begin this examination in the next chapter when we
look at individual adjustment as one of the two components
allegedly constitutive of the mechanism leading to spontaneous
order. And secondly, Hayek's views on rules should alert us to a
naturalist undercurrent in his social thought that may again
surface elsewhere.

2

Spontaneous Economic Order: Individual Adjustment and the Market's Epistemic Role

Like all spontaneous orders, the web of exchange relations forming in the market is, Hayek says, the outcome of a two-part mechanism. Spontaneous economic order develops when the members observe certain rules and adjust to their local situation. Put forward in such generality, this assertion is hardly comprehensible and its relevance for liberalism beyond grasp. A detailed reconstruction is needed if we are to understand what Hayek has in mind here. This chapter explores the sense in which individual adjustment may be said to contribute to the emergence of a spontaneous economic order.

Whenever Hayek talks about the mechanism conducive to spontaneous order, he gives individual adjustment much less prominence than rule-following, the other element of that mechanism. There is a reason for such unobtrusiveness. The idea that spontaneous economic order is, partly, the result of the members adapting to the specific circumstances of their individual situation is the by-product of, and is usually only mentioned in connection with, a claim to which Hayek consistently attaches much greater significance. This is the contention, central to his defence of the market, that spontaneous orders are far better able than the hierarchically structured organizations to utilize knowledge (e.g. 1973: 51; 1978: 75). Turning to individual adjustment means, therefore, above all addressing Hayek's views on the informational capacities of the market. Accordingly, the structure of the argument in this chapter will be the following. The chapter opens with an exposition of Hayek's views on the epistemic role of the market. Hayek claims not merely that a market system manages to gather and utilize the knowledge relevant for efficient economic activity yet dispersed across society. Crucially, he also maintains that only markets can generate the facts and the information needed if such activity is to be organized efficiently. Hayek believes these informational considerations help to answer important institutional questions about what the property arrangements and the role of government should be if an economic system is to work. The second section examines whether such considerations can really be expected to provide substantial guidance in these practical matters. In the third and final section, we shall see how the epistemic role Hayek attributes to the market connects with, and presupposes, individual adjustment. It will be argued that by describing such adaptation solely in informational terms as people's responsiveness to economic change signalled by the price-system, he tends to underestimate the dramatic effects adjustment can have on their welfare. We shall learn that sometimes even the most strenuous adaptive efforts will not suffice to bring people back into the market nexus and to save them from economic disaster. In conclusion, the chapter criticizes Hayek's move to link the notion of adjustment to a systemic holism and calls in question his notion of economic order.

THE EPISTEMIC ROLE OF THE MARKET

If a modern economy is to be successful at all, Hayek declares, it must cope with the 'division' (1949: 50; 1960: 26) or 'fragmentation of knowledge' (1973: 14) characteristic of contemporary mass society. The economic problem society faces, he explains, is

not merely a problem of how to allocate 'given' resources—if 'given' is taken to mean given to a single mind which deliberately solves the problem set by these 'data'. It is rather a problem of how to secure the best use of resources known to any of the members of society, for ends whose relative importance only these individuals know. Or, to put it briefly, it is a problem of the utilization of knowledge which is not given to anyone in its totality. (1949: 77–8)

The fragmented knowledge Hayek has in mind is a knowledge of preferences and production factors. Nobody, he says, neither individual agent nor collective authority, can know what the members' preferences all are and how they rank. Nobody can, in his words, know 'which kinds of things or services are wanted, and how urgently they are wanted' (1978: 182, footnote omitted). Such knowledge is dispersed throughout society. Analogous limitations apply to the information about the resources and other production factors available. Even if a central authority knew in the required detail what individual preferences were and, hence, what should be produced, it would not be able to organize the economy efficiently. The knowledge of what means of production exist and of the various uses to which they may be put often depends on a familiarity with local circumstances. Lacking this knowledge and unable to gather it, any central co-ordinating agency must fail to secure efficient production.

The Hayekian division of knowledge also has a temporal dimension further rendering central economic co-ordination impossible. Over time both preferences and the conditions under which production takes place change, sometimes rapidly. Thus even the most painstaking attempt at collecting the information needed centrally would always lag hopelessly behind reality. It is this *dispersion* and *fugacity* of economic knowledge that leads Hayek to define the economic problem confronting society as that of 'the utilization of the . . . knowledge of particular circumstances of time and place which exists only as the knowledge of . . . different individuals' (1978: 136).

There is yet another dimension to economic knowledge, its *latency*. Hayek believes that often economically relevant knowledge does not exist already and must first be discovered or generated, and he believes it is this fact that tells most forcefully against the possibility of a planned economy. We shall return in a moment to this aspect of economic knowledge and to the argument he draws out from it against central co-ordination. First, an account must be given of Hayek's claim that the market is the only co-ordination mechanism capable of dealing with dispersed and fugacious economic information.

In order to understand how Hayek can claim that only the market fully utilizes dispersed and transitory knowledge we should start by looking at his view of economic activity and his conception of economic agents. Economic activity is, for Hayek, always instrumental, serving ends which lie outside the sphere of production, in people's private world. Given the extensive division of labour typical of advanced societies, the individual depends for the satisfaction of his preferences on others. Others provide him with most of the things he deems necessary for his private ends. Likewise, the results of his productive efforts serve others as the means for their own purposes (1967: 229). It is by engaging in economic activity that the individuals get access to the things they want but are unable to produce themselves.

Now Hayek sees the members of society not merely as productive agents but as *entrepreneurs*, that is, as persons entirely responsible for the positions they occupy in the division of labour and for the advantages they get out of it. It is the economic world's opaqueness, he thinks, which forces everybody to behave entrepreneurially. Unable to pierce through the fog of economic ignorance and partial knowledge, everybody must become active on his own and try as hard as possible to be useful to others. As Hayek puts it: 'in discovering the best use of our abilities, we are all entrepreneurs' (1960: 81). Only if someone is able to offer a product attractive to others will he be in a position to induce others to provide the things he regards as the means for his ends.

In such responsiveness to others' preferences lies, for Hayek, the solution to the problem of dispersed and fugacious economic knowledge. Its utilization becomes feasible, he argues, because the decisions about what to produce and how to do it are maximally decentralized, and the market price-system indicates as quickly and accurately as possible what preferences people have and how they are met most economically. What in an uncertain world the individual needs, he writes,

are signals in the form of known prices he can get for the alternative services or goods he can produce. Given this information, he will be able to use his knowledge of the circumstances of his environment to select ... the role from which he can hope for the best results. It will be through this choice ..., for him merely a generalized means for achieving his ultimate ends, that the individual will use his particular knowledge of facts in the service of the needs of his fellows ... (1976: 9)

It would be wrong to assume that Hayek thinks a market price-system brings about an asymptotic approximation to a stable equilibrium where everybody occupies a permanent niche enabling him somehow to serve others and thereby to earn a living. As Hayek emphasizes, much economic knowledge is fleeting and involves the perception and anticipation of changes in preferences and other parameters. The price-system mirrors these changes, signalling how the individuals should redirect their productive efforts if they are not to lose their incomes.[1] In this way, he concludes, it continually co-ordinates anew individual economic activities when unforeseen changes have disturbed established patterns of co-operation (e.g. 1976: 115–20). Still, the picture given so far might be taken to suggest that economically relevant knowledge is a knowledge of facts which, though frequently of a transitory character, do exist already and need only be grasped. Yet this is not Hayek's view.

Given Hayek's entrepreneurial perspective, economic knowledge is primarily knowledge of profitable opportunities, that is, of how to produce a particular commodity more cheaply than has been done before. Now his point is not merely that such knowledge is widely dispersed and often soon becomes outdated. Hayek draws attention to what he thinks is an important further aspect. That a particular thing can be produced at a certain low cost is a fact and is known, he says, only because in the market an entrepreneur *does* offer it at that low price. In other words, market prices embody the latest information about how cheaply the goods and services offered can be produced, and they serve the competing producers as provisionally fixed points for their future decisions and activities. Here the *latency* of much economic knowledge becomes relevant.

To produce as cheaply as possible is not only a technological problem whose solution presupposes a knowledge of the alternative production methods available. What is also required is the realization of which of the alternative factor combinations imaginable is the most economical one. In Hayek's view, such realization amounts to a veritable discovery:

the method which under given conditions is the cheapest is a thing which has to be discovered, and to be discovered anew, sometimes almost from day to day, ... and ... it is by no means regularly the established entrepreneur ... who will discover what is the best method. (1949: 196)

---

[1] This tells us something about the nature of market prices as instruments of economic co-ordination. Being inherently dynamic, modern market economies are always, to some degree, in disarray (a theme expounded by Shackle 1972). That means their price-system does not reflect the equilibrium prices of cleared markets. Rather, it is exactly because the prices relevant to co-ordination are *dis*equilibrium prices that they indicate who should reorient his productive activities, and in which direction. For more on this, see Kirzner (1984).

However, two different types of 'discovery' must be distinguished here. That the cheapest production method has to be discovered can mean that it is the result of continuous alertness and adaptation to fluctuations in the prices of the known production factors (e.g. 1976: 117–18). Yet sometimes Hayek has in mind a more specific and more genuine sort of discovery. Often, he suggests, production can be made cheaper not by recombining known factors in a novel and still more cost-saving way but by finding new productive uses for familiar things. It is in this respect that he considers the term 'discovery' particularly apt. Nobody can know in advance all the manifold purposes for which a thing may be employed. Only market competition, he argues, induces people to try out new uses for the resources at their disposal:

Provisional results from the market process at each stage alone tell individuals what to look for. Utilisation of knowledge widely dispersed in a society with extensive division of labour cannot rest on individuals knowing all the particular uses to which well-known things in their individual environment might be put. Prices direct their attention to what is worth finding out about market offers for various things and services. (1978: 181–2)

Hayek implies here that the knowledge of economically relevant facts is frequently latent. The things that are the furniture of the world, he seems to say, are given and largely known. But what we do not know fully, because it is not a matter of perceptual recognition, is the great potential for further uses still inhering in all these things. Bringing more of these latent facts to light requires a continuous search process. Thus, for Hayek, it is not merely the dispersion and fugacity of knowledge but, importantly, also the necessity to *generate* new knowledge about new facts that lies at the heart of the economic problem society faces.

Society can solve this problem only, Hayek maintains, if it avails itself of the market and market competition. It is especially its ability to prompt people again and again to explore anew their situation in order to find still more beneficial uses for the things they command that gives the market, in his view, a unique *epistemic* role and leads him to describe competition as 'a procedure for the discovery of such facts as, without resort to it, would not be known to anyone, or at least would not be utilised' (1978: 179, footnote omitted).[2] Or, as somewhat differently we may also say: the market is *not* a *regulative* mechanism merely administering resources whose relative scarcities are already given but a *constitutive* process in the course of which those scarcities are alone established and continually re-established anew.

Hayek's view of market competition as a procedure discovering the most productive uses to which a society's resources may be put forms the basis of his argument against the theory and politics of the planned economy. Efficient production, the argument runs, is impossible if competition is absent or market prices are stiffened by administrative decree, for the market cannot then play its epistemic role. Now Hayek does not only claim that the market can play this role, he also explains why a planned economy cannot. He argues that the planners, if they want to imitate the market, can take recourse neither to science nor to entrepreneurial functionaries.

Hayek insists that the market cannot be replaced by science. The relevant economic facts, we saw, are facts about the most productive uses of a society's resources. These facts, he says, are contingent in two respects. They are transitory in so far as changes in demand or supply or technology may alter them and show other factor combinations and uses to be more efficient. And they are local since they always apply only to a given society with its given specific endowment of resources. Their contingent nature makes them *particular* facts. As such they defy being systematized by, and integrated into, scientific theory (1949: 80; 1960: 25). Describing the differences between economic competition and science, Hayek writes that 'the former is a method of discovering particular facts relevant to the achievement of specific, temporary purposes, while science aims at the discovery of what are sometimes called "general facts", which are regularities of events' (1978: 181). His conclusion, directed at central planning, is that no economic or other theory will ever exist from which the planners could deduce the most efficient productive arrangements.

---

[2] Hayek regards the market as a discovery procedure in yet another respect. By perpetually bringing forth novel goods and services, he argues, the market helps consumers to discover preferences of which they have not been aware before (e.g. 1960: ch. 3; 1967: ch. 23). For a brief discussion of this view, see Kukathas (1989: 98–100).

Hayek's explanation why planned economies fail has another side to it. Neither can scientific theory replace competition nor can, as he also argues, state functionaries take over from the entrepreneurs. The reason for this he sees in the specific nature of the entrepreneur's ability to perceive more productive and profitable opportunities. This ability, he suggests, is a sort of *practical knowledge*, a *skill* resistant again to theoretical statement.[3] Two points in Hayek's account deserve particular mention. First, the exercise of entrepreneurial skills is context-dependent and, moreover, inseparably linked to entrepreneurial autonomy. These skills allow the person possessing them 'to find new solutions rapidly as soon as he is confronted with new constellations of circumstances' (1949: 155). Yet somebody will be capable of practising them only if it is also within his discretion to choose how to exploit an opportunity: 'all the information accessible to (. . .) the individuals can never be put at the disposal of some other agency but can be used only if those who know where the relevant information is to be found are called upon to make the decisions' (1979: 190 n. 7). This renders entrepreneurial activity incompatible with anticipative planning and central co-ordination. Second, entrepreneurial skills come to flourish only in a competitive climate (1979: 76). They cannot, Hayek claims, be learned by formal instruction. Nobody can 'pass on all the knowledge he commands and still less all the knowledge he knows how to ac- quire if needed by somebody else' (1979: 190 n. 7). This means

---

[3] Any analysis is hampered here by the fact that Hayek fails to clarify how this entrepreneurial ability relates to practical knowledge and tacit skill as he discusses them at considerable length elsewhere, particularly in his essay 'Rules, Perception and Intelligibility' (1967: 43–65). In his general approach to skills—'a very com- prehensive phenomenon' (1967: 43)—Hayek is influenced by Gilbert Ryle's (1945/ 46; 1949) distinction between 'knowing that' and 'knowing how', that is, between propositional and practical knowledge, and by Michael Polanyi's (1958; 1967) notion of 'tacit knowledge'. (References, explicit or implicit, of Hayek's to Ryle and Polanyi are numerous. See, for example, 1960: 25, 426 n. 4; 1967: 44 n. 4; 1973: 72–8, 99, 163 n. 4, 164 n. 15; 1978: 38.)

I take Hayek's standard view to be that the successful exercise of a skill depends on the observance of certain rules. What makes an ability a *tacit* skill and an instance of *practical* (versus propositional) knowledge is, he appears to assume, the fact that the person applying the skill (or anyone else, for that matter) cannot, if asked, articulate these rules. Yet he does not seem completely to exclude the possibility of skills which are not based on rule-following. Nor does he appear unequivocally to claim that in the case of rule-based skills those rules cannot be articulated in principle (1967: 43–5; but cf. his sweeping claims to the contrary in 1978: 7, 38– 9). For a circumspect recent discussion of practical knowledge, see Nyiri (1988).

that even if a central authority orders its functionaries to behave as entrepreneurs, they cannot secure an efficient use of resources since the necessary competitive environment does not obtain.

This completes the exposition of Hayek's views about the informational role of the market and of his economic objections to the planned economy.[4] We must now examine how far this epistemological perspective carries *practically*.

THE PRACTICAL IMPLICATIONS OF THE EPISTEMOLOGICAL ARGUMENT

The fundamental economic problem societies face, Hayek says, roots in the fact that the knowledge required for efficient economic activity is dispersed, fugacious, and often latent. He firmly believes that, once the informational nature of this problem has been recognized, important practical conclusions about the structure of a viable economic system suggest themselves almost naturally. His premier conclusion, as we already know from the last section, is that only a market system, but not a planned economy, is a feasible option. Yet he obviously thinks that informational considerations have force beyond deciding the choice of the basic co-ordination mechanism. He also expects the same considerations to yield an answer to the more specific question of what the proper scope of state action should be. He again adduces informational considerations when, in his later writings, he rejects interventionist economic policies. Thus, Hayek's epistemological argument seems extremely powerful. Now it must of course be admitted that to ask what role government should play and whether it should be allowed to correct the economic process makes sense only if the

---

[4] The epistemological role played by the market is perhaps Hayek's single most important theme, and he has returned to it time and again. Apart from the three articles on 'Socialist Calculation' (all repr. in Hayek 1949), the essays most relevant are 'Economics and Knowledge' (orig. 1936/37), 'The Use of Knowledge in Society' (orig. 1945), 'The Meaning of Competition' (orig. 1946), all repr. in Hayek 1949 and 'Competition as a Discovery Procedure' (orig. 1968, repr. in Hayek 1978).

The importance of entrepreneurial alertness to new profit opportunities, though touched upon by Hayek, has been worked out fully only by Kirzner (1973). In an instructive historiographic account Kirzner (1987) describes the unfolding in Austrian economics of the discovery view of the market, showing how the Austrians gradually refined their own position in the course of, and in response to, the socialist calculation debate.

initial question about the basic co-ordination mechanism has already been settled in favour of the market and against central planning. Even though the three issues are in this way related, the practical relevance Hayek ascribes to those informational considerations is nevertheless extraordinary and calls for critical inspection. However, our discussion will be confined to observations of a rather general nature since, as we are only interested here in its directly practical implications, we shall not assess Hayek's epistemological economics in any comprehensive fashion.

In its original form, the epistemological argument aims at a defence of the market—a market, however, of a specific institutional shape. When Hayek maintains that only the market can cope with the manifold fragmentation of economic knowledge, he never leaves a doubt that he has in mind a market based on private property in the means of production. That the market should rest on comprehensive private ownership if it is to play its epistemic role seems to follow inescapably from the kind of problem the fragmentation of knowledge represents. This problem, as we saw, Hayek describes—from the angle of the individual member of society—as the problem of constantly trying to find and exploit 'a better use of things or of one's own capacities' (1960: 81). In the light of this individualist and entrepreneurial conception of economic agents the institution of private property appears as an indispensable precondition of the utilization of fragmented knowledge. That, at least, is the impression Hayek's reasoning conveys. 'If each man is to use his peculiar knowledge and skill', Hayek says, 'it is ... necessary ... that he should have a clearly delimited area of responsibility' (1949: 17, emphasis omitted). What is needed are 'rules which, above all, enable man to distinguish between mine and thine, and from which he and his fellows can ascertain what is his and what is somebody else's sphere of responsibility' (1949: 18).

Perhaps the weakest element in Hayek's reasoning is the individualist and entrepreneurial conception of economic agents. Declaring everybody responsible individually for the position held in the division of labour and the advantages acquired, this conception is not of a universal, anthropological character.[5] It

---

[5] Hayek qualifies this individualist perspective by recognizing heads of family and considering them responsible for the welfare of the family members (see e.g. 1978: 299; 1983: 34). Leaving out this minor complication will not affect the substance of the objection presented here.

introduces into Hayek's account of the problem of fragmented knowledge right from the beginning the idea of self-co-ordination among individuals. This idea seems to leave no solution other than a market of individual owners, making private property appear the obvious and only remedy. But even if one grants Hayek the argument that competition alone can discover the relative scarcities of resources, establish a price-system reflecting them, and in this way generate and spread the information required for an economy that is to be efficient and responsive to people's preferences, one is not thereby logically compelled to regard the institution of private property as the only conceivable solution. At least in theory, market competition may be grounded in property arrangements other than individual ownership in the means of production. Yet, to my knowledge, Hayek contemplates alternative arrangements only once, in the second of his three essays on 'Socialist Calculation' where he discusses competition in market socialism (1949: 148–80). We need not review the more specific reservations he has about such socialism. It suffices to note that the scope of his analysis is unduly restrictive as, on his account of market socialism, the means of production are owned by society, and hence it does not really differ from the planned economy. Hayek never considers genuine alternatives such as a market system in which the principal economic agents are worker-owned co-operatives[6] or a system of mixed property arrangements.

The discussion so far has identified an important limitation of the practical relevance Hayek attributes to his argument about the epistemic role of the market. Contrary to what he implies, that argument cannot by itself establish a case for comprehensive private property, and we must take it for what it is: a brilliant demonstration of why markets are indispensable. What their institutional framework and, especially, their ownership system should be must be decided by other practical, or normative, considerations.[7]

Occasionally, Hayek seems to suggest that, in a second and somewhat different capacity, the epistemological argument might

[6] For a defence of such a type of market socialism, see Miller (1989).
[7] Hayek's individualist and entrepreneurial conception of economic agents does not only prejudge the solution to the fragmentation of knowledge but is too strong in another respect as well. It makes it difficult for Hayek to explain why there should be corporations at all rather than merely clusters of workers trading partly finished products among themselves until they are complete. In other words, that conception does not seem to allow for a theory of the firm. For a discussion of the issues involved here, see Hodgson 1988: ch. 9.

also 'enable us to distinguish between the agenda and the nonagenda of government' (1949: 17). In this Benthamite formula Hayek gives expression to what for liberals is an important concern, namely, the principled demarcation of the proper range of state action. Observing that '[n]either the . . . much misunderstood phrase of "laissez faire" nor the still older formula of "the protection of life, liberty, and property" . . . do . . . tell us what are and what are not desirable or necessary fields of government activity' (1949: 17), Hayek goes on to hint that this demarcation problem may be solved by rules which allow each person to use his knowledge for his own purposes (1949: 17–18). But this suggestion is of doubtful value.

Whatever practical orientation one may be able to derive from the epistemological view of the market, it will be of a far too general nature to give specific guidance as to how the scope of government activity should be delimited. Two problems may illustrate this. The first concerns the definition of consumer freedom. The fragmentation of knowledge can be overcome, Hayek says, if everybody makes himself useful to his fellows, tries as hard as he can to anticipate their preferences, and produces the things they want. This view takes it for granted that the individual is naturally entitled to engage in whatever sort of exchange he deems profitable. It leaves no room for an authority that might rightfully declare certain types of transactions inadmissible. Yet liberals, and others, have long been divided over the extent to which government should be allowed to curb or suppress the production and consumption of things individually or socially damaging and morally dubious. This question of how far the 'free choice of the consumer' (1949: 158) should extend remains to be answered even if in principle one does espouse the market for its epistemic role. In other words, the definition and institutionalization of consumer freedom require antecedent political deliberation and decision. The reasons for adopting a more libertarian, or a more paternalistic, version of consumer freedom cannot be provided by the epistemological view of the market but must derive from elsewhere, for example, from a certain normative conception of individual autonomy.

Another problem illustrating that Hayek's epistemological perspective on the market cannot contribute much to defining the proper scope of state action is the problem of public goods. When

Hayek claims that the market can deal with the fragmentation of knowledge because everybody behaves as an entrepreneur responding to the preferences of others, he presupposes that the things demanded and supplied are all private goods, that is, goods giving the individual exactly the benefits he pays for. Yet not all goods people actually want are of this type. Some are public goods of various sorts, from roads to national defence. These the market does not provide, because a prisoners' dilemma obtains. Everybody would like to see certain public goods supplied and would be willing to pay his share. But fearing that others might withhold their contributions while nevertheless enjoying the benefits, nobody pays, and the good is not provided at all.[8] The practical lesson this dilemma is meant to teach is that there is a role for the state beyond the mere enforcement of the rules of property, contract, and tort. Only the state, the lesson goes, can make everybody pay and thus guarantees the provision of these goods. Hayek is quite prepared to assign to the state the task of supplying a considerable range of public goods (see e.g. 1960: 223; 1979: 43–6), at least as long as the democratic decision to have them does not violate the pre-existing general rules and the principle of proportional taxation (1960: ch. 20; 1979: ch. 14). Yet such pragmatic recognition of the indispensability of the state's role in providing certain goods contradicts his theory which depicts the market as the universal remedy to fragmented economic knowledge. The public goods problem, we may say, reflects more fragmentation than the market can cope with on its own.

Now one might conclude that private goods should be provided in the market and public goods by the state. Yet this suggestion is not particularly helpful because in reality a sharp dividing line between private and public goods does not exist. The intrinsic nature of goods does not tell us very much about their 'publicness'. Goods such as education, health care, and opera houses (which could be, but mostly are not, provided strictly on a market basis) demonstrate that to some degree the identification of certain goods as 'public' ones is a matter of political definition and is influenced by further considerations such as distributional concerns.[9] The

[8] For a concise account of this dilemma, see de Jasay (1989: 60–6). Serious objections to this standard view of the public goods problem are put forward by de Jasay (1989) and M. Taylor (1987).

[9] A point stressed especially by de Jasay (1989).

implication of this appears obvious enough. Which goods, and how much of them, should be provided by the state and financed through taxes cannot be decided on grounds of the informational role of the market. The conclusion is, again, that the 'agenda' of liberal government must be determined largely by considerations other than the epistemic ones on which Hayek places his hopes.

Finally, Hayek wishes to enlist basically the same epistemic considerations against a particular type of state action in the area of economic policy. I have in mind here his argument against the kind of interventionism that grew out of the war economies after 1945 and has, to varying degrees, since come to be relied upon by Western governments. The gist of Hayek's criticism lies in his claim that interventionist economic policies, designed to improve or correct the results produced in the market, fail to achieve their objectives because they must resort to commands, which are incompatible with the market's rule-based co-ordination mechanism and harmful to its information-processing capacities. As he sums up the argument:

The spontaneous order arises from each element balancing all the various factors operating on it and by adjusting all its various actions to each other, a balance which will be destroyed if some of the actions are determined by another agency on the basis of different knowledge and in the service of different ends. (1973: 51)

The practical conclusion Hayek draws is that, as a matter of principle, the market must be left to itself if major co-ordination failures are to be avoided.[10] Now the proper role of government in economic policy is one of the perennial questions of liberal economic theory, and here we cannot even attempt to do justice to its complexity. Two elemental observations throwing, perhaps, some light on the potential force of Hayek's argument must suffice. The first is the concession that government intervention may indeed distort the price-system, sending the wrong signals and encouraging productive activities which are not in the longer run viable. At the same time, and this is the second observation, nothing Hayek says excludes the possibility of endogenous market disturbances and informational uncertainties which only government action can abate. Together these observations suggest that Hayek's

---

[10] Sometimes (1960: 264; 1979: 59) Hayek himself seems to doubt that markets are inherently self-stabilizing.

epistemological considerations are by themselves inconclusive and do not furnish a general argument against any interventionism.[11]

Let us take stock. Hayek's views about the epistemic role of the market have important practical implications. These, however, do not carry as far as he thinks. Contrary to what he suggests, his informational considerations alone do not suffice to justify a claim to the effect that a market only works when it is exclusively based on a system of comprehensive private property. Nor are they of much help in defining the tasks and limits of the liberal state. Nor do they tell decisively against any policy of economic interventionism. Still, Hayek's argument—essentially the contention that only market competition can discover the relative scarcities of resources, establish a price-system mirroring them, and thus provide the information needed for an economy efficient and sensitive to people's wants—represents a genuine insight into the rationale of modern markets and constitutes a powerful explanation of their indispensability.

We can now return to the question that prompted the discussion of this argument in the first place. As will be recalled, the starting-point of our current enquiry was Hayek's highly abstract and not immediately graspable assertion that the fabric of exchange relations developing in a market society is the result of general rule-following and individual adjustment to local circumstances. The present chapter focuses on individual adjustment and aims to elucidate its part within the mechanism of spontaneous order. Making sense of the Hayekian notion of adjustment, I suggested, requires an understanding of the epistemic role he ascribes to the market. Having expounded this role and assessed the practical implications he sees follow from it, we are now able to reconstruct how individual adaptation might be said to conduce to the spontaneous formation of economic order.

INDIVIDUAL ADJUSTMENT AND SPONTANEOUS ECONOMIC ORDER

To comprehend Hayek's claim that spontaneous economic order arises in part from individual adjustment to local circumstances,

---

[11] Hayek's epistemological argument against government intervention is discussed at greater length in Gray (1989: 131–5).

and to see how such adjustment connects with the decentralized utilization of fragmented knowledge, we must look to his entrepreneurial conception of economic agents. On Hayek's view, such agents constantly redirect their activities according to the demands and opportunities of the market. As labourers they untiringly watch for better jobs, and as capitalists they always try to find still more profitable uses for their machines and land, or more promising ventures in which to put their money. They do so because only by being useful to others can they hope to secure for themselves an income. Such permanent adjustment to the exigencies of the market is made possible by the price-system. It informs the participants about what the actual demands and opportunities of the market are. Market prices tell everybody 'in coded form . . . what ought to be done in the present circumstances' (1976: 117, 116). Fragmented knowledge is utilized when economic agents take the right decisions about where to employ their services and resources. These decisions are 'right' if the occupations and forms of investment chosen prove to yield high returns.

It is this continuous reorientation in response to changing price signals that furnishes Hayek with the idea of spontaneous economic order springing from individual adjustment to local circumstances. Market co-ordination, as Hayek writes already in *The Road to Serfdom*, 'leaves the separate agencies free to adjust their activities to the facts which only they can know, and yet brings about a mutual adjustment of their respective plans'. Such decentralized co-ordination, he explains, depends for its success on 'arrangements which convey to each agent the information he must possess in order effectively to adjust his decisions to those of others'. What he terms 'arrangements' here is of course the market price-system, and this he characterizes in not unfamiliar fashion as an 'apparatus of registration which automatically records all the relevant effects of individual actions, and whose indications are at the same time the resultant of, and the guide for, all the individual decisions'. The price-system, he thus goes on to say, 'enables entrepreneurs [i.e. economic agents generally], by watching the movement of comparatively few prices, . . . to adjust their activities to those of their fellows' (1944: 36).

These passages give an account of what I have called individual responsiveness to market prices. In this account, the price-system plays a central role, and any notion of order is absent. This changes somewhat when in his later writings Hayek discusses the market as an instance of spontaneous order. Now he tends to leave out altogether the price-system and its co-ordinating function, and his focus shifts to the formation and preservation of the 'overall order'. So he writes: 'order is achieved by the individuals adjusting themselves to new facts whenever they become aware of them' (1973: 106; similarly in 1976: 11).

Placing earlier and later passages side by side enables us to discern what Hayek exactly means when he identifies individual adjustment as one of the two sources of spontaneous economic order. His idea is this. Economic order, conceived as a web of exchange relations, develops and persists if the participants read the information embodied in market prices correctly and reshape their economic connections accordingly. New opportunities, signalled by the price-system and perceived and exploited by watchful individuals, lead to new exchange relations when altering economic constellations render established business links obsolete. In this sense, individual adjustment and readjustment may be said to generate and maintain economic order. Adjustment, it appears, is indeed a crucial factor of the spontaneous formation of such order.[12]

Hayek portrays individual adjustment largely as an informational process. Individuals adapt to changing market constellations, and preserve the spontaneous economic order, when they react to price signals and take appropriate decisions. This epistemic perspective tends to screen out an important further aspect of the adjustment process: its repercussions on individual welfare. The redirection of productive efforts suggested by the price-system and enforced by the market may affect people seriously, even dramatically. Occasionally, Hayek shows an awareness that the market may make life difficult. Competition, he acknowledges, 'confronts those who depend for their incomes on the market with the alternative of imitating the more successful or losing some or all of their income' (1978: 189). And:

Not only continuous increase, but in certain circumstances even mere maintenance of the existing level of incomes, depends on adaptation to unforeseen changes. This necessarily involves the relative, and perhaps even the absolute, share of some having to be reduced ... (1978: 186–7)

---

[12] 'Individual adjustment' must, in Hayek's social thought, be carefully distinguished from another type of accommodation to which he attaches no less significance. In his theory of cultural evolution, he claims that incessant natural selection leads to some societies being better 'adapted' than others to their environment, thereby increasing their chances of survival and growth. I discuss Hayek's evolutionist adaptationism in Chapter 7.

Severe though the adjustments exacted by 'the hard discipline of the market' (1949: 24) may be, Hayek does not appear to think that they will push many near or below the level of subsistence. He concedes that the 'high degree of coincidence of expectations is brought about by the systematic disappointment of some kind of expectations' (1978: 185) and goes furthest when he allows for a welfare safety net cushioning the most serious consequences (e.g. 1944: 90; 1960: ch. 19; 1967: 175; 1979: 54–6). Yet Hayek never considers the possibility that massive market changes may leave large parts of a population suddenly without access to the most basic goods. But, as Amartya Sen has argued, this is precisely what happened in various famines. People died not because the aggregate availability of food had fallen but because huge price shifts had put it above their reach.[13]

Martin Ravallion has analysed one such case, the 1974 famine in Bangladesh, and concludes that the rice prices were high and unstable largely as a result of speculation. Expected production losses led private stockholders to over-react and hoard rice excessively. Such over-reaction to new price information, Ravallion explains, is not only a general characteristic of rice markets in Bangladesh but was also not countered in the 1974 famine by credible public action. For traders believed that neither the government nor foreign agencies would actually be able to make up for the anticipated shortfall.[14] Now, to be sure, market situations of this sort may be exceptional in various ways. Still, the example drastically demonstrates that there is more to individual adjustment than the informational side Hayek stresses. Moreover, it points to limits of adjustment, showing that sometimes no amount of individual flexibility will suffice to enable people to link up again with the existing web of exchange relations. Finally, it also warns against making the claim about the market's informational capacities an article of faith. As speculative markets illustrate, spontaneous orders may collapse simply because people get the price signals wrong.

Hayek sees individual adjustment not only at the centre of the market's informational function but wants it also to be the core notion in a systems-theoretic account of spontaneous economic order. In various passages, he depicts economic order, the network

---

[13] Sen (1981).   [14] Ravallion (1987).

of exchange relations in a market, as a social entity of its own constantly 'adjusting itself'. Yet in his espousal of such holism or functionalism he simply goes astray.

In Hayek's view, it is the individuals' dependence on a market income that makes them utilize fragmented knowledge and adapt to changing circumstances (e.g. 1976: 75–8, 116–17; 1978: 62–3, 187). This dependence, he suggests, can also be described as a feedback mechanism generating and maintaining economic order. The 'mutual adjustment of individual plans', he thus writes, 'is brought about by what, since the physical sciences have also begun to concern themselves with spontaneous orders, or "self-organising systems", we have learnt to call "negative feedback" ' (1978: 184). It is not implausible to regard the incentives and punishments the market has in store as parts of a method of corrective regulation; in a world where everybody is struggling to make a living, nobody will sustain his specific productive efforts if they remain unrewarded. Yet, tempted perhaps by the seemingly universal applicability of systems theory, Hayek goes on to characterize spontaneous economic order as an entity with a life and reproductive capacities of its own:

we are led to utilise more relevant information when our remuneration is made to depend indirectly on circumstances we do not know. It is thus that, in the language of modern cybernetics, the feedback mechanism secures the maintenance of a self-generating order. (1978: 63)

In similar fashion, he speaks of the 'constant adaptation of the comprehensive order to particular facts' (1978: 11) and of our ignorance of the facts 'to which the whole of social activity continuously adjusts itself in order to provide what we have learned to expect' (1960: 25). However, any holist or functionalist overtones are entirely out of place here. As mentioned, in the individuals' dependence on an income we may indeed see a kind of feedback mechanism explaining why they incessantly engage in exchange transactions, thereby maintaining the web of economic relations Hayek calls spontaneous order. But it is difficult to recognize how this 'economic nexus' (1976: 113) could be a 'self-generating order' that 'continuously adjusts itself' to new particular facts. A pattern of exchange relations, even if it ceaselessly fluctuates, does not contain in itself a capacity either for reproduction or for self-adjustment. Its preservation and renewal is entirely the result of human choice and adjustment, of individuals reading, and reacting to, the facts of their economic situation.

This criticism of Hayek's holist and functionalist vocabulary amounts to more than the mere insistence on terminological precision. There is a fundamental problem lurking here, and it concerns his conception of economic order. 'Order' as understood by Hayek is unable to serve as a standard of comparison, yet he needs such a standard if his claim about order being maintained or restored spontaneously is to make sense. As we already know, Hayekian economic order—the 'economic nexus'—consists in the society-wide pattern of exchange relations entertained between, usually, two parties. Conceived as the total of economic links existing at any one time, such order is amorphous and lacks an ascertainable identity. The most to be said of an actual order is, it seems, that it encompasses more, or less, exchange relations as compared to an earlier point in time. Not being an organic unity with clearly defined contours and internal structures, it cannot be said to re-generate and readjust itself. Some 'nexus' will, in a market economy, always obtain. Lacking a criterion distinguishing order from disorder, Hayek cannot in functionalist fashion talk of individual action tending 'to secure the preservation or restoration of that order' (1973: 39).

This problem, to anticipate a topic discussed in more detail later, remains even if he sheds all functionalist and holist language. The idea of a spontaneous economic order lives on an unexpressed contrast with 'disorder', implying that the distinctness of order lies in its being a *well*-structured, or an especially dense, pattern of economic interactions. Yet Hayek's definition of order as an 'economic nexus' contains nothing that would specify just how well structured or dense a fabric must be if it is to count as 'order', and not as 'disorder'. Thus, however he conceives the process of its unprompted emergence, 'order' is an idea too amorphous to give discriminatory force to his claim about the spontaneous main-tenance of economic order.[15] Even a depressed market economy

---

[15] We also arrive at the same conclusion if we take Hayek's somewhat different though still closely related definition of order as a 'correspondence of expectations' (see e.g. 1973: 36, 38). Order consists in a matching of expectations, he says, but it will always be achieved only at the cost of a systematic disappointment of some expectations (e.g. 1973: 106; 1978: 185). Thus, order is where expectations are and are not met—and the same conceptual haziness ensues.

is, on Hayek's account, still a spontaneous order since some web of exchange relations will always exist.

Examining the idea of a spontaneous economic order, we have now analysed individual adjustment as the first of two components which, Hayek says, together make up the machinery producing such order. The results of the enquiry so far determine the problems to be tackled next. Adjustment, we saw, is vital. Alertness to the price signals of the market and appropriate reorientation of one's productive efforts are essential preconditions of spontaneous economic order. This raises the question of what role there remains for rules, the second component distinguished by Hayek. Seeking an answer is the aim of Chapter 3. Another result concerns the nature of adjustment. We found that individual adaptation to the exigencies of the market involves more than the informational responsiveness in terms of which Hayek usually describes it. Adjustment may be painful. If sometimes spontaneous economic order inflicts severe hardship, we must then ask what the virtues of such order still are. The answer cannot be that it is the fact of its representing order rather than chaos that should make us want it. Clearly, Hayek's conception of economic order is too indefinite to serve as such a value. Nor can the answer lie in the utilization of fragmented knowledge. For the informational capacities of the market are of instrumental significance only and not valuable in themselves. Thus we must find out what, for Hayek, renders spontaneous economic order something uniquely advantageous. This will be the task of Chapter 4. But first we turn to the role of rules.

3
Spontaneous Economic Order: Its Rules

Hayek thinks order in the market is the result of the individuals observing certain rules and adjusting to their specific situation. The significance he accords to rules can hardly be overrated. Often, he does not mention individual adjustment at all, implying that the observance of rules suffices to bring about economic order. He writes, for example, that it is '[t]he obedience to purely abstract rules of conduct that leads to the formation of a social order' (1983: 42) and, similarly, that the order 'into which individual actions are integrated results not from the concrete purposes which individuals pursue but from their observing rules' (1978: 84). In this chapter, we shall discuss the role and nature of those rules.

The first section specifies the rules which, for Hayek, are the 'rules of just conduct' and lead to spontaneous economic order. It shows how those rules may be said to contribute to the emergence of order and describes the institutional form which he thinks they usually take. It explains why in this supposedly social theoretic context he resorts to moral philosophical language and calls them rules of *just* conduct. And it looks at the abstractness and other formal properties that are, in his view, characteristic of those rules. The second section expounds a contrast Hayek draws between rule-governed conduct and purposive action. It presents and criticizes his argument that in modern mass society only rule-guided economic conduct succeeds and purposive behaviour—epitomized in 'economic altruism'—fails. Also, it discusses his view of the market rules as a device for coping with the unknowable consequences of individual economic action. The third section asks how the idea of a spontaneous economic order accommodates the state. Hayek's talk of economic order being the result of rule-following (and adjustment) portrays markets as entirely self-sufficient and self-regulating systems. The section demonstrates that in the idea of such an order the social theorist Hayek denies what the economist Hayek takes for granted: that the state must in various ways supervise and supplemenent the market if instability and collapse are to be avoided. Hayek is again in two minds about another question, giving different accounts of the rules necessary for order in the market. His position usually is the parsimonious one that the required rules are those of 'just conduct'—for him the rules of private property, contract, and tort. Occasionally, however, he insists that additional rules such as 'the rules of the family' must be observed as well, should spontaneous economic order obtain. The final section looks at this comprehensive account, that is, at the further institutions, attitudes, and beliefs which (at least sometimes) he considers no less important for a stable market system. It concludes that the endorsement of such a comprehensive account would force him to abandon his universalist social theoretic ambitions.

One more preliminary remark. Though aiming to offer a detailed analysis of the function and nature Hayek ascribes to rules, the present chapter does not aspire to discuss his views on rules and rule-following exhaustively. Again they are a subject to be taken up later when we discuss Hayek's thesis of tacit rule-following and, in the chapter on cultural evolution, his idea that the market rules embody a social wisdom inaccessible to the human mind.

THE RULES OF JUST CONDUCT

'[T]he importance of the rules of just conduct', Hayek says, 'is due to the fact that the observance of these values leads to the formation of certain complex factual structures' (1973: 110), structures constituting a spontaneous economic order. Yet it is not immediately obvious exactly what rules he has in mind here, why they should be regarded as rules of *just* conduct, and what is special about them.

What do those rules of just conduct—rules whose observance is alleged to bring about spontaneous economic order—consist in? For an answer, we must look to Hayek's analysis of the basic economic problem modern society faces. This, as we saw in the last chapter, is the problem of how to make the fullest possible use of society's dispersed, temporary, and latent economic knowledge. The solution he discerns in the demarcation of 'spheres of responsibility'. Rules should for every member of society define a guaranteed area within which he is free to utilize economic information as he sees fit (1949: 17–18). It is the task of those rules 'to tell each what he can count upon, what material objects or services he can use for his purposes, and what is the range of actions open to him' (1976: 37). Once such a system of rules is established, a spontaneous order will unfold. 'The maximal coincidence of expectations', Hayek thus writes, 'is achieved by the delimitation of protected domains' (1973: 106). It is by creating the necessary institutional preconditions, then, that rules of just conduct may be said to contribute to the formation of spontaneous economic order.

When Hayek says that above all the rules of just conduct 'make it possible . . . to distinguish between the *meum* and the *tuum*' (1973: 107; similarly in 1949: 18), one might infer that they are merely the rules of private property defining exclusive rights over things. For Hayek, this is too narrow a view of the matter. He admits that the rules of just conduct do define property, yet wishes property to be understood 'in the wide sense in which it is used to include not only material things, but (as John Locke defined it) the "life, liberty and estates" of every individual' (1973: 107; similarly in 1967: 167). So property comprises, on Hayek's account, a whole bundle of individual liberties.

The Hayekian rules of just conduct extend beyond property, not only defining the control over things (and one's person) but also regulating the transfer of such control via contract (1976: 37–8, 123; 1988: 30). Moreover they specify entitlements and procedures in cases of tort and restitution. Hayek unambiguously spells out the core content of the rules leading to spontaneous economic order himself when he writes that such order is 'produced . . . through people acting within the *rules of property, tort and contract*' (1976: 109, emphasis added).

What institutional form do the rules of just conduct take? Most of the time, Hayek discusses them as if they were identical with law. This, however, is only his view in a qualified sense.

1. Hayek distinguishes between public law (which he calls 'thesis'), and private and criminal law ('nomos'). Public law defines the organization and activities of government and resembles directives, whereas private and criminal law provide the legal framework of the market. The rules of just conduct, needless to say, he subsumes under the latter category (1976: 34).

2. Not all rules of just conduct manifest themselves in positive law. For Hayek, law is a 'system of rules' comprising 'not only articulated but also not yet articulated rules which are implicit in the system or have yet to be found to make the several rules consistent' (1976: 159 n. 4). Sometimes, as he explains, the existing body of explicit rules is unable to settle a case, and the relevant rules must first be discovered. Recourse may have to be taken to practices already observed but not yet codified legally, or certain rules may be 'found to be required complements of the already established rules if the order which rests on them is to operate smoothly and efficiently' (1973: 123).

3. Not 'every single rule which forms part of a system of rules of just conduct is by itself a rule defining just conduct' (1976: 31). Hayek does not seem to mean here rules of enforcement or rules specifying the procedures by which the rules of just conduct can be altered. Rather, he appears to think of rules that have merely the status of legal definitions or prescribe formal conditions which are binding if certain types of contract are to be valid and to enjoy the protection of the law (1976: 34–5).

4. Rules of just conduct need not, according to Hayek, be part of the legal system but may be adhered to as the result of effective social sanctions. The reason why not all rules of just conduct exist in codified form he sees in their origin. He believes that the rules conducive to spontaneous economic order emerged in a long process of cultural evolution by natural selection and that the consciously legalistic culture characteristic of modern society is only a relatively recent development. That is why, he argues, not all those rules have already been converted into explicit law (e.g. 1976: 34).

So Hayek offers a differentiated picture of the institutional forms the rules of just conduct may take. Still, we will not go wrong if for the purposes of our present discussion we regard those rules as identical with law. Some of the qualifications mentioned above will be examined later, in the chapters on tacit rule-following and cultural evolution.

At first sight, it appears puzzling that he consistently speaks of 'the rules of just conduct' when in fact he means 'the rules conducive to spontaneous economic order'. Why should these rules, whose principal notion is the idea of private property, be seen as the precepts of justice? Hayek's answer interweaves systematic considerations with the effort to uphold the intellectual tradition of the Scottish Enlightenment.

Order, Hayek says, arises from the partition of the world into spheres of individual responsibility. Self-co-ordination operates and order develops once the institution of private property is established. With these observations Hayek wants to remind us of what he believes was, in the past, common knowledge, particularly among the thinkers of the Scottish Enlightenment: that civilization, prosperity, and progress rest on private property (e.g. 1988: 33–5). Now for anyone wishing this insight to have practical import, the problem is obviously how to ensure that the institution of private ownership, and behaviour conducive to economic order in general, receive the attention and allegiance they deserve. For Hayek, the solution consists in declaring them morally sacrosanct. Justice, he explains, 'is an attribute of human conduct which we have learnt to exact because a certain kind of conduct is required to secure the formation and maintenance of a beneficial order of actions' (1976: 70). The protection of private property, in particular, must thus be the foremost demand of justice and the supreme task of government. This view Hayek already finds in the writings, especially, of David Hume and Adam Smith. Indeed, for Hume and Smith, as Hont and Ignatieff note, '[t]he proper province of justice was the enforcement of *suum cuique*, "to each his own", i.e. the rules of property'.[1] And it is from Hume and Smith that Hayek borrows the term 'rules of just conduct' (see e.g. 1976: 185 n. 6).

Behind Hayek's reference to the thinkers of the Scottish Enlightenment we can glimpse his systematic motive for consistently speaking of 'rules of just conduct'. The rules leading to spontaneous economic order are rules of just conduct, he suggests, not because the behaviour they enjoin is to be prized in itself but because great moral value attaches to the prosperity and progress which the conduct specified by those rules brings about. This is instrumentalist moral reasoning, to which we shall return later.

Occasionally, one gets the impression that Hayek regards the rules indispensable for spontaneous economic order as rules of just conduct because they seem to embody a kind of impartiality constitutive of justice. He thus claims that as rules conducive to

---

[1] Hont and Ignatieff (1983: 24).

spontaneous order they necessarily possess certain formal features distinguishing them from other norms.

Hayek thinks that the rules leading to spontaneous economic order—the rules of just conduct—possess three distinctive characteristics: that they are negative, end-independent, and abstract. Apart from a few exceptions, these rules, he says, are *negative*. Negative rules define certain constraints which the individual agent must not overstep, but they leave him otherwise free to pursue whatever goals he wishes. As Hayek explains, 'practically all rules of just conduct are negative in the sense that they normally impose no positive duties on any one, unless he has incurred such duties by his own actions' (1976: 36). Only a few rules of just conduct are not negative. Among the examples Hayek mentions are the duty to assist in danger on the high seas and certain obligations between parents and children (1976: 36).

The paradigm case of negative rules, from which Hayek probably drew his inspiration, are the rules of private property, and the category of 'negativity' may capture an aspect of their nature. But apart from wondering why in the context of a discussion about rules conducive to spontaneous economic order he suddenly talks of the seafarers' duties and of family obligations, we cannot but question his assertion that 'practically all rules of just conduct are negative'. As will be recalled, these rules are, for Hayek, basically the rules of private property, contract, and tort. Considering the rules of contract, we must find it difficult to understand how they could be described as being 'negative'—or 'positive', for that matter. Unlike the rules of property, they do not really constrain freedom of action. Though defining and structuring the legal options available to the individual agent, they constitute provisions enabling him to shape and modify his personal situation. The rules of contract do not disallow certain courses of action but institute certain standard forms of how transactions are to be carried out. An important group of rules conducive to spontaneous order cannot therefore plausibly be said to be 'negative'.

Another feature Hayek considers characteristic of the rules leading to spontaneous economic order is their *end-independence*. The rules of just conduct are 'general purpose tools' (1976: 21) serving the pursuit of a vast range of different individual ends. Observance of these rules, Hayek says, does not in itself promote some particular goal. Being end-independent, they can 'never fully determine a particular action but only limit the range of permitted kinds of action and leave the decision on the particular action to be taken by the actor in the light of his ends' (1976: 37). End-independence may be a feature typical of the rules of private property. Yet, again, it is implausible to characterize the rules of contract primarily as free from, or indeed tied to, specific goals. The institution of contract as a whole, to be sure, may be regarded as a 'multi-purpose instrument' (1976: 4). The various rules together forming that institution, however, are neither end-independent nor goal-oriented. Rather, they specify certain formal and other conditions that must be satisfied should a particular contract be valid and the obligations stipulated be legally enforceable. As such they increase the predictability and certainty in the parties' dealings with one another. While contracts may be subservient to many individual ends, the rules constituting the different types of contracts have specific functions, and 'end-independence' does not contribute to illuminating their character.

Finally, the rules of just conduct, Hayek maintains, are *abstract*. 'What is meant by the term abstract', he writes, 'is expressed in a classical juridical formula that states that the rule must apply to an unknown number of future instances' (1976: 35, footnote omitted).[2]

Hayek believes that negativity, end-independence, and abstractness 'are all necessary characteristics of those rules of just conduct which form the foundation of a spontaneous order' (1976: 36) and that they are important each in its own right. This must be doubted. As we have seen, negativity and end-independence fail to say anything meaningful about the rules of contract, rules vital for spontaneous economic order. Also, contrary to what Hayek assumes, they are not distinct properties. He regards a rule as negative if it does not contain a specific duty to undertake some particular action. Now actions are, in his view, always geared

---

[2] In Hayek's social thought, 'abstract' has at least two further, more specific meanings. In his theory of cultural evolution, the abstractness of rules is intended to signify the idea that rules of conduct do adapt us to the world but do not tell us how their observance intervenes in, and enlists to our advantage, the causal interdependences governing the world (for more on this idea, see Ch. 7, pp. 158–60). When predicated of spontaneous orders, their abstractness is meant to denote the fact that such orders possess certain holist properties which they retain even if the identity and number of the elements constituting the order change. One instance of such abstractness is discussed in Ch. 4, pp. 100–10.

to some goal or purpose or end. Therefore, if a rule is negative, it prescribes neither specific actions nor, hence, specific ends. The conclusion is, unavoidably, that negative rules are necessarily end-independent.

'Abstractness' is problematic in a different way. For Hayek, a rule is abstract when it applies 'to an unknown and indeterminable number of persons and instances' (1973: 50). Abstractness thus understood does not add anything to what we know already. Admittedly, the concept of a rule is not a clear one. But it seems incontrovertible that rules 'cannot be particular and must in some sense be general'. 'What is necessary', Geoffrey Marshall writes, 'is that a rule deals with a class of cases (whether persons, objects, or occasions) and that the necessary degree of generality, whatever it is, can be acquired in any of these dimensions.'[3] This suggests that abstractness is a definitional element of rules. At least once, Hayek explicitly endorses this view himself. In the course of a discussion of 'terminological issues' (1976: 12), when contrasting 'rules' with 'commands',[4] he himself describes rules precisely as 'refer[ring] to an unknown number of future instances and to the acts of an unknown number of persons' (1976: 14). Thus, that the rules leading to spontaneous economic order are abstract is analytically true and says nothing of substance about them.

What remains, then, of Hayek's claim that the rules conducive to spontaneous economic order are negative, end-independent, and abstract? End-independence collapses into negativity, negativity does not apply to all rules, and abstractness is part of the definition of rules. Hence, the most that can be predicated of these rules is that some of them are negative. This, however, is hardly a momentous insight.[5]

RULE-GUIDED CONDUCT AND PURPOSIVE ACTION

So far Hayek's explanation of why rules are a prerequisite of spontaneous economic order is a fairly straightforward one.

---

[3] Marshall (1983: 183–4, emphasis omitted).
[4] Hayek thinks a command 'regularly aims at a particular result', at determining a particular action (1976: 14). Van Loon (1958) argues that a distinction between rules and commands along the dichotomy between generality and particularity does not work because commands too may be general.
[5] For further critical discussion of the formal properties that Hayek thinks render a norm a legal rule of just conduct, see Haakonssen (1988).

Self-co-ordination works and an order of exchange relations develops, he says, if rules demarcate for every person a sphere within which he is free to choose his own productive role and to trade with others. Yet Hayek's belief in the indispensability of rules is rooted also in considerations of a more fundamental nature. So we find him arguing that individuals must exhibit some predictability in their conduct if reliable and mutually beneficial forms of co-operation are to develop in social life; complete behavioural capriciousness would render any division of labour and any spontaneous order impossible. Some rule-following, it seems, is necessary (1960: 153). But Hayek's emphasis on rules is also founded on an argument much more pretentious and complex than this elementary observation. The argument revolves round the instrumental nature of rules and, as far as one can see, has three parts. It starts from a contrast between rule-guided conduct and purpose-oriented action; it then attempts to buttress the case for rule-governed behaviour by trying to show that purposive action in the guise of 'economic altruism' fails; and finally it seeks to make plausible that the rules of the market are a device for coping with the unknowable consequences of individual economic action. This argument we shall now consider.

Human action, Hayek says, is dominated either by purposive orientations or by the observance of rules (1978: 84–5). Purpose-oriented action is led by an 'understanding of the causal connections between particular known means and certain desired ends' (1978: 7), rule-governed action characterized by an unconditional commitment to follow the guidance laid down in the rule, irrespective of specific goals. Purposive action, he thinks, is informed by a kind of instrumentally rational calculation alien to rule-oriented behaviour. Hayek insists that a clear recognition of this difference is vital if disaster is to be avoided in constitutional politics and economic policy. For various reasons, he argues, a purpose-oriented approach instructed by the precepts of instrumental rationality will fail if the desirable end to be realized is the generation of economic order (e.g. 1973: 57–8). To grasp these reasons, we must further work out the differences he sees between purpose-directed and rule-guided action.

There are several important differences. Purposive action aims at achieving short-term results; the rules of the market must be 'applied through the long run' (1976: 29) if they are to generate economic order. The goals envisaged by purposive action are usually definite end-states, whereas a spontaneous economic order represents a complex, fluctuating, process-like state of affairs. Purposive action uses specific means; rule-governed action relies on the guidance embodied in abstract values. Finally, purposive action attains its ends by applying means whose instrumental nature can easily be demonstrated. In contrast, a direct instrumental relation between the observance of the rules of just conduct and the emergence of a spontaneous economic order is not perceivable. People, Hayek says, frequently do not know the function—the 'purpose'—of those rules, sometimes not even their content (e.g. 1973: 11).

Stressing these differences, Hayek strongly implies that the rules of just conduct possess a rationality distinct from the instrumental rationality manifest in purposive action. Yet he believes the nature and value of rule-governed action are not appreciated easily, leading people to dismiss such action as irrational and to regard as rational only action guided by specific purposes and employing specific means. The characteristic contributing most to the air of irrationality is the absence of a visible causal link between the adherence to the rules of just conduct and the development and maintenance of a spontaneous economic order. He thinks this undermines more than any other feature of rule-following the public's allegiance to the market society, as it creates a constant temptation 'to reject all general values whose conduciveness to particular desirable results cannot be demonstrated' and to let oneself 'be guided only ... by explicit particular purposes which one consciously accepts' (1973: 58).[6] His fear is that people fail to recognize what the rules of just conduct accomplish and that, in consequence, they discard the market system, espousing an interventionist regime or, worst of all, a planned economy, whose system of central direction and tight control resembles the structure of purposive action most closely.

However, in spite of Hayek's efforts to distance rule-following from the rationality of purposive action, both purposive and rule-guided action share, on his own account, an important feature.

[6] In addition, Hayek believes that the lack of a manifest causal connection between the observance of the rules of just conduct and the emergence of spontaneous economic order also limits their moral justifiability. For more on this, see Ch. 8, pp. 187–90.

The rules of just conduct no less than the specific means used in purposive action are basically of an *instrumental* nature. That purposive action embodies an instrumental perspective is trivially true since the means are chosen, of course, for their conduciveness to achieving certain specific ends. But in the case of the rules of *just conduct* such a perspective is far from inescapable. Those rules are usually supposed to be observed primarily for other than merely instrumental considerations. One may honour them, for example, because this is simply the right thing to do or because, by following them, a person expresses his nature as a moral being. Yet any notion of rules being observed for intrinsic, moral reasons is alien to Hayek. By insisting that the rules of just conduct are important because they bring about economic order he reveals a plainly instrumentalist perspective. Thus, however he may wish to contrast purposive and rule-guided action, they do not, on his account, differ in their basic orientation, which is one of instrumental rationality.[7]

To strengthen the case for his rules of just conduct, and to expose the inadequacy of any purposive action designed to improve the economic situation of specific people, Hayek puts forward an argument about the self-defeating nature, under modern conditions, of 'economic altruism'. Hayek starts from the assumption that altruism was a moral attitude indispensable in the prehistoric bands and the tribal societies succeeding them. These groups and societies survived because in his productive activities every member was led by an immediate concern for his fellows'

---

[7] Emphasizing the instrumental nature of the Hayekian rules of just conduct does not imply an assertion to the effect that they are the product of human intelligence and inventiveness. They could, as Hayek believes, still be the result of cultural evolution. It hardly needs elaboration that Hayek's purposive action is a crude version of the notion of action used in rational-choice theory, where the individual is conceived of as 'the artificer . . . who fashions the fabric of the social world' (Hollis 1987: 1) according to his desires and in the light of his beliefs. More difficult is the question (which we cannot discuss here) how far his rule-guided conduct can, or cannot, be accommodated in rational-choice theory. While the instrumental nature of those rules does appear to allow an account in terms of rational choice, the unconditional, almost Kantian commitment to follow the rules regardless of specific outcomes suggests otherwise. For a concise statement of explanatory rational-choice theory, see Elster (1985b), for a broad survey and useful guide to the literature Elster (1986). But compare also Elster (1989a; 1989b), where he gives social norms an explanatory role of their own. A subtle philosophical account of how, in social theory, the relation between *homo oeconomicus* (the rational calculator observing rules if this pays off) and *homo sociologicus* (the pure rule-follower or role-player) should be seen is given in Hollis (1987).

needs. But, says Hayek, such economic altruism achieves its aim of creating material circumstances favourable for everybody only under two conditions. The number of people involved must be small, and the individual members' needs must be known (1983: 30–1). In modern society, Hayek argues, these conditions no longer hold, and their absence renders economic altruism anachronistic as 'the individual can no longer know whose needs his efforts do or ought to serve' (1988: 81). In Hayek's view, economic altruism becomes even positively obstructive. '[T]he old impulse to follow inborn altruistic instincts', he warns, 'actually hinders the formation of more extensive orders' (1988: 81), disrupting the social division of labour and depriving society of the advantages of specialization. Under the circumstances of modern society, Hayek maintains, only the observance of the rules of just conduct will guarantee that the members' wants and needs are met. Modern man is able to bestow huge benefits upon his fellows 'not because he aims at or intends to serve the concrete needs of others, but because he observes abstract rules' (1988: 81).

This argument fails doubly. It demonstrates neither the obsolescence, in spontaneous economic order, of purposive action, nor does it succeed in discounting other-regarding motivations and behaviour. The reasons for such failure are the following. The observance alone of the rules of just conduct brings about neither a spontaneous economic order nor the advantages Hayek associates with it. For such order to develop, further activity on the part of the economic agents is required—activity which, as we have seen, he calls individual adjustment and describes as everybody's continuous efforts to anticipate how he could be useful to others. Such responsiveness to the wants and needs of others is exactly of the type of conduct Hayek characterizes as purposive action: everybody must try to find specific means to meet a specific demand. Ironically, Hayek's argument thus shows not the inappropriateness of purposive action but rather its crucial importance for the market process.

The same argument also miscarries in its polemic against 'economic altruism'. To be sure, there is a genuine issue here that must be taken seriously. This is the question of what role self-interest plays within the spontaneous order of the market. Hayek's position is ambiguous. On the one hand, he repeatedly (1944: 44; 1949: 13–15; 1973: 56; 1976: 110, 145, 153 n. 7) and emphatically denies that spontaneous economic order depends on people being selfish. On the other, he recommends individual self-interest as a recipe for economic prosperity. He describes the market, for example, as 'a method of providing benefits for others in which the individual will accomplish most if, within the conventional rules, he pursues solely his own interests' (1978: 65). Elsewhere, he states laconically that 'we generally are doing most good by pursuing gain' (1976: 145; similarly in 1978: 62; 1979: 70). However, the success of a market economy cannot be traced back to the fact that its members seek above all their self-interest. A society is held together not only by the 'economic nexus' but also by a whole web of other social relations and institutions. These may nourish motivations and attitudes which in turn significantly influence the members' economic behaviour and, in the end, the overall performance of an economy. As Sen observes, 'the success of a free market does not tell us anything at all about what *motivation* lies behind the action of economic agents in such an economy. Indeed, in the case of Japan, there is strong empirical evidence to suggest that systematic departures from self-interested behaviour in the direction of duty, loyalty and goodwill have played a substantial part in industrial success.'[8]

Now Hayek not only wants to establish, negatively, that under modern conditions purposive action cannot achieve economic order and prosperity but also, positively, that rule-governed conduct can. We find an argument to this effect adumbrated in his view that the rules of just conduct are 'a device for coping with our ignorance of the effects of particular actions' (1976: 29, similarly on 8–9 and 20–1). The general idea seems to be that economic activity has consequences which, being unknowable, must be contained or channelled by appropriate rules. 'Man has developed rules of conduct', Hayek writes, 'not because he knows but because he does not know what all the consequences of a particular action will be' (1976: 20–1). Still, it is unclear what consequences he actually has in mind, and how he thinks the rules enable us 'to cope' with them.

In modern society, Hayek notes, 'the individual can no longer know . . . what will be the effects of his actions on those unknown persons who do consume his products or products to which he has

---

[8] Sen (1987: 18, footnote omitted).

contributed' (1988: 81). Hayek says here that in an extensive, highly specialized division of labour the individual economic agents cannot usually know who will buy the goods in whose production, at some stage, they were involved, and that they can know even less in which ways the owner will benefit from those goods. It is difficult to recognize how the rules of just conduct would enable us to cope with this ignorance or even why anyone should bother about it at all. As he realizes himself, the market rests on the fundamental tacit convention that its 'economic nexus' represents only a 'means-connected' (1976: 110, 112) order, leaving the individual parties free to make whatever use they want of the things acquired. And Hayek himself argues that the ignorance of how people will use the goods is an indispensable precondition for the market to work. If in every single transaction the parties' personal ends and values would have to be balanced too, most contracts would fail to materialize. But, says Hayek, agreement on means is possible. It 'can to a great extent be achieved *precisely* because it is *not known* which particular ends they [those means] will serve' (1976: 3, emphasis added). So the view of rules as a device for coping with the unknowable consequences of economic activity is, on Hayek's own account, unconvincing, and it is hard to see how it could be made plausible. Other considerations may still show the rules of just conduct to be crucially important. Even if the argument as such founders, it demonstrates again Hayek's instrumentalist perspective. The rules of justice he deems valuable not in themselves but for certain outcomes to which they contribute.

SPONTANEOUS ECONOMIC ORDER AND THE STATE

The idea of a spontaneous economic order portrays the market as a system of co-operation establishing and maintaining itself autonomously, without assistance from an external agency; for a complex division of labour to develop and be preserved, the members of society must only observe the rules of just conduct and adapt to changes in their individual situation. This picture, offered by the social theorist Hayek, diverges radically from the views the political economist Hayek has about the market, as we shall now see.

In his discussion of spontaneous economic order Hayek grants the state a conspicuously subordinate role, tending to treat government as just another of many organizations:

> in all free societies . . . the co-ordination of the activities of all [the] separate organizations, as well as of the separate individuals, is brought about by the forces making for a spontaneous order. The family, the farm, the plant, the firm, the corporation and the various associations, and all the public institutions including government, are organizations which in turn are integrated into a more comprehensive spontaneous order. It is advisable to reserve the term 'society' for this spontaneous overall order . . . (1973: 46–7)

Occasionally, he even banishes the state completely from the scenery of modern market society, for example when he flatly alleges that '[i]t is because it was not dependent on organization but grew up as a spontaneous order that the structure of modern society has attained that degree of complexity which it possesses' (1973: 50). The most he concedes is that in society the organization called government 'occupies a very special position' comparable to 'a maintenance squad of a factory' (1973: 47).[9] Still, the idea of a spontaneous economic order presents the market society largely as a self-organizing and self-stabilizing system.

When discussing the market from an economist's viewpoint, Hayek does not regard it as a mechanism capable of running on its own. Rather, he acknowledges that a market system requires monitoring, correcting, and supplementing if it is to perform acceptably and that such regulation falls to the government. Nowhere does he offer a comprehensive account of the role of the state, but in his writings we may discern six different tasks of government, each reflecting, and responding to, a different kind of potential market instability or market deficiency. These tasks are the following.

1. The state must enforce the rules of just conduct. '[I]n most circumstances', Hayek explains, 'the organization which we call government becomes indispensable in order to assure that those rules are obeyed' (1973: 47). Without the protection of the

---

[9] The spontaneous *economic* order we are talking about seems to differ from the 'spontaneous overall order' of *society* discussed by Hayek. However, a discrepancy does not really exist for he thinks society is held together 'mainly by what vulgarly are called economic relations' (1976: 112). Thus, society and economy are, on his account, largely coterminous.

individuals' spheres of self-determination, he seems to fear, social order may degenerate into civil strife.

2. Legislature and courts must adapt the existing system of rules to the social and technological changes inevitably brought about by the dynamics of modern market society. Mostly such adjustment consists in a modification of the right to property and aims at internalizing as far as possible the negative spill-over effects resulting from particular uses people make of things they own. Yet sometimes, Hayek says, no such internalization is feasible, 'and altogether new conceptions of how to allocate control ... may have to be found' (1973: 109). One must assume that the administration of such 'alternative forms of regulation' (1960: 369) again requires some involvement on the part of the state.

3. It is a task of the state to facilitate the market process in various ways. Interestingly, Hayek thinks this applies especially to the provision of information. '[T]hough one of the most efficient instruments for coveying information', the market, he admits, will 'function more effectively if the access to certain kinds of information is free' (1979: 60). Hayek wants the state not only to offer a good general education (1979: 60–2) but also to collect and provide 'many kinds of information ranging from land registers, maps, and statistics to the certification of the quality of some goods or services offered in the market' (1979: 44, similarly on 62). Also, the state should set the standards for weights and measures (1960: 223; 1979: 44).[10] As Hayek recognizes, the market will not on its own produce these services, even though they are essential for its smooth functioning (1979: 44). To enable the state to carry out some of these tasks he even entitles it to override the rules of private property (1979: 62–3). Moreover, Hayek admits that frequently the rules of just conduct alone do not suffice to guarantee statisfactory outcomes, and he argues that the government should introduce additional rules such as '[b]uilding regulations, pure food laws, the certification of certain professions, ... restrictions on the sale of certain dangerous goods (...), as well as some safety and health regulations' (1979: 62).

[10] Concerning the issue of money, Hayek's position changed. While he once saw 'the provision of a reliable and efficient monetary system' (1960: 223) as an important function of government, in the 1970s he argued vehemently in favour of a *Denationalisation of Money* (London: Institute of Economic Affairs, 2nd edn., 1978), that is, for a system of competing private currencies.

4. The state must keep in check potentially self-destructive tendencies inherent in the market process. It must arrange for a social safety net, a uniform minimum income for those unable to make a living in the market (1944: 28, 90; 1960: 285–305; 1967: 175; 1976: 87, 136; 1978: 64, 92; 1979: 54–6, 142). The market society has a moral duty to help the poor, Hayek declares, for it was its dynamic that broke up the traditional family ties and the social security they offered (1960: 285; 1979: 55). Yet he also suggests that sheer prudence dictates the implementation of a safety net, arguing that some such arrangement might not least be 'in the interest of those who require protection against acts of desperation on the part of the needy' (1960: 285). Left to itself, it seems, the spontaneous order of the market may produce a measure of 'discontent and violent reaction' (1979: 55) that could jeopardize even its institutional foundations.[11]

The market harbours another self-destructive or, at least, self-inhibiting tendency. Though not opposed to monopolies in principle, Hayek wants the state to intervene if a monopoly uses its power to coerce other economic agents into a specific behaviour or to deter potential competitors from entering the market. Monopolistic misconduct 'clearly ought to be curbed by appropriate rules', and people affected by it should be granted the right to claim damages (1979: 84–5).

5. The state must provide certain goods which the market does not supply because it cannot overcome the free-rider problem and fully exclude from the benefits those unwilling to pay. Among those public goods Hayek counts not only national defence and roads but also such things as theatres and sports grounds. He thinks it is not necessary that the state should actually produce all those goods itself. As far as possible, that is to be left to the market. What is crucial is that the state should use its coercive power to establish and enforce the compulsory system of financing them, thereby ensuring that everybody contributes (1979: 41–64).

6. Finally, the state may have to intervene in times of market contraction. As Hayek remarks, '[n]obody will deny that economic

---

[11] Hayek insists that a social safety net would be entirely compatible with the functional requirements of a market system (e.g. 1944: 28; 1976: 136). What he objects to, and regards as inimical to the very rationale of the market, is the attempt to subject the income distribution as a whole to some criterion of 'social' or 'distributive' justice (e.g. 1960: 289; 1976: 136; 1979: 55).

stability and the prevention of major depressions depends in part on government action' (1960: 264). What such action might consist in Hayek describes as follows:

> it is merely common sense that government, as the biggest spender and investor whose activities cannot be guided wholly by profitability, and which for finance is in a great measure independent of the state of the capital market, should so far as practicable distribute its expenditure over time in such a manner that it will step in when private investment flags, and thereby employ resources for public investment at the least cost and with the greatest benefit to society. (1979: 59)

The only problem with 'this old prescription' is the inertia of the government machine '[t]o bring about the required changes in the rate of governmental investment promptly enough to act as a stabilizer, and not, as is usually the case, with such delays that they do more harm than good' (1979: 59). By allowing such intervention Hayek concedes that the spontaneous order of the market is not a self-stabilizing system or, if it is, that it reaches a stable condition only after prolonged and socially costly adjustment processes.[12]

As this catalogue of governmental tasks reveals, for the economist Hayek the market is not the self-regulating system of social cooperation that the social theorist Hayek wants us to see. When in his idea of a spontaneous economic order he ranks government merely as one among numerous other organizations, he contradicts a core message of his own political economy: that an outside agency, the state, must supervise, correct, and supplement the economic process and mend its institutional framework if a modern market system is to produce acceptable outcomes. When he explains the complexity of modern Western society as entirely the result of spontaneous self-correction, he forgets that in his own agenda for state activity he argues for a considerable measure of central direction. There are empirical and analytical reasons why the social theorist Hayek cannot be right. As historical sociology shows, the state[13] has everywhere had a major part in the rise of capitalist

---

[12] I leave out of consideration Hayek's early views on the possibilities of governmental interventionism, contained in his books of the 1930s (1931; 1933a; and 1939). For more on these, see Barry (1979: ch. 8).

[13] 'State' here means the type of state as it developed in Western Europe from the Middle Ages onward. The state conceived as a comprehensive organization, controlling a certain geographic area and holding a monopoly of power, has

society.[14] And it is hard convincingly to counter the essentially Hobbesian argument that the state cannot be on a par with firms and individuals if it is not to become embroiled in their quarrels, thereby losing its authority. The state cannot be just another player in the market game but must be its organizer and umpire.

Its failure to accommodate the state drastically diminishes the explanatory force of the idea of a spontaneous economic order. Emphasizing the observance of the rules of property, contract, and tort, this idea points to important background institutions of the market society. Yet it does not offer a conceptual framework that is sufficiently differentiated to explain how in modern Western society a complex division of labour came about and how it is sustained. Self-co-ordination, though vital, is only part of the answer. Elements of co-ordination by central direction are equally indispensable. Only a theoretical account recognizing the interplay between self-co-ordination *and* central direction can hope to achieve an adequate understanding.

MORE RULES

The idea of a spontaneous economic order lacks analytical strength quite apart from the fact that it ignores the state. The only background institutions it considers necessary for an economic order to form are the rules of property, contract, and tort. Such parsimony makes it a highly ambitious social theoretic notion, suggesting a universal range of application. Whenever and wherever those rules of just conduct are established and enforced, the claim seems to be, a complex modern division of labour will ensue.

Occasionally, however, Hayek makes the spontaneous formation of economic order dependent on the existence of further social institutions and the observance of additional rules and attitudes.

evidently a much richer historical morphology. Regarding the relationship between state and economy, the two features most clearly distinguishing the European state from its counterparts in Imperial China and in the Islamic culture are, according to Hall (1985; 1986; 1988) and Mann (1986), the limited arbitrariness and the relatively high degree of infrastructural penetration. Hall and Mann employ these notions in their explanations of why capitalist economies developed only in the West but not in the oriental world.

[14] There is a vast literature on how the modern Western state has been interacting with the economic system in order to keep it going. Hall (1985) gives an account and provides a short bibliographical essay.

This presents him with a dilemma. In its parsimonious version the idea of a spontaneous economic order appears too abstract to say very much about the nature of, and the conditions required for, a successful market society. Yet if he introduces too many further rules and qualifications into the idea, it may no longer hold universally, losing in theoretical scope. This section expounds those amplifications and briefly discusses how they bear on Hayek's theoretical enterprise.

Though Hayek does not always distinguish them clearly and nowhere presents a comprehensive account, we find him talking about at least five different groups of social and cultural background conditions required should a market system be stable and flourish.

1. Hayek assumes that the members of a market society must possess certain capitalist and competitive attitudes. They must, he says, be economical, save and reinvest rather than consume the fruit of their labour. Hayek conceives of the capitalist attitude as a 'responsibility' of the individual and describes it as the 'duty . . . to build up capital, both for his family and for his business' (1983: 34; similarly in 1979: 164–5). The market requires not only a capitalist but also a competitive mentality. The 'morals of . . . exchange' (1987b: 231) include 'the practices of finding customers, of competing with other sellers, of having to find an occupation' (1983: 34) and of 'money lending with interest' (1983: 31). Moreover, individuals must be economically rational, 'normally prefer[ring] a larger return from their efforts to a smaller one, and . . . increas[ing] their efforts in a particular direction if the prospects of return improve' (1973: 45). This also means that prices are not to be fixed according to custom but should be set in anticipation of what the market will yield (1979: 161).

2. The members of a market society must hold fast firmly to specific moral conceptions of individual responsibility and economic justice (1967: 231–2). Let us look first at responsibility. Hayek believes a market society cannot last if its members do not accept that they are wholly responsible themselves for their position in the distribution of incomes (1960: 71; 1978: 299). He sees the significance of such responsibility in its socially beneficial consequences. To make the individual member accountable for his economic situation 'forcefully directs his attention to those circumstances that he can control as if they were the only ones that

mattered' (1960: 71). Explaining the function of economic responsibility retrospectively, Hayek notes that '[t]he aim was to make it worth while for people to act rationally and reasonably and to persuade them that what they would achieve depended chiefly on them. This last belief . . . had a wonderful effect in developing both initiative and circumspection' (1967: 232). For Hayek, then, this conception of responsibility forms part of an overall moral and institutional design by which man, who 'was by nature lazy and indolent, improvident and wasteful' (1949: 11; 1960: 61), could be induced, even forced, 'to contribute as much as possible to the need of all others' (1949: 13; likewise in 1976: 74).

One would assume that a moral conception of responsibility holds individuals accountable only for what the average person can control. Yet Hayek wants individuals to be made responsible for something largely outside their powers, as he frankly admits. Hayek speaks here of a 'real dilemma' (1976: 74). On the one side, he treasures the discipline which the belief in economic responsibility exercises. On the other, he concedes that the underlying presumption that a person's economic situation depends solely on his own efforts is 'not entirely correct' (1967: 232), is 'partly erroneous' (1976: 74), and possibly even 'largely false' (1960: 83). For it is one of Hayek's recurring themes that the distribution of incomes in the market is analogous to a 'game' and its outcome determined by effort, skill, and, importantly, luck (e.g. 1976: 71, 115, 126).

The stability of an economic system must be doubted if its morality rests on knowably wrong factual assumptions about the control people can have over their lives. Moral exhortation designed to improve the system's performance may easily have the opposite effect and generate outrage once wider parts of the population, and especially the underprivileged, realize its ideological falsity. Yet Hayek appears to hope that the deceit simply goes unnoticed. The question of 'whether without such partly erroneous beliefs the large numbers will tolerate actual differences in rewards which will be based only partly on achievement and partly on mere chance' (1976: 74) he obviously answers in the negative, fearing that without those 'partly erroneous beliefs' the whole machinery of individual exertion induced by the market incentives would break down and leave everyone worse off.

The morality of the market society, Hayek says, must also

include a specific conception of economic justice. It must be every-body's moral conviction that an economic system is just if it allows the individual 'to keep what his fellows are willing to pay him for his services' (1967: 233). In other words, everybody has to accept as just what is the result of voluntary exchange. Hayek is undoubtedly right when he thinks that the members' moral beliefs about what is just should not consistently be disappointed by the way in which the social system they belong to actually distributes benefits. Otherwise that system will deplete its legiti-macy. He thus concludes that in the market society any notion of 'distributive' justice in line with some premeditated principle is dysfunctional, and he regards as particularly inept the view that justice requires rewarding people according to moral desert (1960: 93–9; 1967: 231–3; 1976: 62–100). Still, at best Hayek is here making a moral-psychological observation. As he occasionally does not seem to realize, the question of whether a market system *is* just must be approached differently.

3. Hayek believes a market society will survive and prosper only if the family is a well-entrenched institution. One of the functions he attributes to the family is that of passing from one generation to the next not only material property but also behav-ioural patterns indispensable in a market society (1960: 90–1). Also, Hayek mentions the beneficial effects the institution of the family has on children as well as on the whole of society. A person raising his children himself (and not leaving their education to some sort of Platonic communism) feels more responsible for, and is more directly concerned about, their life prospects. Hayek trusts that such a person will therefore be inclined to adopt a long-term perspective not only generally but also, and especially, in his eco-nomic decisions. In this way, he thinks the institution of the family introduces into economic reasoning a measure of circumspection and foresight advantageous not only to the individual child but ultimately also to the market society as a whole, for it will con-tribute to reducing the misallocation and waste of resources (1976: 9–10). Finally, Hayek thinks the market society cannot do with-out the family because it serves to domesticate male sexuality. He compares the institution of the family to the right of private prop-erty, suggesting that both demarcate a protected area upon which third parties must not infringe (1987a: 37–8).

4. Hayek maintains that the mechanism of self-co-ordination

characteristic of the market society works only if its members show 'a high degree of voluntary conformity' (1960: 62) to the established conventions and traditions. Hayek argues that beyond the rules of just conduct there are rule-based arrangements— conventions—whose observance greatly facilitates the market process because it introduces a degree of predictability which is generally beneficial (1949: 23; 1960: 62). The unwillingness to submit to such conventions may take various guises. People may follow a misconceived ideal of a fulfilled life, obsessed with the development of their individual personality and thereby posing 'a grave obstacle to the smooth working of an individualist system' (1949: 26). Or, he says, they may have succumbed to a rationalistic ideology recommending that conventions and traditions should be observed only if their usefulness has been proved (1949: 22–7; 1960: 63–5).

Conventions may not only be important because their observance makes everybody's behaviour more predictable. As Hayek does not seem to see, they may also considerably increase the extent to which a market system is open to informally directed stabilization. G. L. S. Shackle has graphically described the market as being

subject to sudden landslides of re-adjustment to a new, precarious and ephemeral, pseudo-equilibrium, in which variables based on expectation, speculative hope and conjecture are delicately stacked in a card-house of momentary immobility, waiting for 'the news' to upset everything again and start a new dis-equilibrium phase.[15]

Such capriciousness is not, however, a natural condition of market societies in general. Economic self-co-ordination always operates against the background of specific social and cultural attitudes which may curb, or favour, the market's volatility. Social conventions may exclude certain dynamic business practices regarded as 'disruptive' and channel competition by clearly delimiting the areas within which it is 'free'. Government may be seen as an authority whose recommendations, even if issued only informally, ought to be followed. Such conventions may be backed by a system of social sanctions so powerful as to deter any potential freerider. Conventions of this kind are to be found in societies like Japan's, where the degree of conformity, not only in life generally

---

[15] Shackle (1972: 433).

but also in the economic sphere, seems to be much higher than in Western European and North American societies. The submission to such informal norms greatly increases the possibilities of governing and stabilizing social order. A society with a high degree of conformity and a subtle system of 'non-interventionist' direction is better able to cope with the shifts and fluctuations inherent in the market than the more 'anarchic' or 'individualist' societies of the West.

5. Lastly, Hayek claims market society will survive only if its members adhere to their inherited religious beliefs. It was religious convictions, he thinks, that made groups stick to certain economic practices long enough to give cultural evolution time to select those most beneficial. Without the support some religions gave to the institutions of the family and of private property modern market society would not have arisen (1983: 48; 1987b: 231–2; 1988: 56–7, 136–7). Such support, Hayek insists, is still significant; even today many people do not recognize the market's uniquely beneficial character. Therefore, he concludes, we still need religion as an element of stability: 'the loss of these beliefs... creates great difficulties' (1988: 137).[16]

We have already seen how in his advocacy of individual responsibility Hayek is prepared to endorse as ideologically indispensable a belief which he thinks is in fact false. He exhibits a similar tendency with respect to religious convictions. Taking an agnostic stance himself (1988: 139–40), Hayek declares that these beliefs are 'not true—or verifiable or testable—in the same sense as

[16] Hayek's account of the link between people's religious convictions and the rise and persistence of the market society seems to suffer from a basic contradiction. As we have seen, Hayek claims it was religious beliefs favouring the family and private property that kept market systems 'alive' long enough to become those selected by cultural evolution. In *idealist* fashion, he thereby assumes that religious ideas crucially determine whether or not a particular type of social system survives. That is also why he attributes an important role to religion, even in today's world in which market systems are safely established. At the same time, Hayek offers an explanation of why certain religions spread and became world religions. 'Among the founders of religions over the last two thousand years, many opposed property and the family. But the only religions that have survived are those which support property and the family' (1988: 137, emphasis omitted; similarly in 1987a: 42–3 and in 1983: 48). Hayek implies that on its evolutionary path forward the market society took with it only religions granting the family and private property important roles, and pushed aside all religions functionally incompatible with market institutions. The underlying assumption here is that it is the market society and the unfolding of its institutions in the course of history that determines which religious beliefs people will hold. This is an unambiguously *materialist* position.

scientific statements' (1988: 137), that they are even 'myths' (1987*a*: 42), ranking with 'superstition' (1988: 157), and actually 'false' (1988: 57). Again we can only doubt the stability of a type of society that manages to secure the allegiance of its members only if it relies on beliefs which under modern conditions of religious pluralism and secularism are no longer shared by a majority.

We have identified five clusters of social and cultural background conditions which, according to Hayek, are required beyond the rules of property, contract, and tort if a spontaneous economic order is to develop and last: capitalist and competitive attitudes, specific moral conceptions of individual responsibility and economic justice, the institution of the family, a psychological and intellectual disposition unreservedly to accept the established conventions and traditions of social intercourse, and finally certain religious creeds.

Hayek's belief in the indispensability of these conditions gets his theoretical enterprise into trouble. Contradicting his own idea of a spontaneous economic order, Hayek does not actually think that the observance of the rules of property, contract, and tort suffices to explain the formation of order in the market; on his own account, the idea is too parsimonious to serve its theoretical purpose. Hayek might eliminate this inconsistency simply by building those social and cultural conditions into the idea as well. Its claim would then be that spontaneous economic order depends on a unique set of specific legal norms, social institutions, economic orientations, religious beliefs, and cultural attitudes. Indeed, at least once we find Hayek surmising that '[t]here may exist just *one* way to satisfy certain requirements for forming an extended order' (1988: 17, emphasis added). Yet such a claim is implausible.

While the legal system of a market society must in itself certainly be more or less consistent, the cultural and social background conditions need not, and probably never do, form a functionally tight framework that is tailored in its entirety exactly to the functional demands of the market process. In modern market societies (that is, in modern societies where markets play an important role), there exists a pluralism of partly conflicting, partly compatible social practices, beliefs, and attitudes, many of which are undoubtedly supportive of the market system while others are neutral and still others subversive of it. Also, as a look across the globe reveals, markets work under social and cultural conditions that vary greatly. Even if one concedes that the operation of a market system is not compatible with any sort of social practices, moral convictions, and religious beliefs, this does not warrant the conclusion that it works only if certain specific conditions exist.[17] Hayek's claim about the necessity of particular background conditions has the appearance of a somewhat disguised description in abstract terms of a historically and geographically specific type of market society, perhaps that of Western European and North American societies in the 1950s and 1960s.

What if Hayek relinquishes his specific list of indispensable background conditions, acknowledging that they can vary considerably? Such a move would bring him somewhere near the older German Historical School of Wilhelm Roscher, Bruno Hildebrand, and Karl Knies. This school of economic thought emphasized the individuality of each single national economy and stressed the important role specific institutions, habits, customs, and beliefs must play in any satisfactory explanation of economic life. Of course, an economic science more sensitive to the peculiarities of several national economies is to be had only at the cost of renouncing the universalist ambitions epitomized in the idea of a spontaneous economic order. This is a price Hayek is not willing to pay. Though feeling at one with what he regards as the Historical School's main critical thrust,[18] he strongly opposes its 'anti-theoretical bias' (1952a: 65). Hayek clearly fears that too much explanatory emphasis on specific background conditions would deflect the focus from the fundamental, and basically simple, 'causal' relation between the rules of private property, contract, and tort and the emergence of order, replacing social and economic *theory* by turning it into social and economic *history*, a discipline (in his view) essentially narrative, not interested in systematically recurring causal relations, and not teaching any lessons that are universally valid.

[17] For more on Hayek's functionalism, see Ch. 7.
[18] While commonly considered a reaction against the universalism, abstractness, and cosmopolitanism of English classical economics, in Hayek's somewhat idiosyncratic interpretation the older German Historical School objects above all to what he calls 'French Rationalism', the view that social and economic institutions are, or should be, the product of conscious design (1952a: 64–5, 84–5).

4

Spontaneous Economic Order:
Its Beneficial Nature

Having in the last two chapters reconstructed and discussed the mechanism of spontaneous economic order, we shall now consider Hayek's claim about the inherently beneficial character of such order. Hayek does not confine himself to an explanatory perspective, merely giving an account of how in the market society individual adjustment and rule-following bring about and sustain economic order. He never leaves room for doubt that he also regards such order as uniquely advantageous, writing, for example, that 'the maintenance of a spontaneous order of society is the prime condition of the general welfare of its members' (1976: 6). Hayek, it seems, offers two arguments destined to lend force to this claim. The first, more hinted at than spelled out, is the argument from the mutually advantageous nature of uncoerced exchange, the second the argument from the market's efficiency.

MUTUAL GAIN FROM UNCOERCED EXCHANGE

Hayek nowhere explains in any detail how, based on the idea that uncoerced exchange is mutually advantageous, spontaneous economic order can be shown to be generally beneficial. Yet without question there is, in his work, an argument to that effect. Roughly, it runs as follows.

The things in the world are often not yet with the person who wants them most. Hence, everybody can improve his situation if there is room for exchange. This, Hayek says, is an insight already attained long ago: 'It was the simple recognition that different persons had different uses for the same things, and that often each of two individuals would benefit if he obtained something the other had, in return for his giving the other what he needed' (1976: 109). Exchange, as he elsewhere states with aphoristic brevity, 'is productive; it does increase the satisfaction of human needs from available resources' (1988: 95). In order that exchange should become possible and its benefits could be reaped, two institutions were needed, private property and contract: 'All that was required to bring this about was that rules be recognized which determined what belonged to each, and how such property could be transferred by consent' (1976: 109, footnote omitted). These rules, as we know, Hayek calls 'rules of just conduct'.

In outline we can now see what Hayek's argument must be. It starts from the premiss that voluntary exchange is mutually beneficial, the supposition being that a person only engages in exchange if on balance the transaction is to his advantage. The enforcement of the rules of just conduct prevents[1] coercion among the trading parties, guaranteeing that any exchange relation is entered into voluntarily—and, hence, is advantageous on all sides. What holds for each single market transaction, the argument then goes, must equally hold for any aggregate of exchange relations. So the conclusion is that if each single market relation is advantageous, the whole web of exchange relations existing in a market society— its spontaneous economic order—must be advantageous too. I take Gray to be referring to the same argument when he writes approvingly that '[s]pontaneous order generalizes the insight contained in the theory of peaceful trading, that voluntary exchanges . . . are to mutual benefit'.[2]

If this is an argument intended to show that, for its members, a spontaneous economic order is systematically beneficial, it fails. The most obvious deficiency concerns the tacit assumption that everybody is integrated into the economic web. This assumption is vital for the inference that, since participating in that web is advantageous, membership in the market society and, thus, the market society itself are beneficial. It is an empirical and contingent matter whether all members are really woven into the economic nexus. We do not find it difficult to imagine people who, though formally subject to the rules of the market, remain outside the economic web because of their inability to offer anything the market would reward. That such disconnectedness is no mere possibility

[1] Or, at least, enforcement of the rules precludes the more serious forms of coercion. Hayek says he knows 'of no way of preventing coercion altogether and that all we can hope to achieve is to minimize it or rather its harmful effects' (1967: 348; similarly in 1960: 138–9).   [2] Gray (1986: 124).

but a hard fact of life Hayek himself acknowledges when he advocates a minimum safety net for the old, the disabled, and the unemployed (e.g. 1960: 285–305). Contrary to what the argument assumes, he thereby concedes that the market society often fails to make everybody part of its economic fabric. This amounts to the admission that economic self-co-ordination and spontaneous economic order are not always beneficial generally.

Hayek might object by saying that a market society creates enough wealth to permit it to look after those unable to earn a living on their own. He may have this in mind when he remarks, for example, that '[a] society relying on the market order . . . is likely fairly soon to reach an overall level of wealth which makes it possible for this minimum to be at an adequate level' (1978: 92). Whether true or not, this claim cannot rescue the argument. The institution of a social safety net, the provision of benefits for those falling outside the market, requires collective action, something a system of voluntary exchanges cannot accomplish by itself. It may well be that the market society produces a larger output than any alternative economic system. But should the benefits of such abundance reach all members systematically, society must resort to a mechanism other than economic self-co-ordination. Since on Hayek's own admission a market society is advantageous for all its members only if it also pursues redistributive policies, its general beneficence cannot be traced back to the principle that voluntary exchange is mutually rewarding.

As we have seen, the pure market society cannot be said to be beneficial for everybody because there will always be members who, incapable of linking in to the web of exchange relations, have no access to the things they would need for a minimally tolerable life. To those outside the market fabric the premiss that voluntary exchange is mutually advantageous simply does not apply. Yet this premiss can hardly say anything at all even about the well-being of those who do form part of the spontaneous economic order.

Remember: the Hayekian argument is that the spontaneous order of the market society, consisting in innumerable voluntary exchange relations, is beneficial for everyone participating in it because it embodies in generalized form the principle that uncoerced exchange is mutually advantageous. Stressing the cumulative acquisition of advantages through reiterative exchange, the argument crucially assumes that the web of exchange relations is so closely knit, and so shot through with manifold opportunities, as to make it possible for all to attain a satisfactory level of welfare. But by making this assumption it banks on rather improbable circumstances.

Hayek is quite clear that some market expectations will regularly be frustrated (e.g. 1976: 107, 124–5)—he even regards such disappointment as functionally indispensable if the market is to fulfil its co-ordinating role and continuously eliminate the misallocation of resources. Hayek accepts that this can cause individual hardship, though he thinks it will usually be merely of a temporary nature. For he firmly believes that ' "on the whole" and in the long run' (1976: 115) the market will work out to everybody's advantage. Hayek's belief is informed by the idea that participation in the market is akin to a game which, if played often enough, will distribute luck (and misfortune) more or less evenly, giving everybody a fair share. Indeed, the idea of the market being a game is one of his favourite metaphors (e.g. 1976: 70, 115–20, 126; 1978: 60–5).

Now it cannot be denied that market success depends partly on chance and thus does resemble a game. Even so, the metaphor is profoundly misleading. In a game, after every round the cards are reshuffled anew, giving each player the opportunity for a fresh start from the same base-line. In the market process, however, the chances of success are very much determined by the initial distribution of wealth, which is hardly ever equal or near-equal and which tends to become even less so with each further 'round'. As Hayek himself observes, 'we do not at every moment have to start from scratch, but can begin with equipment which is the result of past efforts' (1976: 124). And, most explicitly, he concedes that '[i]n a sense it is even true that such a system gives to those who already have' (1976: 123, similarly on 130–1). Such a system is hardly a game. For why should those who start without an adequate initial endowment and are thus on the losing side right from the beginning want to play it at all? With Hayek's rare and always oblique admission that, unavoidably, there exists 'inequality' (1960: 42), even 'great inequality' (1976: 83),[3] the argument deriving the universally beneficial nature of the market society from the

---

[3] Economic inequality is, according to Hayek, not only unavoidable but also indispensable. It is inequality, he thinks, that spurs the members of the market society on to achievement, growth, and progress (e.g. 1960: 42–5).

premiss that voluntary exchange is mutually advantageous lacks an essential empirical link. The generalizing inference on which the argument relies would be valid only if the opportunities were roughly the same for all members. On Hayek's own account, this condition does not obtain.

We do not have to pursue this argument further as its flaws are too obvious. The principle that voluntary exchange is mutually advantageous not only says nothing about how well off overall a trading party is, it cannot say anything definite either about the institutional structure and the 'mix' of co-ordinating mechanisms an economic system beneficial for all its members should adopt. To be sure, markets must be given ample scope. But as the public goods-problem reminds us, certain preferences cannot be met over the market. And, in the end, Hayek is (as we know from the last chapter) quite prepared to allow the state to step in where the market fails. Finally, we should only mention, but need not further probe, the difficulties besetting the initial premiss itself. The applicability of the principle that voluntary exchange is mutually advantageous depends on an unambiguous notion of uncoerced choice, and that means on a consistent definition of coercion. Yet Hayek's view of coercion is notoriously problematic.[4] Not least, it leaves room for the prospect that certain market transactions are coercive.[5] If this possibility is admitted, the argument never gets off the ground, for then not all market exchange can be said with certainty to be mutually beneficial.

MARKET EFFICIENCY

Hayek advances a second argument designed to redeem the claim that the economic order forming in the market society is, for its members, uniquely advantageous. This is the argument from the market's efficiency. Its starting-point is the assumption that market economies are more productive than alternative economic systems, and its core contention the claim that in a spontaneous economic order 'the chances of anyone selected at random are likely to be as great as possible' (1976: 132). One problem with

[4] See Hamowy (1961: 28–31); Barry (1979: 71–5); Rothbard (1982: 219–28); Demsetz (1988: 281–92); Kukathas (1989: 149–53).
[5] For illustration and a brief discussion, see Kukathas (1989: 152).

this argument is that the claim issuing from it is far from clear. There are two questions in particular calling for an answer. What sort of opportunities is 'chances' intended to mean? And, in which sense can an economic system maximizing the chances of 'anyone selected at random' be said to be beneficial for each of its members?

While the argument pivoting on the mutual gains of voluntary exchange attempts to derive the beneficial nature of spontaneous economic order from the benefits of the individual transactions constituting that order, the present argument locates the value of such order in some irreducibly holist property. This comes out most clearly when Hayek speaks of the abstractness, or abstract character, of spontaneous economic order. When he describes such order as having certain 'abstract features' (1967: 72),[6] he wants to say that it invariably possesses certain enduring properties irrespective of its particular shape. The property foremost in Hayek's mind is its beneficial nature, which he outlines as follows:

the common welfare or . . . the public good of a free society can . . . be defined . . . only as an abstract order which as a whole . . . provides . . . the best chance for any member selected at random successfully to use his knowledge for his purposes. (1967: 163)

In almost identical fashion, he elsewhere declares 'that the common good . . . consists in an abstract order . . . which will increase everybody's chances as much as possible . . . [but which] . . . must leave undetermined the degree to which the several particular needs will be met' (1976: 114).[7]

Hayek's contention is, then, that spontaneous economic order is beneficial because it 'increases' (1976: 107, 114, and elsewhere) and even makes 'as great as possible' (1976: 132, similarly in 1967: 163) 'the prospects or chances of every one' (1976: 107) taken at random.

How should we understand this claim? Gray thinks it indicates Hayek's espousal of a probabilistic form of preference-utilitarianism.[8] It is true that when speaking of 'chances' Hayek characterizes them as the chances of the individual 'to achieve his ends'

---

[6] See also 1967: 92; 1973: 39, 105; 1976: 14; 1978: 137.

[7] Additional passages further varying the theme that spontaneous economic order offers only chances for, but not the certainty of, success include 1960: 29–30; 1976: 23, 107, 122, 126, 129–30; 1978: 62.   [8] Gray (1986: 60).

(1978: 184) and, somewhat differently, 'to have a certain range of opportunities' (1976: 130). However, in my view such a preference-utilitarian interpretation is too charitable, and I shall argue that 'chances' ultimately boils down quite simply to 'average individual income' or 'average individual share in the social product', and that any probabilistic connotation is irrelevant and misleading. Hayek himself provides support for such a reading when he specifies those 'chances' as an individual's 'chances . . . of earning a particular income' (1976: 188 n. 23) and says that spontaneous economic order increases 'the prospects or chances of every one of a greater command over the various goods' (1976: 107). Nevertheless, though committing himself to 'income', he still talks here of 'chances' and even makes an explicit attempt to state them in probabilistic terms (1976: 130–1, 188 n. 23). So let us see first how we can make sense of those probabilistic overtones.

Hayek's seemingly probabilistic perspective is most conspicuous, of course, in those passages where he says that spontaneous economic order is beneficial because it increases, or makes as great as possible, the prospects of anyone selected *at random* (1976: 23, 129–30, 132; 1978: 62, 184). Thus formulated, the claim implies that the beneficial nature of spontaneous economic order reveals itself in a comparative test. Take the two basic types of economic systems, market society and planned economy, Hayek seems to instruct us. Now pick from each of them an individual, compare their incomes—that is, the baskets of goods at their disposal—and you will see (Hayek appears to suggest) that the member of the market society is consistently better off.

Yet there is a problem with this test. Since we are to take the two persons at random, it may well happen that from the market society we select a low-paid unskilled worker while at the same time we choose a highly salaried bureaucrat from the central planning board. So, if carried out only once, the test may easily put the market society in second place. To get sound results the random test has to be repeated a number of times, and one must compare what the average incomes in the two samples (the first consisting of members of the market society, the second of people living in a planned economy) are. The more often the test is carried out and a couple of individuals selected, the larger the two samples and the more reliable the test results become, increasingly approximating the average incomes earned in the two economies.

The inevitable conclusion is that, if the test of picking individuals 'at random' is to make sense, it must be understood as a test comparing average individual incomes. This means the probabilistic connotations in Hayek's formulations are out of place. We do not need to elaborate on the comparative dimension of this test. It suffices to be aware that Hayek makes his claim about the beneficial nature of spontaneous economic order against the background of the planned economy; spontaneous order makes the individuals' prospects 'as great as possible' in comparison with what a planned economy would achieve under identical circumstances.

The discussion so far suggests that Hayek's claim about the beneficial nature of spontaneous economic order *is* the claim that such order maximizes average individual income. But more must now be said to strengthen and explain this interpretation. This we shall do by analysing various Hayekian passages, all of which comprise in some form the idea of average income being maximized.

That spontaneous economic order is beneficial because it maximizes average individual income Hayek formulates most succinctly as follows:

The individuals have reason to agree to play this game because *it makes the pool* from which the individual shares are drawn *larger than it can be made by any other method.* But at the same time it makes the share of each individual subject to all kinds of accidents . . . (1978: 137, emphasis added)

In this passage, Hayek neatly identifies the two elements characteristic of the average-income view. He asserts that the output per head is maximized, and he concedes that nothing can be said about how the total social product is distributed among the members.

He goes a step further and, as I believe, already a step too far in another passage. Again we find him talking about the two elements of the average-income view, but now he adds a proposition about the improvement of the chances of *everyone*. The operation of a market economy, Hayek writes,

is *likely to increase everybody's chances.* Though the share of each will be unpredictable, because it will depend only in part on his skill and opportunities to learn facts, and in part on accident, this is the condition which alone will make it the interest of all so to conduct themselves as to make as large as possible the aggregate product of which they will get an unpredictable share. Of the resulting distribution it . . . [can only] . . . be claimed . . . that it is the result of a process which is known to *improve the chances of all* . . . (1976: 122, emphasis added)

The claim that spontaneous economic order increases or improves everybody's chances is a curious one. If the distributional pattern is unpredictable because partly determined by luck, nothing guarantees that in the longer run everybody's prospects of getting a greater share increase. A necessary link between the growth of the average output per head and the improvement of an individual's economic situation does not exist.

There is, I think, a specific idea leading Hayek to make that strange claim about the improvement of everybody's chances. This idea is adumbrated in the following two passages. In both of them, he once more subscribes to the two elements constituting the average-income view: that average output per head is maximized, and that individual shares partly depend on chance. And again we read about the market game increasing every individual's prospects. Yet this time Hayek puts that proposition somewhat differently:

of that particular combination of commodities and services which will be produced more will be made available than could be done by any other known means; . . . in consequence, though the share in that product which the different individuals will get is left to be determined by circumstances nobody can foresee and in this sense to 'accident', *each will get for the share he wins in the game (. . .) as large a real equivalent as can be secured*. We allow the individual share to be determined partly by luck in order to make the total to be shared as large as possible. (1978: 91, emphasis added)

This competitive game, at the price of leaving the share of each individual in some measure to accident, ensures *that the real equivalent of whatever his share turns out to be, is as large as we know how to make it*. The game is, to use up-to-date language, not a zero-sum game, but one through which, by playing it according to the rules, the pool to be shared is enlarged, leaving individual shares in the pool in a great measure to chance. . . . The so-called 'maximum' which we thus reach naturally cannot be defined as a sum of particular things, but only in terms of the chances if offers to unknown people *to get as large a real equivalent as possible for their relative shares, which will be determined partly by accident*. (1978: 186, emphasis added)

These passages enable us to find out what the idea must be that tempts Hayek into his claim about the improvement of everybody's chances. This idea revolves round the metaphors of the aggregate output as a 'pool' and of the market process as a 'game'. Together these metaphors evoke the following scene.

Another round of the market game has been played, and the members of society stand in front of the new heap of goods which, as in every previous round, they should now distribute among themselves. The criterion along which the distribution must be carried out is evidently this: a player has entitlements to the total product to the extent to which he was successful in the game and has earned an income. The size and composition of the basket of goods (the 'real equivalent') a member gets out of the pool depends on the relative size (the 'share') of his income as compared to the incomes of all others.

With this scene in mind, we can grasp the meaning of Hayek's reformulated proposition 'that the real equivalent of whatever [an individual's] share turns out to be, is as large as we know how to make it' (1978: 186). Implicitly, Hayek invites us to undertake a fictional comparison. Look at this scene, he seems to say, and imagine that the heap of goods supplied by the market system would be replaced by what under otherwise the same circumstances a planned economy, or 'any other method' (1978: 137) of economic co-ordination, is capable of producing. Given the fact that a market system is the most productive 'method', Hayek would argue, the output of any type of economy other than that of the market would be smaller. What conclusion, he would then ask us, must be drawn from this? If we accept his premiss about the unrivalled productive efficiency of the market, we will say that under a market regime the pool of goods is largest, and that *taken together* the members get as much as possible. Yet in his own answer Hayek goes further and believes that he can specify the market's beneficial nature for *every* single member in the following way: 'each will get for the share he wins in the game (. . .) as large a real equivalent as can be secured' (1978: 91). In other words, Hayek claims that the market *maximizes* not only the aggregate product but *also the quantity of goods every individual receives*. However, he can make this claim only if he subscribes to the idea that the distribution of incomes across the members is given and independent of the type of economic system employed to produce the pool of goods. Hayek's assumption must be that the relative size of each person's income remains unaffected by the type of economy in operation. Only then can he maintain that it is the market economy which allows 'people to get as large a real equivalent as possible for their relative shares' (1978: 186).

This idea is implausible, nor does Hayek endorse it elsewhere. Hayek makes much of the inseparability of production and distribution, insisting that the market owes its unsurpassed productivity to the fact that the distribution of incomes is not interfered with.

The 'maximisation' of the total product . . . , and its distribution by the market, cannot be separated because it is through the determination of the prices of the factors of production that the overall order of the market is brought about. (1978: 92, similarly on 91 and 64–5)

Therefore, the introduction of a system other than the market economy, even if undertaken merely to use a different 'method' of producing the pool of goods, unavoidably changes the distributional mechanism and the profile of the resulting income distribution. We have to think here only of the most obvious case: on Hayek's own account a planned economy denies chance any role and makes the income distribution exclusively a matter of political will, assigning incomes in accordance with some predetermined principle (e.g. 1976: ch. 9).

If production and distribution are interdependent in the way indicated, the thought experiment implied by Hayek, of comparing how much each individual's relative income share would buy under the various economic systems, loses its basis. In all likelihood, the distribution of those shares—and that means of individual entitlements to the social product—would vary from system to system. So it cannot be said that under a market system a particular individual would for his income share 'get as large a real equivalent as possible' (1978: 186). Any talk by Hayek about the spontaneous order 'increas[ing] everybody's chances as much as possible' (1976: 114) is therefore unwarranted.

If taken seriously, Hayek's own views about the interdependence of production and distribution subvert his proposition that spontaneous economic order maximizes every member's prospects or chances. Dropping this untenable claim brings us back to the average-income interpretation, the two basic components of which Hayek affirms throughout all the passages quoted: that spontaneous order maximizes average individual income, and that nothing definite can be said about the distribution of incomes across the population. But how far can an economic system merely maximizing average income be said to be beneficial for its members?

The argument from the market's efficiency has a striking similarity to average utilitarianism. The utilitarian principle demands that, in society, well-being per capita must be maximized. Now Hayek is not a utilitarian and criticizes it for its assumption that a felicific calculus could determine the amounts of utility which alternative courses of action or alternative institutional arrangements would produce and that on this basis the option to be preferred could be identified (1976: 17–23).[9] Still, there is an important parallel. Just as average utilitarianism ignores the problem of how the sum of satisfactions is distributed among the individuals,[10] Hayek is indifferent about the distribution of incomes. Only a planned economy, he says, but not a spontaneous order, can make that distribution conform to some predetermined principle of justice (1944: 74; 1976: 69), and it can do so only at the price of a massively lower output (1978: 92).

Now given his view about the income distribution depending on luck, and in the light of his frank admission that ' "to those who have will be given" ' (1976: 131),[11] it is difficult to see how he can in earnest believe that in the long run (1976: 115) the market system has a tendency to benefit all. What John Rawls writes of F. Y. Edgeworth's utilitarianism equally applies to Hayek. Hayek too must presume 'that men move from one social position to another in random fashion and live long enough for gains and

[9] For more on Hayek's views about utilitarianism, see Ch. 8, pp. 216–20.

[10] For criticism of this neglect, see e.g. Rawls (1971: sects. 5–6, 28, 30). Yet compare James Griffin's (1986: 168, footnote omitted) rejoinder that '[i]t is just a modern muddle to contrast sharply distributive and aggregative principles, as if an aggregative principle could not also be fully deliberately distributive.'

[11] Hayek's views about the distributional effects of a market system contradict and invalidate the justification he advances elsewhere of economic inequality. Hayek asserts that a society needs the rich to pull the poor out of their misery. The reasoning adduced in support of that claim, however, is heavily metaphorical and not easy to reconstruct in more analytical terms: 'the over-all speed of advance will be increased by those who move fastest. Even if many fall behind at first, the cumulative effect of the preparation of the path will, before long, sufficiently facilitate their advance that they will be able to keep their place in the march. . . . At any given moment we could improve the position of the poorest by giving them what we took from the wealthy. But . . . it would, before long, slow down the movement of the whole and in the long run hold back those in the rear' (1960: 48–9).

losses to average out'. But, comments Rawls, 'society is not a stochastic process of this type'.[12] We cannot trust that time will reduce, let alone even out, distributional disparities. Whether, in view of the possibility that some people end up very badly, spontaneous order can still plausibly be said to be 'beneficial' or, in one of Hayek's own formulations, to represent 'the prime condition of the general welfare of its members' (1976: 6) depends on the moral semantics of 'beneficial' and 'general welfare of its members'. Taking a quasi-utilitarian stance, Hayek may counter the criticism of being inattentive to distributional aspects simply by reasserting that the only relevant fact is average income. Or he may say it is an unavoidable and therefore tragic feature of the world and the economic laws governing it that in the endeavour to improve life as much as possible some people do lose. Spontaneous order, he may argue, is still as beneficial a mode of economic co-ordination as there can be.

However, it may be remarked that economic co-operation will always benefit certain parties and that for this reason spontaneous order, like any alternative mechanism of co-ordination, is somehow beneficial anyway. In order to be 'really' beneficial, one might insist, spontaneous order would in some qualified sense have to be advantageous for everyone. In other words, a counter-argument can be formulated to the effect that any claim about the beneficial nature of a particular type of economic system must comprise a distributive dimension or at least a particular concern for the worst off. Hayek concedes this point, yet only implicitly. Recognizing that, on its own, spontaneous economic order may not offer everybody an acceptable standard of living, he advocates the institution of a minimum safety net. He thereby admits (what his rhetoric often conceals) that such order and the mechanism of self-co-ordination generating and maintaining it become advantageous for each only if they are supplemented and corrected by appropriate redistributive principles.

It should also be evident by now that a spontaneous economic order as described by Hayek does not satisfy Rawls's famous difference principle. What makes such order beneficial in Hayek's view is, as we know, that it maximizes the prospects of everyone 'selected at random'. V. Vanberg sees this criterion as open both

[12] Rawls (1971: 170).

to a utilitarian and a Rawlsian–contractarian interpretation.[13] Going further, B. L. Crowley discovers close affinities between Hayek and Rawls and finds they disagree merely about matters of methodology.[14] And there is, of course, Hayek's own remark that his differences with Rawls seem 'more verbal than substantial' (1976: xiii). However, any tendency to align Hayek with Rawls and to regard the former's view about the beneficial nature of spontaneous economic order as congenial to the latter's difference principle is misguided.

True, there is in Hayek's writings one passage where he appears to follow the same reasoning that leads Rawls to the difference principle. Like Rawls, Hayek asks us to consider in which type of society we would prefer to live 'if we knew that our initial position in it would be decided purely by chance' (1976: 132). Rawls argues that taking into account the grave consequences of such a choice we would pay overriding attention to what is in each alternative the most underprivileged position. As one of the principles that are to govern the preferred economic system we would therefore, Rawls thinks, choose the difference principle, which requires that, *inter alia*, those at the bottom are made as well off as possible or, in his words, that inequalities are 'to the greatest benefit of the least advantaged members'.[15] Hayek on his part is interested primarily in identifying the type of society that would be favoured, and he believes we would opt for an 'industrial society', the underlying assumption being that such a society is a spontaneous order.

Does the similarity of their reasoning mean that the spontaneous order of Hayek's 'industrial society' meets the demands of Rawls's difference principle and maximizes the prospects of the worst off? There are at least three facts strongly militating against such a conclusion. First of all, there exists to my knowledge only one passage where Hayek adopts a view reminiscent of the Rawlsian choice behind a veil of ignorance. This passage is too narrow a basis to render that view representative of Hayek's thought. Secondly, and most importantly, that view stands in sharp contradiction to Hayek's average-income conception which I have identified in his argument deriving the beneficial nature of

[13] Vanberg (1986: 79. n. 3).   [14] Crowley (1987: 201).
[15] Rawls (1982: 162). Rawls presents his argument most fully in 1971: chs. 2, 3, and 5.

spontaneous economic order from the market's efficiency. While the difference principle is above all concerned about the economic situation of the least favoured members of society and enjoys explicit priority over 'the principle of efficiency and . . . that of maximizing the sum of advantages',[16] Hayek merely demands the maximization of income, or output, per head. Finally, in the light of Hayek's repeated admission that in a spontaneous order the distribution of incomes is in a great measure determined by chance, it is not easy to comprehend why such chance should show clemency to the underprivileged and spare them the worst forms of economic hardship it is capable of inflicting. Mistrusting the spontaneous order's beneficent hand himself, Hayek argues for a 'certain flat minimum income if things go wholly wrong' (1979: 143).

The contrast with Rawls's difference principle once more highlights Hayek's neglect of distributive considerations. It is this deficiency which makes it impossible for the argument from the market's efficiency to be an argument about the generally beneficial nature of spontaneous economic order. Its core assumption— that market-oriented economies produce an output superior to that of centrally directed economies—may, if qualified appropriately, be sound. Still, it does not suffice to render plausible the claim that spontaneous order and the market mechanism generating it are beneficial for everybody. For that claim to acquire plausibility, additional assumptions would be needed about the distributive patterns markets engender. But Hayek's metaphor of the market as a game and the concomitant idea of the distribution being largely determined by luck rule out any such assumptions. We must therefore conclude that spontaneous order becomes reasonably advantageous for everyone only if its distribution is corrected by external institutions counteracting the economic misfortune which will otherwise befall some.

[16] Rawls (1971: 302).

5

The General Idea of a Spontaneous Social Order

The last three chapters examined the idea of a spontaneous economic order, analysing the mechanism of adjustment and rule-following to which Hayek attributes the generation of such order, and discussing the features that render it, in his view, uniquely valuable. Now I want to explore what further applications the idea of a spontaneous order may have in the social world. That there exist many spontaneous social orders other than that of the market is, for Hayek, beyond doubt. He defines social theory as the systematic study of spontaneous orders (1949: 67; 1952a: 39; 1967: 71–2; 1973: 37), maintaining that an individual may often be a member not only of the comprehensive spontaneous order of society but also 'of numerous other spontaneous sub-orders' (1973: 47). He advances the same thesis in different form when he describes spontaneous economic order as just one 'instance of a general method of indirectly creating an order in situations where the phenomena are far too complex to allow us the creation of an order by separately putting each element in its appropriate place' (1967: 92). By making these claims Hayek implies that the fact of its wide applicability proves the theoretical power of the idea of a spontaneous social order and that this, in turn, once more confirms the soundness of his endeavour to explain the market process in terms of such order. It is for this reason that we must examine the general idea of a spontaneous order.

To keep the discussion carefully focused and to avoid confusion, a distinction should be recalled that I made earlier between two basically different categories of unprompted social orders, a distinction whose importance Hayek and his commentators have usually failed consistently to observe. This is the contrast between order as a network of interactions among numerous parties and order as an established system of rules or norms. An awareness of this distinction is imperative if we are to make progress in our understanding of the idea of a spontaneous social order. On Hayek's own account, the logic explaining the formation of the two kinds of order must be different. Order as a web of interactions, he says, is brought about by individuals adhering to certain rules and adjusting to their local situation. The evolution of law, language, morals, and other systems of rules, however, cannot itself be explained in terms of rule-following should an infinite regress be averted. In this chapter we shall only discuss orders of the first type, and I suggest that it is for these alone that we reserve the term 'spontaneous social order'. The allegedly spontaneous, unplanned nature of market rules will be considered later, in the chapter on Hayek's theory of cultural evolution.

Even if thus clarified and narrowed, the idea of a spontaneous social order remains elusive. Hayek nowhere gives an account of what the general features shared by all spontaneous social orders are. Nor does he, except for some far-fetched illustration from the animal world (e.g. 1967: 69–70), give any examples other than that of order in the market. Nor, as we saw earlier, does the secondary literature agree on what the core content of the idea is. This state of affairs will inevitably render the analysis undertaken in this chapter less rigorous and more speculative than one might ideally wish it to be.

I begin by offering various semantic and other reflections exploring the concepts of 'social order' and 'spontaneity' to be found at the bottom of the idea of a spontaneous social order. In the second section, five claims will be identified which I take to represent the substance of the notion of a spontaneous economic order, and we shall examine how far they may be applicable to a wider range of phenomena loosely qualifying as spontaneous social orders too. The conclusion will be that under close scrutiny Hayek's general idea of a spontaneous social order crumbles, that it is unable to furnish the focal point of a social theory, and that social theoretic discourse will achieve more if it is conducted in a vocabulary and within a conceptual framework less abstract and more attuned to the peculiarities of the individual phenomena it studies.

SOCIAL ORDER AND ITS SPONTANEITY

It will help our approach to the general idea of a spontaneous social order if we begin with a tentative exploration of the underlying notions of 'order' and 'spontaneity'. Let us first turn to the concept of 'order'.

Its manifold connotations seem to deprive 'order' of the discriminatory force needed if it is to serve as a concept capable of identifying and designating a distinct category of social phenomena. For social 'order' can mean many things: inexistence or repression of conflict, absence of change, uniformity, static equilibrium, fluctuating equilibrium, or systemic unit.

It does not require much effort to see that most of these meanings do not apply even to the spontaneous order of the market, Hayek's paradigmatic example of a spontaneous social order. Economic rivalry in the market involves conflict and disruption; progress (1960: 39–53) is change; the market process depends on individual diversity and on people having widely differing aims and preferences (1976: 109, 111); and market equilibria (as he would say) are never static. Also, the market process cannot be conceived in functionalist terms.

So there remains the economic notion of a fluctuating equilibrium which, to be sure, is almost coterminous with Hayek's idea of a spontaneous economic order. Yet is this notion applicable to other social patterns as well? G. L. S. Shackle thinks so:

Despite history's record of ferocity and evil, which seems so vividly to bear out Macbeth's assessment of life, there is a vast contrary evidence: the all-encompassing web of markets and diplomacy, the fabric of laws and contracts, the international basis of calendars and navigation. If humanity tries, however erratically, to organise itself, it tries for equilibrium.[1]

But if conceived thus broadly, 'equilibrium' has no more discriminatory power than 'order' itself, and we are left with the same problem of narrowing its scope to give it teeth.[2] If we take, as I think we should, 'equilibrium' in its economic meaning, it hardly applies to any social fact other than the network of market relations. 'Equilibrium', it appears, does not offer any way of specifying social 'order'. But which of the other meanings could we allow in when we move away from 'economic order' towards the broader concept of 'social order'?

If in functionalist fashion we conceive of social order as a system—something Hayek occasionally does (1967: 77; 1973: 28,

[1] Shackle (1981: 254–5).   [2] See, however, Elster (1989b: 101–12).

39)—then one of the problems becomes how to delimit the over-all systemic unit. We must know the boundaries separating the endogenous systemic processes from the external world should we be able to distinguish internal functional adjustments from exogenous disturbances impairing the system. The difficulty with a functionalist approach is notoriously that lacking reliable criteria we can construe almost any change as a mere internal adaptation if only we define the overall unit comprehensively enough. This vagueness disqualifies the systemic interpretation from giving the term 'social order' a more specific content.

There are problems with the other meanings too. How much conflict and how much change is normal for a social pattern still to be an 'order'? Once it is conceded that orders may exhibit a certain measure of disruption, the distinction between order and disorder begins to blur. One man's order may be another man's chaos. There is a telling example. While in Hayek's eyes the market is a spontaneous *order* of exchange relations, it appears to Shackle as a 'kaleidic' world of incessantly fluctuating expectations, valuations, and beliefs.[3] Hayek tends to overlook that competition does not go easily with 'order'.

Hayek himself does make an attempt to specify 'social order' when he defines it as 'a matching of intentions and expectations' and an interlocking of productive activities (e.g. 1973: 36). Still, this definition fails to give us a firmer grasp of 'social order'. Such matching and interlocking are the very stuff of which social relations are made generally, be they co-operative or antagonistic ones.

'Order' not only has numerous descriptive connotations but also an implicit normative dimension. This dimension becomes visible when 'order' is set off against 'disorder'. 'Order' then usually appears as positively valuable. Hayek shares this normative per-spective. He thinks social order is useful because it enables human beings to achieve aims which would otherwise remain outside their reach (1952a: 82). Instituted as an organization, 'social or-der' allows people jointly to pursue and attain a goal which as individuals they could not realize, and in the form of a spontane-ous order it 'serves the multiplicity of separate and incommensur-able ends of all its separate members' (1976: 108, and similarly elsewhere).[4]

---

[3] Shackle (1972).
[4] In a somewhat different way, order plays an equally important role in German philosophical anthropology as represented by Arnold Gehlen and Helmuth Plessner.

But on reflection, we cannot consider 'order' always to be unequivocally valuable. Whether an organization is a good thing or not crucially depends on the goals it seeks to realize. In recent history, some goals and the organizations set up to implement them have often been simply abhorrent. The bureaucracy established by the Nazis to administer and oversee the Jewish genocide is certainly the most infamous example, yet not by far the only one. Whether spontaneous orders can be similarly perverted is difficult to say for we still do not know what social arrangements other than the web of market relations might count as such orders. However, if (as Hayek seems to assume) for all social orders, organizations as well as spontaneous orders, a 'matching of intentions and expectations' and an 'interlocking of activities' is constitutive, such orders need not be beneficial, at least not for all those involved. In a caste society or a slave state, there may on everybody's part exist well-established role-expectations, and a system of submissive collaboration may be working smoothly, yet such social orders are, not only from a liberal point of view, highly objectionable.

Now let us leave the concept of social order and see what the 'spontaneity' consists in that renders certain orders *spontaneous* social orders. Often, Hayek seems to locate the source from which spontaneous order springs in certain energies flowing freely in the social universe. The idea implied appears to be that if channelled appropriately these forces will unfailingly produce social order. Whenever we face an organizational task exceeding our individual intelligence, especially when we try to cope with the perennial problem of maintaining order in society, we have, Hayek suggests, no option other than to have recourse to those energies. '[T]he only possiblity of transcending the capacity of individual minds is', writes Hayek, 'to rely on those super-personal "self-organizing" forces which create spontaneous orders' (1973: 54).[5] The implication, stated expressly at least once (1978: 75), is that those forces will release their ordering energies as soon as a regime guaranteeing 'the rules of individual conduct' has been established.

In this philosophical tradition, man is not seen primarily as a purposive being in need of order for the successful pursuit of his goals but as an animal lacking inborn survival instincts and therefore dependent on institutional order as a framework of orientation. For a tendentially highly conservative exploration of this line of thought, see Levy (1987).

[5] Similar passages in 1960: 25, 160; 1967: 74; 1973: 38, 41, 42, 63; 1976: 114.

Any such talk, even if it is only metaphorical, is out of place. There are no such things as 'spontaneously ordering forces'—only human beings acting singly or collectively within the social and institutional structures in which they find themselves. People simply take their fate in their own hands, be that in the market economy where, as Hayek says (e.g. 1967: 232–3), it is up to the individuals to make themselves useful to others and thereby earn an income, or in their personal lives in their choice of a mate and of a place to live; be that under the reasonably favourable conditions of a Western society or under the most antagonistic circumstances of a POW camp.

Antagonistic conditions, in particular, induce people to organize themselves in all sorts of groups and networks. A few examples may be mentioned of such co-operative patterns. In a fascinating paper, Diego Gambetta explains how the Mafia (Sicily) and its sister organizations, the Camorra (Naples) and the 'ndrangheta (Calabria) can be seen as a response to certain specific political and economic circumstances prevailing in southern Italy.[6] In order to secure their regimes, the Spanish, Austrian, and Bourbon powers which successively dominated southern Italy in the seventeenth and eighteenth centuries resorted to a whole bundle of strategies aimed at dividing and ruling the local population.[7] What they left was a system of justice nobody considered reliable and effective and—again resulting from the strategies of sowing distrust—an utterly fragmented economy: 'the unpredictability of sanctions generate[d] uncertainty in agreements, stagnation in commerce and industry, and a general reluctance towards impersonal and extensive forms of cooperation.'[8] It was in such an environment that the Mafia could establish itself as a 'coalition of clusters' (Gambetta) based on personal rather than publicly institutionalized relations. In the absence both of an impartial system of justice and a social climate of trust, durable relations were possible only if they were private, maintained by private favours and, if necessary, private violence. Moreover the Mafia was able to overcome the economic fragmentation by enforcing and thus guaranteeing extensive co-operation in areas where it could achieve exclusive control. These areas included 'land, cattle, sources of water in a dry land, markets,

---

[6] Gambetta (1988).   [7] See also Pagden (1988).
[8] Gambetta (1988: 162).

auctions, ports, building, transport and public works', in short: areas accessible to monopolization.[9]

Being an unforeseeable response to specific historical conditions, why not see the Mafia as a 'spontaneous social order'? This seems all the more plausible since, as Raimondo Catanzaro has expounded in his article 'Enforcers, Entrepreneurs, and Survivors: How the Mafia has Adapted to Change', its history, especially over the last few decades, can be written as the story of how it adjusted to altering economic conditions and exploited new 'market opportunities'.[10] In other words, the story of the Mafia can be told in terms closely resembling those Hayek uses to describe the spontaneous formation of order in the market.

Take another example of orders formed 'spontaneously', without anybody having devised them. Could not the youth gangs existing in large cities be interpreted as spontaneous social orders? Such gangs, as the sociological literature explains, are a response of young low-class people to the conditions of poverty and unemployment surrounding them, without the prospect of ever embarking on a successful middle-class career. Not only may each gang be regarded as a spontaneous order. A precarious equilibrium also exists among competing gangs, and between the gangs and the police. To make the analogy with Hayek's spontaneous economic order even more striking: internal gang life is based on specific rules, and territorial demarcations akin to the rules of private property govern the coexistence of rival gangs.[11]

Let us return to economics. Economic order develops 'spontaneously' even where the rules of private property are not recognized by the state. Planned economies of the former Soviet communist type, incapable of providing basic goods and services, notoriously generated (and, where they persist, still generate) black markets. Usually, these markets work even though the property rights in the goods produced and traded illegally are publicly not acknowledged and cannot be enforced. Similarly, excessively bureaucratic economies (as they exist, for example, in various Southern American countries) are typically paralleled by informal economies in which inhibiting regulations are either ignored or made

---

[9] Ibid. 164, with reference to Th. Schelling.   [10] Catanzaro (1985).
[11] See the account of female gangs in New York, and the biographical sketches of three gang members, in A. Campbell (1984). Campbell also provides a useful survey of the existing sociological literature on gangs generally.

'workable' by bribing state officials. Finally, in a richly documented study Jack Hirshleifer shows how economic order emerges, again 'spontaneously', under conditions of extreme political or natural disaster. Particularly instructive among the cases he discusses are war communism in Russia (1917–21), the American Confederation (1861–5), the reconstruction of the Japanese economy after Hiroshima and Nagasaki, and Germany's recovery from collapse (1945–8).[12]

Considering all these cases we are, I think, forced to conclude that eventually the 'spontaneity' Hayek discovers in certain social orders and co-operative arrangements simply reflects the responsiveness human beings exhibit *vis-à-vis* their life conditions. Responsiveness means: people are mostly active on their own. They need not usually be told what to do, but try themselves to protect and further their interests, taking into account, and reacting to, the specific circumstances they face. This will often result in co-operation with others.

'Spontaneity' interpreted as 'responsiveness' has two implications. First, the distinction Hayek draws between spontaneous orders and organizations collapses further.[13] Over longer stretches of time, organizations are no less the result of people's 'spontaneous' responsiveness to a changing environment than Hayekian spontaneous social orders proper. This also applies especially to the firm, for Hayek the archetype of an organization (1973: 46). It suffices here to recall the classic success stories of those corporations, multinationals today, which half a century ago began as one-man firms in the backyard of some suburban house. The growth of such corporations, their present size and structure, though in part stemming from a series of strategically adroit managerial decisions, was not planned in advance, was unforeseen and unforeseeable. The second implication is that its 'spontaneity' does not necessarily make a social order generally valuable—as the examples of the Mafia and the street gangs vividly demonstrate.

Our discussion has shown 'order' and 'spontaneity' to be exceedingly indeterminate analytical concepts. That on their own such concepts are somewhat indefinite is to be expected and need not be a point of special concern. For they owe their power to categorize the many phenomena of the social world largely to the

---

[12] Hirshleifer (1987: 3–141).   [13] See Ch. 1 pp. 31–2.

specific empirical hypotheses the social theorist formulates about them. This also applies to those Hayekian concepts. We can (if we can) decide whether a certain pattern is a spontaneous order when we know the various claims Hayek makes about the emergence and nature of such orders. Unfortunately, as we shall see in the following section, these claims do not add up to an integrated whole. When 'order' and 'spontaneity' are highly indeterminate *and* the specific claims intended to explicate those terms lack coherence, any thorough examination of the wider applicability of Hayek's idea of a spontaneous order becomes rather problematic. The trouble is simply that we can never really be sure whether or not a certain pattern looking like a spontaneous order counts as such for Hayek. This difficulty we will have to bear in mind when we look now at the versatility of this idea and probe the empirical claims he associates with it.

THE WIDER APPLICABILITY

Hayek nowhere spells out the claims which taken together constitute the idea of a spontaneous social order. There are in his writings numerous discussions, under various headings, of spontaneous economic order, and it is in the course of these discussions that he puts forward several major and minor propositions about the formation and nature of such order. These we analysed in Chapters 2, 3, and 4. Obviously, when now we want to know what the content and range of the broader idea of a spontaneous *social* order is, we cannot simply extrapolate from the Hayekian notion of a spontaneous *economic* order and just generalize all those specifically economic claims. A choice has to be made. The core of the idea must undoubtedly still be that a spontaneous order develops when in their dealings with one another the agents observe certain rules and when, within the confines of those rules, each agent adjusts to the specific circumstances of his particular situation. I suggest, but shall not elaborate further, that in addition to this basic mechanism we regard five claims as capturing the essence of the idea of a spontaneous social order. Since, as I believe, a concise and tightly integrated account of this idea cannot be given, these claims are best seen as vistas on spontaneous social order from various different, though partly overlapping, ranges and angles. They are as follows.

1. Spontaneous orders are much better able than organizations to utilize dispersed, fugacious, and latent knowledge.

2. Spontaneous orders have an inherent tendency to self-correction and stability.

3. For an order to form spontaneously it suffices that within appropriate rules individual adjustment is informed by rational self-interest.

4. If the rules are to be conducive to spontaneous order, they must not be coercive or, at least, not more than minimally coercive.

5. Spontaneous order and the co-ordination and co-operation it embodies require the pre-existence and universal observance of certain rules.

The idea of a spontaneous social order to which these five claims give expression is not a value-neutral explanatory concept. Without always saying so, Hayek consistently takes spontaneous orders to be beneficial (e.g. 1952a: 82–3) and, hence, valuable. Clearly, their beneficial nature depends on the presence of certain institutional preconditions as they are mentioned in the fourth claim, that is, on rules that are not more than minimally coercive. The minimization of coercion, as we remember, plays a crucial role in Hayek's argument deriving the value of spontaneous economic order from the voluntariness of the exchange relations possible under a regime of private property. That argument, though making use of various social theoretic and, especially, economic insights, is ultimately a moral philosophical argument, relying in the last resort on a premiss about the moral badness of coercion. Equally, any broader assertion about the value of spontaneous social orders in general must rest on similar moral reasoning. To predicate of spontaneous social orders that they are valuable is to presuppose considerations showing that it is a morally good thing that spontaneous orders have the systematic effects they actually have.

Once the partly moral philosophical nature of its basis has been recognized, the idea of a spontaneous social order can no longer be seen as a social theoretic notion advancing our understanding of order in the social world, but must be regarded as a normative ideal of social coexistence and co-operation. Its character as such an ideal becomes most evident when Hayek applies the idea to the spontaneous order of society as a whole. Often he then treats it as synonymous with Adam Smith's notion of the 'Great Society' and Karl Popper's 'Open Society' (e.g. 1973: 2), evaluative concepts serving as signposts in liberal political thought. Such ideals do not have their place in explanatory social theory but in the province of normative social and political philosophy. Still, this does not rule out a critical analysis of Hayek's idea of a spontaneous social order and of the claims he associates with it. A social theoretic examination remains still possible. We only have to keep in mind that due to the vaguely normative nature of certain presuppositions of that idea the results will unavoidably be of a tentative and conditional character.

We shall now consider the five claims which I think together form the general idea of a spontaneous social order. The aim is to examine their wider applicability and to reach a conclusion about the theoretical fertility of this idea. The strategy will be the following. We shall concentrate on each of those five claims in turn while keeping the others constant. Against each claim I shall try to adduce counter-examples, social phenomena, which, though they can plausibly be seen as spontaneous orders, do not confirm that claim and deny it general validity. Limitations of space do not permit a discussion as detailed as one would wish it to be. In particular, I shall neither describe these examples in game theoretical terms, though such an account might often be illuminating, nor even distinguish between two-person- and many-person-situations. Also, I shall take it to be obvious and shall not work out in detail for whom a particular spontaneous order is, or is not, advantageous. Any more extensive discussion would have to pay careful attention to how such an order distributes benefits and burdens. Hayek's important implicit assumption that in the long run spontaneous orders are unreservedly beneficial for each participant is undoubtedly too simple, if not wholly wrong, since it does not hold even in his paradigmatic case of the order in the market.

These qualifications notwithstanding, I believe the counter-examples given will suffice to subvert Hayek's idea that in the social world there exists a clearly identifiable category of 'spontaneous orders' resting on the same mechanism of rule-following and adjustment and possessing the same informational capacities and self-stabilizing tendencies.

1. *Spontaneous orders are much better able than organizations to utilize dispersed, fugacious, and latent knowledge.* Here we shall only look at the alleged ability of spontaneous orders to exploit

dispersed knowledge. An obvious group of phenomena calling in question this claim are epidemics (such as cholera, typhus, and tuberculosis), the analysis of their causes, and the introduction of measures to contain them. Coping with an epidemic cannot be left to the free play of a society's spontaneous forces. Usually individuals are unable to acquire the information necessary for an adequate response to the risks posed by such diseases. For this reason, it has always been seen as a task of government to fund medical research, warn the public, and issue directives about how to combat such threats to public health. Only a cynic could regard the extinction of large parts of the population as a process of spontaneous adjustment towards a new order.

Even the spontaneous order of the market does not always guarantee an optimal utilization of dispersed knowledge. Frequently there exists between sellers and buyers an informational imbalance. In a well-known article, George Akerlof has presented a model of how the market for used cars may break down because dishonest salesmen cheat their customers, selling them 'lemons', cars whose defects come to light only later. Once buyers become aware that a certain percentage of used cars are lemons, they start systematically to make an allowance for this possibility in the prices they are prepared to pay. This, in turn, makes decent owners reluctant to sell their cars at the current price level because they are undervalued. In this way, dishonest salesmen trigger a dynamic process at the end of which reliable cars disappear and the market collapses,[14] although, as Thomas Schelling remarks, 'institutional arrangements like guarantees, or the certification of cars by dealers who exploit a reputation for good cars, may keep the used-car market alive'.[15] Other informational imbalances may be found in the market for life insurances or in the relationship between psychoanalyst and patient.

2. *Spontaneous orders have an inherent tendency to self-correction and stability*. It is almost impossible to examine this claim because it is not clear where it applies. We can judge its validity only if we know exactly the boundaries delimiting a particular spontaneous order, for otherwise we are not able to distinguish internal self-correcting processes from external changes transforming the whole order. Where the boundaries of a social phenomenon

---

[14] Akerlof (1970).   [15] Schelling (1978: 100).

are to be drawn often depends on one's perspective or on certain values to which one feels committed. A few sketchy examples may illustrate this.

An earthquake has struck. The survivors start to salvage whatever remnants of their possessions they find under the rubble; slowly they begin to rebuild their houses, and after two decades life has returned to normalcy. Was the earthquake simply a disaster, or does its occurrence and the subsequent recovery point to some self-stabilizing tendency? Another example. Does the increasing use of drugs threaten the fabric of Western society, or is it merely a self-correcting process, providing people with new excitements at a time when life in these highly regulated societies has become boring? And are the rising divorce rates and growing numbers of single-parent families the result of a self-adjusting process adapting the individuals' private lives to modern society's high social, economic, and geographic mobility, or do they reflect a decay of the morals of an orderly society? These contrasts, to be sure, are overdrawn. Yet they drastically illustrate the problem the claim and its examination pose.

3. *For an order to form spontaneously it suffices that within appropriate rules individual adjustment is informed by rational self-interest.* Clearly, Hayek does not advocate the straightforward pursuit of what is advantageous only to oneself. Hayek does suggest, however, that a spontaneous order beneficial to each will form if each pursues his own interest *within the rules given* (e.g. 1978: 65). In this respect, he differs from the economic approach to human behaviour according to which any choice and also, therefore, any decision about whether to follow or to defy a given rule is made in the light of the expected individual benefits.[16] Hayekian individuals have a kind of Kantian ethos.

Hayek's claim is hard to assess because, when looking at the patterns he might regard as spontaneous orders, we do not know what the appropriate rules are. If they are consistently those of private property and contract, they do not preclude prisoner's dilemmas. In social life, there are not only private goods, goods that can be parcelled out and whose use or consumption can be made dependent on the individual's willingness to pay for the advantages received. Social life has also many features with public-goods

---

[16] See e.g. Becker (1976).

character, arrangements beneficial even to those who do not contribute to their provision or maintenance. Those contributions can,
but need not, be financial; they may also consist in co-operative
efforts or in the exercise of self-restraint.[17] In the case of public
goods, the rules of private property are unable to guarantee beneficial outcomes. The pursuit within those rules of their self-interest
leads individuals directly into what Derek Parfit calls a 'contri-
butor's dilemma' because it can be better for each if he does not
help to provide a particular public good and worse for each if he
does. Two of the examples mentioned by Parfit may suffice to
show this dilemma. Each commuter goes faster if he drives, but if
all drive each goes slower than if all take buses. And, when the
sea is overfished, it can be better for each if he tries to catch more,
worse for each if all do.[18]

Hayek might propose to solve these dilemmas in the following
way. We must, he might say, introduce just one further rule. The
commuters have merely to observe a rule optimizing existing
transport facilities and allowing individuals to use their cars in
rotation on certain days while on others consigning them to public
transport, and the fishermen avoid depleting the sea when they
observe certain maximum quotas. However, in each case the new
'rule' does not merely supplement the existing system of rules but
replaces an (unsuccessful) self-co-ordinating mechanism by central
direction—and the whole process is no longer a spontaneous order
based on private property at all.

The argument so far against the claim that for a beneficial spontaneous order to develop it suffices if individuals' pursuit of their
own interests is bounded by appropriate rules has rested on the
assumption that those rules are the rules of private property and
contract. Any further examination of this claim is impossible and
seems unnecessary: impossible because nowhere does Hayek give
the slightest hint at what other content 'appropriate' rules might
possess, and unnecessary since, as I indicated, the claim does not
hold even for spontaneous economic order.

4. *If the rules are to be conducive to spontaneous order, they
must not be coercive or, at least, not more than minimally coercive.* This claim too has to be discussed against the background
of Hayek's assumption that spontaneous orders are inherently

---

[17] Parfit (1984: 61).   [18] Ibid. 61–2.

advantageous. Counter-examples must show that less coercive rules lead to a less beneficial order or, conversely, more coercive ones to a more advantageous outcome.

One category of cases includes the elimination or containment of 'neighbourhood effects' (e.g. 1960: 341, 365, 369), the internalization of external effects. People will take measures to reduce harmful car exhausts and stop polluting lakes and rivers if they are made to bear the full costs of such damaging behaviour. They may give up such behaviour if the state offers a tax allowance for owners of cars with an air-pollution abatement device and imposes a tax on industrial pollution. Such tax arrangements can be interpreted as rules. Even though their implementation constrains choice and adds a measure of coercion previously absent, the overall outcome is more beneficial than it was before, under a less coercive regime of rules.

Another example nicely illustrating that less coercion does not necessarily lead to more satisfactory outcomes is given by Gambetta and has certain parallels with the case described by Akerlof and mentioned earlier of the market of 'lemons', used cars with hidden defects. In his essay on the Mafia, Gambetta tells the story of a Neapolitan coachman (in the 1860s) complaining about the jailing of a *camorrista* whose previous services he is missing bitterly. Payed adequate protection money, the *camorrista* made sure the coachman got horses worth their price. Now that he is in prison, the coachman has promptly been saddled with a 'lemon', a bad horse. In a world where distrust is the norm, the *camorrista* exercises coercion useful both to seller and buyer. Not only does he save the buyer from an unfavourable deal, he also acts in the seller's interest, for in the absence of any authority guaranteeing the quality of the horses traded, buyers are disinclined to enter on any deal at all and the market may soon collapse. This leaves all three parties worse off.[19]

That more rather than less coercion can generate better results may also apply to constitutional politics. Gus diZerega interprets

---

[19] For an extended analysis of this example, cf. Gambetta (1988: 171–3). Gambetta also explains why it is still not in the interest of the Camorra to guarantee quality across the whole horse market and thereby to act as a kind of 'private' state offering the public good of general trust to everybody. The answer is that the Camorra's services are regarded as most valuable by the 'public' in a climate of pervasive distrust.

democracy as a Hayekian spontaneous order. Its rules, he says, are purely procedural and abstract, and it is not established to serve some particular purpose.[20] Now in their pure form, the rules of democracy declare political decisions subject to simple majority voting. However, a fully democratic polity would be highly unstable. 'A small majority might', as Jon Elster writes, 'easily be reversed, by accidents of participation or by a few individuals changing their minds. More importantly, the majority might be persuaded by the passions of the moment to act rashly and to override individual rights granted by earlier decisions.'[21] For these reasons, the rules of democracy have always been considerably restricted. In modern democracies, the most important restrictions are 'substantive rules protecting privacy, property, civil liberties etc. and . . . procedural rules that require more than a simple majority to change the constitution.'[22] Any such restriction unavoidably narrows the scope of simple majority voting. From a strictly democratic point of view, a democracy curbed by constitutional safeguards such as individual rights and qualified majority requirements must, if compared to unbounded democracy, appear as less uncoercive. Still, as the theory and practice of democracy largely concur, these safeguards usually produce superior political outcomes. Democracy, if interpreted as a spontaneous order, may be seen as a further instance of more than minimally coercive rules leading to more beneficial results.

5. *Spontaneous order and the co-ordination and co-operation it embodies require the pre-existence and universal observance of certain rules.* According to this claim, self-co-ordination and voluntary co-operation are possible only within an institutionalized framework whose rules have been established beforehand. Yet various examples intimate that such co-ordination and co-operation may develop even while a system of rules guiding the parties' conduct does not exist.

On the Western front there existed during the First World War for shorter and longer periods numerous tacit local truces between British and French battalions on the one side and German ones on the other.[23] Such co-operative behaviour seems astonishing. It contrasts not only with the motivations and intentions one would

---

[20] diZerega (1989: 161–3).   [21] Elster (1987: 80).   [22] Ibid. 81.
[23] Ashworth (1980).

usually ascribe to parties at war with each other but also appears almost impossible, for the battlefield is a place highly inhospitable to co-operation and the kind of communication that requires. Not only is each party commonly expected to take the slightest opportunity for improving its own territorial situation and for harming the enemy, but also, in the absence of established channels of communication and, importantly, of rules securing friendly communication, co-ordinated self-restraint among enemy battalions is difficult to imagine. Still, at times an extensive live-and-let-live system did flourish. Robert Axelrod has explained how such co-operation could emerge.[24]

Co-operation among enemy battalions is hard to imagine because, as Axelrod makes clear, each side finds itself locked in a prisoner's dilemma. Rational deliberation recommends each side to shoot rather than not to. If 'we' think 'they' will not shoot, we should do so because that brings us victory. If, however, we think they will shoot, we should do so too, for otherwise we face defeat. Such reasoning saves both sides from defeat but is deadly for many and, in trench warfare, leaves the strategic positions unchanged. Though avoiding the worst, it makes the two sides miss a much superior outcome. If both sides restrained themselves, they would strategically still get the best they could and at the same time spare the soldiers' lives.

How did self-restraint and co-operation develop in trench warfare? According to Axelrod, verbal agreements between enemy battalions played only a minor role. Usually co-operation emerged accidently and was then sustained deliberately. Non-shooting periods at dinner times and during bad weather were tacitly extended. And by aiming effectively at irrelevant targets one side was able to show the other not only its capability of inflicting damage with great precision but also that its restraint was intentional, and that it would punish any lack of reciprocity on the part of the second side. By exchanging such signals enemies were able gradually to establish co-operative relationships. Such relations were not planned in advance and were not supervised by any authority. They exhibit all the features characteristic of self-co-ordination and spontaneous co-operation. Axelrod is surely right when he takes the live-and-let-live system during the First World

[24] Axelrod (1984: 73–87).

War to demonstrate 'that friendship is hardly necessary for coop-eration based upon reciprocity to get started.'[25] Yet in the context of Hayek's idea of a spontaneous social order, and in view of the emphasis this idea puts on rule-following, another conclusion suggests itself more immediately: co-operative relations may un-fold even though no framework of behavioural rules delimiting the parties' legitimate spheres of autonomous choice does exist in advance. With that conclusion the idea of a spontaneous order loses its most central element.

The same conclusion appears to apply to much international politics. Co-operation among nations is largely achieved under conditions of anarchy: a world government that enforces a firmly established set of rules defining the conduct among states does not exist. True, there are the rules of international law. Some of these are very old conventions and are regarded by almost everybody as sacrosanct. Still, states are not subject to international law in the same way as citizens who must obey the law of the land. Interna-tional co-operation depends only partly on pre-existing rules. To a considerable extent, it is sought although—and even because—appropriate rules are lacking. In other words, spontaneous inter-national self-co-ordination is more often an attempt to attain acceptance for new international norms and institutions than an embodiment of the Hayekian type of co-operation under an exist-ing system of rules.[26]

The examples given clearly contradict Hayek's claim that a spontaneous order emerges, and a beneficial outcome is secured, only if the parties move within a well-established and generally known system of rules that renders much of their behaviour pre-dictable. One final example, however, may remind us that on closer inspection things are frequently as ambiguous as to make an unequivocal finding impossible. This example is about what Robin Fox calls 'the inherent rules of violence', rules defining ritual fight-ing among the members of a community or tribe.[27] Such rules, the standard anthropological argument goes, channel and defuse the violence and aggression which are an ineradicable fact of the human condition. The underlying assumption is that without rules violence

---

[25] Axelrod (1984: 87).

[26] For illustration, see the case studies and essays in Oye (1986).

[27] Fox (1977). Among the cases he mentions, see particularly his detailed report on ritual fighting among the people of Tory, a small Irish island.

may get out of control, eventually destroying a community's social fabric. Rules of ritual fighting seem, then, fully to accord with and support Hayek's claim. Yet there may be a complication. Not implausibly, it can be objected that the mere existence of rules of violence invites violence. Knowledge of the rules allows an individual to anticipate a potential adversary's response and to calculate the costs and benefits of an aggressive act, whereas uncertainty about reactions and outcomes makes people less inclined to engage in violence. Rules of ritual fighting may thus also be cited as evidence against Hayek's claim about the beneficial nature of behavioural rules and of the order emerging from their observance.

We have looked at the five claims which I believe constitute Hayek's idea of a spontaneous order. Against each claim counter-examples can be adduced. We saw that spontaneous orders may be quite unable to cope with dispersed information; that the claim about their tendency to self-correction and stability may be empirically vacuous; that the parties' pursuit, within certain behavioural rules, of their self-interest may not save them from highly unfavourable outcomes; that the least coercive rules need not always guarantee the best results; and that rules may be unimportant for self-coordination. The conclusion our examination suggests is this. Contrary to what Hayek wants us to believe, there is no coherent general idea of a spontaneous social order. The claims he advances are intelligible, though not always entirely plausible, as long as we remain within the economic context in which he developed them. It is Hayek's view of the market that lends them a certain significance and enables us to see them as somehow forming a complex notion. Yet once we leave the market, the idea disintegrates. We find it impossible to imagine spontaneous social orders other than that of the market to which all five original claims apply simultaneously. It appears difficult to avoid the verdict that in the social world a distinct category of spontaneous orders, generated by the same mechanism of rule-following and individual adjustment and exhibiting the same information-processing capacities and self-stabilizing tendencies, does not exist, and that Hayek's generalizing move from the market model to a comprehensive and substantive conception of spontaneous social co-ordination fails.

The Hayekian idea of a spontaneous social order appears flawed even if we strip it of its bolder claims and reduce it to an idea about the mechanism of social self-co-ordination. The idea that certain orders spring from rule-following and individual adjustment is, for the purposes of social theoretic analysis, vacuously abstract. The notion of rules seems not only to be 'an especially messy cluster concept . . . with many debatable members'[28] but also to lack discriminatory force since some behavioural regularity, some rule-following, is involved in almost any human action and social interaction. And adjustment obtains whenever human beings co-ordinate their activities. An account in terms only of rule-following and adjustment will, therefore, rarely suffice to explain the emergence of macro-patterns.[29] Recourse to the reasons, the specific desires and beliefs, that make people do what they do is often indispensable. To focus on the agents' reasons need not mean ending up with the kind of intentionalist explanation Hayek dismissively calls 'psychology' and considers unrevealing (e.g. 1949: 67; 1952a: 39). To explain aggregate patterns (the Hayekian spontaneous orders) by tracing them back to individual actions determined by specific desires and beliefs does not render those patterns the result of human intention. In his book *Micromotives and Macrobehavior* Thomas Schelling gives interesting examples of how 'the relation between the behavior characteristic of the individuals who comprise some social aggregate, and the characteristics of the aggregate'[30] may be explored. What distinguishes him from Hayek is that, while using general models, he is far more sensitive to the specifics of a case, its agents, and the situations in

[28] Lewis (1969: 105).

[29] A comparison with Charles Lindblom's (1965) analysis of self-co-ordinating processes, worked out independently of Hayek, casts further doubts on the unique explanatory power Hayek claims for his mechanism. Lindblom shares Hayek's interest in types of social co-ordination other than by central management and, like Hayek, finds that many people simply refuse to believe that there can really be such co-ordination. Moreover, like Hayek, Lindblom mentions the market, the development of common law, and the evolution of language as instances of self-ordering processes. But here the parallels end. While Hayek thinks self-co-ordination rests both on rule-following and adjustment, for Lindblom the crucial explanatory concept is adjustment alone; Lindblom even explicitly rejects any recourse to rules because he counts them among the means of central direction. And again in sharp contrast to Hayek, Lindblom sees self-co-ordination based on adjustment at work especially also in government, for Hayek the paradigm case of co-ordination by central direction. Now Lindblom's approach may harbour its own problems and cannot be adduced as evidence proving Hayek wrong. Yet the comparison shows *how* differently 'rule-following' and 'adjustment' may in social theoretic explanation be employed, further intimating that they lack in analytical power.

[30] Schelling (1978: 13, emphasis omitted).

which they find themselves. Unlike Hayek, Schelling does not in a grandly abstract social theoretic discourse lose sight of the peculiarities of a phenomenon. Nevertheless, he can in substance still agree with Hayek that the analysis of social aggregates, of their emergence and properties, is 'characteristic of a large part of the social sciences, especially of the more theoretical part'.[31]

Social theory, it seems, will do better without the idea of a spontaneous order. That ambitious planning and central direction frequently do not work, while self-co-ordination and decentralized decision-making do, is no evidence for the ubiquitous effectiveness of some principle of spontaneous order. Rather, it may simply reflect what I called people's responsiveness *vis-à-vis* their life conditions: the fact that usually they need not, and do not want to, be told what to do—that they try for themselves to further their interests, making use of established and novel forms of interaction and co-operation and thereby, sometimes, creating aggregative patterns they did not anticipate.

[31] Ibid. 13.

6

Tacit Rule-Following

Hayek's social theory does not end with the idea of a spontaneous order. Hayek makes further far-reaching claims of a social theoretic nature which we must take seriously even if we reject that idea as untenable. In this chapter, we shall examine his thesis that some of the rules of just conduct, which form the institutional basis of spontaneous economic order, are followed unconsciously.

Hayek thinks that wide areas of human activity are guided by behavioural rules. We are able to orient ourselves in the world, exercise skills, and interact with others, he says, because we observe rules.[1] Yet it would in his view be a misunderstanding to believe that thought, perception, skills, and social interaction are all the result of the deliberate application of known rules. Human conduct, he claims, is also based on unconscious, or tacit, rule-following. Hayek thus talks of 'the uncontestable assumption that we are not in fact able to specify all the rules which govern our perceptions and actions' (1967: 60). Tacit rule-following, he explains, is conduct 'guided by rules (. . .) which the acting person need not explicitly know (be able to specify, discursively to describe, or "verbalize")' (1967: 45, footnote omitted).[2] The claim, then, appears to be that often we are not aware of, and are not in a position expressly to state, the rules which actually direct our behaviour.

Its sweeping generality makes it difficult to examine this claim. In order to reach a reasonably definite verdict about its plausibility one must distinguish between different spheres of human conduct. While not entirely unconvincing with respect to sensory perception or to man's basic linguistic capacities,[3] the claim seems

[1] For more on rules and rule-following, see esp. 1967: chs. 3–4; 1973: ch. 2; 1978: ch. 3.

[2] Other passages on unconscious rule-following include 1960: 62; 1967: 56, 66–7; 1973: 11, 18–19, 72; 1976: 11, 38–9.

[3] One should not think here of the grammatical ability to master a particular language (say, French) but of what Chomsky calls the 'universal grammar', the fundamental human capability to become a member of any language community.

problematic in the case of practical skills such as playing the violin. Yet I shall leave these wider conjectures aside and concentrate on the thesis of tacit rule-following only in so far as it may apply to the rules of just conduct, which, as we remember, are for Hayek the rules leading to spontaneous economic order. Thus restricted, the claim we are interested in may provisionally be formulated as follows. We act, and judge the conduct of others, in the market according to rules of which we are only partly aware. As such this idea hardly strikes us as immediately plausible. Hayek offers three arguments designed to lend it credibility.

The first rests on an inference drawn from natural spontaneous orders. In Hayek's view, examples such as that of the iron filings which on a sheet of paper 'arrange themselves' along the lines of force emanating from a magnet placed below,

clearly show that the rules which govern the actions of the elements of such spontaneous orders need not be rules which are 'known' to these elements; it is sufficient that the elements actually behave in a manner which can be described by such rules. The concept of rules as we use it in this context therefore does not imply that such rules exist in articulated ('verbalized') forms . . . (1973: 43)

The analogy presupposed here between natural and social spontaneous orders does not hold, of course, unless one regards persons in naturalistic fashion as filings held in their economic positions by some powerful social magnet. So one might dismiss the Hayekian claim altogether.

We find a second argument, purporting to demonstrate the plausibility of the thesis that we observe some of the rules of conduct unknowingly, in Hayek's theory of cultural evolution. Hayek believes that at the dawn of history people did not distinguish between purpose-oriented and normative imperatives or—to use Max Weber's terminology—between instrumentally rational (*zweckrational*) and value-rational (*wertrational*) action. There was, says Hayek, 'just one established manner of doing things, and knowledge of cause and effect and knowledge of the appropriate

For more on the idea of such a grammar, see e.g. Chomsky (1980). What distinguishes Hayek from Chomsky, however, is Chomsky's (1980: 28) assumption that the rules of the universal grammar are genetically determined, part of the human biological endowment; Hayek believes they are learned unconsciously in the process of cultural evolution. For a discussion relating Hayek's views on rule-following to modern information theory and linguistics, see J. Campbell (1984: 258–61).

or permissible form of action [were] not distinct' (1973: 18). Lacking the awareness that a particular goal could be achieved by different courses of action and that there could be alternative moral constraints, early man did not possess the ability critically to distance himself from, and evaluate, the rules he followed. In this sense he observed them unconsciously. But how then was progress possible and did civilization develop? The answer to this question lies, for Hayek, in the cultural evolution of the market society and in man's ability to learn new rules blindly.

In the early days of mankind, not every group followed exactly the same rules. Also, from time to time some group would as a result of chance stumble upon new rules. In consequence, depending on the particular rules they observed, certain groups were more successful than others. Less fortunate groups either adopted the survival-enhancing rules followed by the more prosperous ones, or they were doomed to dissolve. Hayek believes it was in the course of such an evolutionary process that the rules of just conduct, chief among them the rules of private property, emerged and markets established themselves. Now given what he regards as the fact that those rules were observed tacitly and nobody was able to spell them out, how could the members of a less successful group learn and adopt them at all? Hayek concedes this is a 'difficult question' but eventually he thinks it was 'by example and imitation (or by "analogy")' (1973: 19), surmising that man possesses 'a kind of "movement pattern detector" ' allowing him to recognize rules without actually knowing them and 'a "movement pattern effector" ' enabling him to act in line with rules without consciously applying them (1967: 45).

Hayek does not maintain that even today we still observe all the rules of just conduct unknowingly. Such a claim would be untenable. Yet he is unclear about *how far* we have become able to identify and formulate the rules which originally our ancestors followed blindly. This vagueness comes out in the third argument he adduces to support the thesis of tacit rule-following. This argument rests on an analogy between the sense of language (the *Sprachgefühl*) and the sense of justice (the *Rechtsgefühl*). Describing the sense of language as 'our capacity to follow *yet unformulated* rules', he sees 'no reason why . . . the sense of justice (. . .) should not also consist in such a capacity to follow rules which we do not know in the sense that we can state them' (1967:

45, footnotes omitted, emphasis added). He parallels the two senses but fails to say whether the sense of justice (like the sense of language) is guided by rules 'yet unformulated' but statable in principle, or whether some of the rules of just conduct will always elude articulation. We encounter the same ambiguity elsewhere when Hayek at first suggests that some of the rules are imperceptible as such:

the capacity to judge actions of our own or of others as just or unjust ... must be based on the possession of highly abstract rules governing our actions, although we are not aware of their existence and even less capable of articulating them in words. (1978: 46)

Yet he goes on to remark that '[r]ecent developments in the theory of linguistics at last make explicit those rules to which older linguists used to refer as the *Sprachgefühl*—which is clearly a phenomenon of the same sort as the sense of justice' (1978: 46, footnote omitted), thereby implying that 'at last' we may be in a position to 'make explicit' all the rules constituting our sense of justice too.

I think this ambiguity does not have a neat solution because in fact Hayek advances *two* different claims. The *first* is a retrospective thesis about how man's previously unconscious moral orientations increasingly became articulated and formalized legally. Hayek thinks this development was an invisible-hand process with the common law judge as its main protagonist. For Hayek, this thesis is not merely of historical interest, but above all of great practical relevance, for he believes this evolutionary process also warrants the conclusion that the institution of the common law judge largely guarantees the preservation and further refinement of the rules of the market. The *second* is a systematic thesis holding that the interpretation and application of the rules of law is always guided by higher-order rules which we are unable ever fully to know. Beginning with the historical thesis, we shall now analyse the two claims.

THE HISTORICAL THESIS

In the history of mankind Hayek discerns a steady tendency towards an ever-growing part of the rules of just conduct becoming known explicitly; rules which had previously been observed

unreflectively were more and more followed consciously and expressed in legal terms. For Hayek, the rise of the institution of law
is the story of the gradual legal formalization of man's originally
intuitive sense of justice. This sense, he declares,

[t]his capacity to act, and to recognise whether others act, in accordance
with non-articulated rules probably always exists before attempts are
made to articulate such rules; and most articulated rules are merely more
or less successful attempts to put into words what has been acted upon
before ... (1978: 81)

There is an obvious reason why men increasingly became aware
of those rules, as Hayek notes himself (1973: 99–100; 1976: 15–
16). Especially in jurisdiction there is an internal dynamic at work
inevitably leading to the rules becoming articulated. Rules of just
conduct serve to prevent and settle conflict. In cases of dispute, the
parties invoke rules they think justify their respective positions. It
is then up to the judge to determine the relevant rules and thereby
to decide the case. In this way, the unconscious observance of
rules of conduct transforms into obedience to the law.

Hayek's thesis about the increasing legal articulation of the rules
of just conduct is implausible in moral philosophical as well as
social theoretic respects. To begin with its moral philosophy, that
thesis is based on a curious conception of man's sense of justice
and lacks any emphatic notion of moral reflection. On Hayek's
account, the sense of justice stores humanity's experience with the
market and with the behavioural regularities its operation requires.
He assumes that at some early stage in history the market, the
result of previous cultural evolution by natural selection, was a
firmly established institution, and he thinks that everybody followed the rules on which it rested long before their articulation
and legal codification started. So the Hayekian sense of justice is
an unconscious heritage of that past and consists in an intuitive
knowledge of, and adherence to, the rules that made, and still
make, the market process possible. These rules, as we remember,
are the rules of private property, contract, and tort.

Let us, for the moment, accept Hayek's assumption that in
the distant past a clearly contoured and substantive sense of justice had taken root. Even if that were true, there is no guarantee
that, in the process of its being handed down through the generations, that sense did not undergo major modifications. Hayek himself mentions various circumstances undermining it. Nowadays,

he explains, more and more people work in large organizations; not themselves exposed directly to the market and its demands, they disregard, even despise, its morals (1979: 165; 1983: 33-4). Also, 'prophets and philosophers, from Moses to Plato and St Augustine, from Rousseau to Marx and Freud' (1979: 166) condemned the very rules on which the market builds. Given those corrosive influences, Hayek's trust in an intuitive sense of justice is unwarranted.

Yet the very idea that people once possessed, and instinctively applied, the precepts of just conduct is difficult to sustain. Hayek defines the sense of justice as 'nothing but that capacity to act in accordance with non-articulated rules', and he describes the endeavour to find just solutions as the attempt 'to express in words the yet unarticulated rules' by which a particular conflict should be judged (1978: 81). This is a merely formal account. It does not entitle Hayek to regard views critical of market morals as the false teachings of false prophets. And it does not explain why the unreflected attitudes constituting the Hayekian sense of justice should by themselves embody what is morally right.

Once people become conscious of a particular rule and thereby aware of other feasible rules, there is no reason why they should unthinkingly cling to it and not seriously consider the alternatives. By identifying the originally tacit rules of just conduct with just law, Hayek makes redundant, indeed leaves no room for, explicit moral principles or other normative criteria against which a particular legal version of a previously unconscious rule could be examined. Hayek's view allows neither independent moral standards nor the kind of fundamental moral reflection in the course of which such standards are to be justified. We cannot, as Hayek does, simply regard moral views critical of the market rules as deviations from what once was, and therefore also now should be, considered right. Rather, we should see them as part of our inescapably diverse ideas about justice among which only moral reflection can provide any orientation.

Equally, Hayek has no sense for the problems posed by the application of rules. His view appears to be that just law is the result of previously tacit rules being transmitted into legal rules (1978: 81-2). This means that the unarticulated rules of the unreflective sense of justice must already possess the format of legal rules. More than that, the rules of the legal system are always only defective replicas at best of the rules which we observe when we follow our sense of justice. '[M]ost articulated rules', Hayek writes, 'are merely more or less successful attempts to put into words what has been acted upon before' unconsciously (1978: 81). Hayekian legislation and adjudication do not seem to require judgement. One must wonder how the sense of justice, acquired long ago, was capable of anticipating, and taking appropriately into account, the social and technological circumstances of modern life. One would think that the rapid changes characteristic of advanced societies call for occasional adjustments in the legal system. Hayek does not deny the need for adjustment (e.g. 1973: 109). But he does not seem to regard it as an endeavour to adapt the legal rules to changing empirical circumstances *while* preserving their moral thrust, and he does not therefore see any role for the faculty of judgement. At best, he envisages functional modifications to make the exchange system work more smoothly.

These criticisms may be summed up as follows. By permitting the tacit moral attitudes to become the legal rules of just conduct, by excluding fundamental moral reflection and independent normative standards, and by denying judgement any role, Hayek *naturalizes* justice. He derives justice directly from routines which, though given to mankind in a process he calls 'cultural' evolution, are (on his own account) none the less the unmitigated result of natural selection and in no way shaped by moral considerations about right and wrong. The intuitive sense of justice he depicts as an incontestably reliable court of appeal. He conceives of it not as a fragile source of moral orientation whose formation and cultivation depend on favourable social conditions but as a faculty not mediated socially, therefore as a quasi-natural, though not genetically based (1979: 159–60), ability of human beings.

So far we have discussed the moral philosophical aspects of Hayek's historical thesis. More important and more interesting, however, are its social theoretic side and the practical lesson he thinks it teaches us. This lesson is about how best to secure the preservation and further refinement of the legal rules of the market. To recapitulate: Hayek's thesis is that there is in the history of mankind a continuous process in the course of which the originally unconscious rules of the market have gradually become explicit and been transformed into today's systems of private law. For Hayek, the principal character of this story is the common law judge. It was independent judges, he believes, who in an invisible-hand process of decentralized adjudication contributed most to laying the legal foundations of the market. In the remainder of this section we shall look at the mechanism Hayek sees at work in this process and consider the plausibility of his conclusion that the future development of the market rules is again best left to the very same mechanism. I only mention, but shall not further comment upon, the fact that Hayek arrives at his universalist thesis by generalizing the historical development of a particular legal culture, that of English common law (1973: chs. 4–6).[4]

Hayek's reconstruction of how the intuitive rules of the market were transformed into private law identifies the common law judges as the principal agents of this process. As we saw earlier, Hayek assumes that essentially these rules are already being observed, even if only tacitly, when the process of their legal articulation begins. In this situation, a judge trying to settle a dispute may reach his verdict in one of the following ways. Depending on the specific features of a case and the degree of explicitness the system of rules has already attained, he may arrive at his decision

- by confirming or modifying or sharpening a particular inter-pretation of an already explicit rule; or
- by articulating and at the same time specifying a rule hitherto followed tacitly; or
- by introducing a new (higher-order) rule that is to resolve conflict among existing explicit rules.

Now what is it that renders the common law judge the ideal per-son to formulate, and translate into law, the intuitively observed

---

[4] Thorough historical scholarship calls seriously in question the Hayekian story of the English common law. Atiyah (1979), in his magisterial study, conceives, first, of the evolution of the English common law not as a process of articulating previously tacit rules but as the conversion of the law of contract into the law of the free market. Secondly, in Atiyah's view the period during which the idea of freedom of contract unfolded and found its strongest expression in law is confined to the years between 1770 and 1870. Before 1770 the law of contract was severely curbed by various regulatory, paternalistic, and moralistic restrictions, while after 1870 (until the 1970s) it was again increasingly subject to a whole range of redistributive measures and to legislation designed to protect contracting parties with systematically weaker bargaining power (such as workers and consumers). Atiyah does not discern a continuous tendency towards ever more market-friendly rules. At times, even Hayek himself seems to have reservations about postulating such an unequivocal trend (1973: 141–3).

rules of the market, which (as we must not forget) are for Hayek at the same time the rules of just conduct?

Hayek's answer has two elements, the first of which is this. Only a judge but no political authority, he says, is free from distorting special interests and immune to the corruption which political power invites (1973: 87–8, 96–8). Hence, only judges could invent, and will maintain, the idea of abstract rules covering an unknown number of future instances and parties. It seems unlikely, he conjectures, 'that any authority with power of command would ever have developed law in the sense in which the judges developed it, that is as rules applicable to anyone who finds himself in a position definable in abstract terms' (1973: 97). This conception of the judge as the politically independent creator and guardian of law Hayek deploys especially against what he regards as the fundamentally mistaken rationalist view of 'legislation [as] the sole source of law' (1973: 91). Legislative bodies, he explains, were originally designed only to decide in matters of public law, that is, in questions concerning the organization of government, but gradually (and deplorably, he believes) they also assumed the prerogative of making and changing the rules of just conduct. Being instruments of political authority and, therefore, liable to interventionist fallacies, parliaments are, Hayek claims, in general not suited for the development and protection of the rules of the market (1973: 89–93).

The second consideration leading Hayek to assert that the legal articulation and systematization of the rules of just conduct had to lay, and must largely remain, in the hands of the common law judge is about the special intellectual capacities required for adjudication. Only the activity of being a common law judge, Hayek believes, generates and cultivates the ability to formulate hitherto tacit rules:

It seems that the constant necessity of articulating rules in order to distinguish between the relevant and the accidental in the precedents which guide him, produces in the common law judge a capacity for discovering general principles rarely acquired by a judge who operates with a supposedly complete catalogue of applicable rules before him. When the generalizations are not supplied ready made, a capacity for formulating abstractions is apparently kept alive, which the mechanical use of verbal formulae tends to kill. (1973: 87)

From these considerations Hayek concludes that the rules of the market developed, and could only develop, in a decentralized process in which they were progressively articulated and refined by independent judges. Hayek sees so close a link between the common law judge and the market system that he repeatedly describes him as an 'institution' and 'organ' of spontaneous economic order (1973: 95, 119). It is Hayek's unqualified contention 'that the judges by their decisions of particular cases gradually approach a system of rules of conduct which is most conducive to producing an efficient order of actions' (1973: 118). In other words, only a common law system and common law judges guarantee that in the long run the rules of the market are maintained and further perfected. We only grasp the full force of this practical claim, Hayek declares, when we realize that the development of judge-made law is merely one particular example of many beneficial evolutionary processes, only a further 'instance of those "products of human action but not of human design" in which the experience gained by the experimentation of generations embodies more knowledge than was possessed by anyone' (1973: 119). However, before falling in with Hayek's evolutionist incantations we ought to examine carefully whether the gradual development of law by independent judges will really always produce the rules required for economic self-co-ordination. In particular, we should look at the conditions that must obtain if this process is invariably to lead to the result Hayek so confidently foresees.[5]

The whole process of unfolding the common law crucially rests on the judges' shoulders. An obvious question naturally posing itself, then, concerns the judges' sense of justice. What are its

[5] Hayek's claim has close affinities with the views of Bruno Leoni (1972). Leoni, like Hayek, wants a large part of the legal framework to be a common law system. He bases his argument on the, he alleges, fundamental parallels between planned economy and legislation on the one side, and between the market process and the development of lawyers' law on the other—parallels extending also to the failures and achievements of the respective co-ordination mechanisms. Analogous to the planned economy, in a legal system based on legislation the decisions are taken centrally, Leoni explains, by representatives with unrestricted power but 'fatally limited' knowledge of the jurisprudential problems at hand, and with an equally limited respect for the citizens' wishes. In contrast, the development of law by independent judges has, he thinks, the invaluable advantage that their power is restricted to finding a solution in a particular case and is further bound by precedent, and that the whole process is 'a sort of vast, continuous, and chiefly spontaneous collaboration between the judges and the judged in order to discover what the people's will is in a series of definite instances' (Leoni 1972: 21–2). However, Leoni (like Hayek, as we shall see) fails to detail the mechanisms that would bear out his claims. Contrary to what Hayek suggests (1973: 168 n. 35), Leoni does not argue that legislation should be completely banned from altering private law (see Leoni 1972: 9, 23, 131–2).

principal ideas? Contrary to what one would expect, this sense does not, on Hayek's account, comprise a genuinely moral orientation but is simply identical with the economic knowledge of the rules and institutions on which a market system depends. This comes out unambiguously in many passages where Hayek describes the reasoning on which the judges must found their decisions. These decisions, he explains, must be guided by the 'general principles on which the going order of society is based' (1973: 87). When they fill gaps in the existing body of law, judges must proceed 'in a manner that will serve to maintain and improve that order of actions which the already existing rules make possible' (1973: 100, footnote omitted). New rules may be introduced when 'they are found to be required complements of the already established rules if the order which rests on them is to operate smoothly and efficiently' (1973: 123).

In the light of this account of judicial reasoning, it is hardly surprising when Hayek's conception of jurisprudence draws its main inspiration from the economic theory of the market: 'Without . . . an insight into what the scoffers still deride as the "invisible hand", the function of rules of just conduct is indeed unintelligible' (1973: 114). Recognition of the market mechanism, Hayek insists, is essential 'in the philosophy of law, in so far as it guides jurisdiction and legislation' (1973: 114). Jurisprudence, he opines, arrives at an adequate understanding of the 'purpose' of law only if it consults economics; that law must serve the formation of a spontaneous order is an idea which the philosophy of law finds difficult to express clearly unless it takes recourse to 'the explanation of that order provided by social theory, particularly economics' (1973: 112).

To maintain that without an insight into how the 'invisible hand' operates the function of law is unintelligible is to say that the judges must possess an extensive knowledge of the market process if they are to master the task Hayek assigns to them. Now the articulation of the rules of just conduct starts when all or most of them are still observed tacitly; the judges are thought to take up their role at a time when nobody is supposed to have any theoretical economic knowledge. So how could they already have any deeper insights into how the market works and what its institutional framework must be? Hayek seems to think that they acquired such knowledge in a process of trial and error while exercising their office. He vaguely writes that the rules would never have been discovered and articulated 'if the existence of a spontaneous order of actions had not set the judges their peculiar task' (1973: 123).

This is not a very plausible explanation. Remember: Hayek puts forward a claim to the effect that *invariably* 'the judges by their decisions of particular cases gradually approach' a body of rules conducive to spontaneous order (1973: 118, and elsewhere). If there were such a process, it would have to contain a mechanism *systematically* (and not only accidentally) steering the development of the rules towards those required for a market. It would have to be a mechanism operating primarily on the judges (for they are the principal agents), instilling into them an economic view of society and making them see it, above all, as a spontaneous order. However, there is nothing in Hayek's account suggesting that they, or anyone else, would necessarily acquire such a view. On the contrary, he assumes that the market rules had developed imperceptibly and were at least for a time observed unconsciously.

I conclude that Hayek manages to get the process of rule-articulation and rule-improvement going only at the price of illicitly equipping the judges with a knowledge they cannot have had. The thesis that the rules of the market took shape in a long decentralized decision-making process in which, Hayek claims, nobody had in mind their final overall design (e.g. 1973: 100) is actually conditional upon the circumstance that right from the beginning the judges must have had a fairly good idea about what the eventual system of rules should look like and how, therefore, they would have to decide the cases before them in order to approach it. This renders his thesis self-defeating.

There is another, related condition again necessary but again officially ruled out by Hayek. This time it is not about the expertise the judges must have if market rules are to emerge but about their basic political outlook. Hayek describes the activity of articulating and modifying rules essentially as the solution of local technical problems, as 'piecemeal tinkering' (1973: 118). He denies that in order to do their job judges would have to follow certain political preferences or know anything 'about any "interest of society" which they serve' (1973: 119; similarly on 100–1). Hayek is here fully in line with his own rejection of intentionalist social theoretic explanations, explanations which regard social outcomes merely as the result of outcome-oriented individual action (e.g. 1949: 67; 1952a: 39).

Yet why should the judges always prefer rules of horizontal co-ordination over forms of hierarchical direction? Even if the rules the judges must find are to be abstract, that is, applicable to an unknown number of future instances, they need not compellingly be the rules of the free market.[6] Moreover the process of rule-articulation and rule-refinement, as Hayek describes it, contains no incentive mechanism inducing judges always to choose solutions and rules as near to the market rationale as possible. It seems that, Hayek's disclaimer notwithstanding, the judges must have a consistent political preference for market rules if such rules are to be the systematic (and not merely accidental) result of the Hayekian evolution of the common law. However, whether judges do have such liberal predilections is, of course, an entirely contingent matter. Thus, a process of decentralized judicial decision-making possesses no inherent teleology towards market institutions and provides no guarantee for the resultant law necessarily to consist of rules of economic self-co-ordination.

This even Hayek implicitly acknowledges. He admits that the gradual development of judge-made law, if left to itself, may run into a dead end. 'For a variety of reasons', he writes, it 'may lead into an impasse from which it cannot extricate itself by its own forces' (1973: 88). Of the reasons he gives, two deserve special mention. The first reckons with the possibility (to which I pointed above) that the judges have a class-bound illiberal bias (1973: 89). The second is about the limited foreseeability of the long-term consequences particular judicial decisions have. Undesirable implications of a specific precedent may become visible only later when judges are no longer prepared to reverse it because they would thereby gravely disappoint people's expectations which in the meantime it has encouraged (1973: 88).

---

[6] It is an established criticism, formulated, among others, by Raz (1979: 220, 226–9), that—contrary to what Hayek (1960: 153–6, 220–33) suggests—abstract rules are not by themselves liberal or minimally coercive and need not be congenial with the functional requirements of a free market. In jurisprudential terms, this is the rejection of the Hayekian idea that the rule of law guarantees individual freedom. Kukathas (1989: 148–64) has a discussion of this idea and its critique, and Waldron (1989) analyses the different conceptions of the rule of law (Hayek's among them) in liberal theories.

By advancing such reasons Hayek concedes that the common law judges cannot be trusted to generate market rules systematically. His admission amounts to nothing less than the nullification of his own claim that we have here an example of a consistently beneficial invisible-hand mechanism with invariably desirable outcomes. Hayek's concession goes even further. As a remedy for evolutionary aberrations he recommends legislation, the very method of creating law of which elsewhere (e.g. 1973: 143–4) he is highly suspicious. '[L]aw as we know it', he admits, 'could never have fully developed without . . . the occasional intervention of a legislator to extricate it from the dead ends into which the gradual evolution may lead it' (1973: 100; similarly on 88–9). Conditions analogous to those required for the development of judge-made law must obtain if legislation is to bring the articulation of the market rules back on track. Legislators must know, first of all, what the overall institutional structure of a market system should look like and, secondly, they must emphatically want to replace judge-made law inimical to the market rationale. Hence, again conditions must hold for which there is no room in an invisible-hand process.

Although Hayek is dimly aware that resort to legislation may introduce an intentionalist element incompatible with a basically evolutionist account, he nevertheless tries to maintain the impression that the development of private law was an invisible-hand process. Seeking to reassure us he declares that

it remains still true that the system of rules as a whole does not owe its structure to the design of either judges or legislators. It is the outcome of a process of evolution in the course of which spontaneous growth of customs and deliberate improvements of the particulars of an existing system have constantly interacted. . . . No system of law has ever been designed as a whole, and even the various attempts at codification could do no more that systematize an existing body of law and in doing so supplement it or eliminate inconsistencies. (1973: 100)

Yet Hayek cannot really convince us that here we still have an 'evolutionary' process before us. Contrary to what he says, the articulation and perfection of law is *not*, on his own account, a process in which judicial decision-making and legislation 'have constantly *interacted*'. Legislation he calls in to correct deficiencies in judge-made law. So legislation becomes the ultimate arbiter of which course the 'evolution' of law should take.[7] Such arbitration must be based on a clear understanding of, and unambiguous preference for, market institutions.

Furthermore it is of course true that a thousand years ago nobody had the slightest idea of what the legal system of a late twentieth-century market society would look like, and that such a system is not the implementation from scratch of a premeditated plan. Only an eccentric would claim so. Yet the rejection of any such view does not commit us, as Hayek appears to think, to an evolutionist perspective and, more specifically, to the idea that the law of the market society is the result of a process which has been necessarily beneficial because it was based on decentralized judicial decision-making and could thereby build on the accumulated experience of all previous generations. Unable to discern any teleologically oriented mechanism and, therefore, disinclined to believe that the Hayekian evolution must unfold the rules of the market with systematic necessity, we should, I suggest, take a more sceptical stance. We see the emergence of those rules better as the historically contingent outcome of *bricolage* and chance, or as—in John Gray's phrase—one of 'the vagaries of mankind's random walk in historical space',[8] a caprice which, once we have begun to realize its significance, we may further cultivate—if we so wish.

In sum, Hayek's historical thesis of tacit rule-following, the idea that originally unconscious rules of just conduct came to be articulated as the law of the market society in an invisible-hand process, is flawed in fundamental moral philosophical and social theoretic respects. It is committed to an indefensible moral naturalism and fails to offer a satisfactory explanatory account. Seeing the common law judge as the principal character of this evolutionary process, Hayek endows him with expertise and political preferences incompatible with a non-intentionalist, invisible-hand explanation.

---

[7] That in the end Hayek relies on legislation also shows in his own model constitution, which gives the judiciary a rather subordinate role and entrusts the further development of the rules of just conduct to a special assembly. Starting from his distinction between *law proper* ('nomos', consisting of the rules of just conduct and indispensable for economic self-co-ordination) and *public law* (law structurally analogous to commands and forming the basis of any governmental activity), Hayek envisages a bicameral parliament. The *Legislative Assembly* has no tasks and powers other than to alter, if necessary, the rules of just conduct. Within those rules and attendant fiscal constraints laid down by the Legislative Assembly the *Governmental Assembly*, the second chamber, decides over the provision of public services (1979: ch. 17).   [8] Gray (1986: 70).

Hayek's practical claim that the development of the market rules is best left to the common law judge definitively collapses when he is forced to give legislation the role of a *deus ex machina* saving the judge-made law from its evolutionary pitfalls.

THE SYSTEMATIC THESIS

Hayek advances a second thesis employing the notion of tacit rule-following. At its briefest, its claim is that the interpretation and application of the rules of law are governed by higher-ranking rules at least some of which we do not consciously know. The thesis, in one of Hayek's own formulations, is that

> no system of articulated law can be applied except within a framework of generally recognized but often unarticulated rules of justice. . . . [T]he whole process of development, change and interpretation of law would become wholly unintelligible if we closed our eyes to the existence of a framework of such unarticulated rules from which the articulated law receives its meaning. (1967: 102, footnotes omitted)

Let us call this the systematic thesis of tacit rule-following because the subject-matter is not now a historical process in the course of which unconscious rules gradually take shape as legal rules but law as a body of already explicit rules whose application systematically (i.e. inescapably) depends on the tacit observance of certain background rules.

How this systematic claim relates to the historical thesis remains unclear. Hayek seems to think that, as all modern Western societies now have comprehensive and explicit legal systems, the process of verbalizing the rules of the market has come to, or is very near, its end (1978: 82). His idea appears to be that even when all the rules which together constitute the law of the land have become positive legal norms, there remains a residue of other, higher-order rules defying articulation in principle.

Hayek's assumption that the interpretation and application of law involves a hierarchy of rules emerges, for example, when he discusses Ronald Dworkin's view that law is a 'collection' of relatively short-lived rules informed by more basic and enduring principles. While professing to be basically in agreement with Dworkin, Hayek has reservations about the term 'collection'.

Instead, he prefers to speak of law as a 'system of rules', that is, as 'a body of rules ... mutually adjusted to each other and possess[ing] an order of rank' and including not only rules in articulated form but also rules 'implicit in the system' or rules not yet found but none the less necessary 'to make the several rules consistent' (1976: 159 n. 4).

We are able to put law into practice, we can in a consistent fashion settle problems of meaning among the legal rules, we can bridge discontinuities and remove contradictions, Hayek believes, only because we rely on higher-order rules of which we are not fully aware. As he explains:

> it seems probable that no system of articulated rules can exist or be fully understood without a background of unarticulated rules which will be drawn upon when gaps are discovered in the system of articulated rules.
> This governing influence of a background of unarticulated rules explains why the application of general rules to particular instances will rarely take the form of a syllogism, since only articulated rules can serve as explicit premises of such a syllogism. (1978: 81–2)

So what should we think of Hayek's idea that the interpretation and application of law—of the legal rules defining just conduct—is governed by meta-rules some of which elude conscious recognition?

Hayek leaves no doubt that beyond the rules of law the systematic thesis also applies to the rules of human action, perception, and thought in general:

> conscious thought ... must ... be assumed to be directed by rules which in turn cannot be conscious—by a supra-conscious mechanism which operates upon the contents of consciousness but which cannot itself be conscious. (1967: 61, footnotes omitted)

That same notion of supra-conscious control he puts forward when he surmises that there exists

> a ... general principle applying to all conscious and particularly all rational processes, namely the principle that among their determinants there must always be some rules which cannot be stated or even be conscious. (1967: 62)

Passages such as these confirm that in Hayek's writings we indeed find the idea that actual rule-following depends at least partly on the tacit observance of higher-order rules.

Returning to the rules of just conduct: what is the systematic thesis really about? Hayek appears to offer a theoretical account of the mental operations occurring when we interpret and apply law, an account comprising two more specific claims. The first is the claim that the interpretation and application of the rules of law is guided by meta-rules, the second that at least some of these meta-rules will always be followed unconsciously. We shall discuss these claims in turn.

Is it plausible to think of judges[9] as resorting to meta-rules when they interpret law, when they fill gaps and resolve contradictions encountered in the existing body of legal rules? This must be doubted. Legal rules often contain generic and other abstract terms calling for specification. Such specification requires determinant judgement. The judge must establish how a rule is to be understood; he must decide whether and in which way the rule in question applies to a particular person or instance. Now Hayek's meta-rules, should they really be rules, again include terms demanding specification. Thus, if the interpretation of rules is thought to depend on higher-order rules, and if rules 'must in some sense be general',[10] such interpretation may rapidly proliferate into an infinite regress: the interpretation of rules requires meta-rules, these meta-rules, being rules in need of interpretation themselves, call for meta-meta-rules, and so forth. Its potential open-endedness is a most serious weakness of the rule-based model by which Hayek seeks to explain the faculty of judgement.

To admit that the abstract terms usually found in legal rules have to be specified in order to be workable does not commit us to the view that only further rules can achieve such specification. When judges pronounce that a certain term and the rule of which it forms part are to be understood in such and such a way, the result of their deliberations should be taken as what in fact it is: a decision. In other words, they must be seen as defining a term (and rule), as fixing its meaning by choosing one among various alternative solutions. Such choice, however, need not be arbitrary but is usually thought to be based on legal and moral reasoning. By presenting the interpretation of law as an entirely rule-governed activity Hayek not only ascribes to it a precision it cannot have

---

[9] I shall concentrate here on judges (and leave out the wider legal public) because judges are expected to interpret the law authoritatively. By doing so I want to make sure that throughout the focus is on the important problem that the meta-rules relied upon cannot be any rules but must be the 'right' ones leading to correct interpretations and, ultimately, just decisions.   [10] Marshall (1983: 183).

but also depicts judges as mere automatons, as executors of a hierarchical order of rules whose origin and nature remain entirely in the dark.

Thus, for Hayek *judgement depends on rules and rule-following*. Further still, judgement as a human faculty of its own does not exist, its function being performed by the mechanical application of higher-order rules. Hayek seems to assume that this faculty (as far as he would allow for it) is formally fully theorizable; in his view, we may not be aware of the content of all the rules on which our judgement builds, but we know for certain that when we reflect about how to apply some rule of conduct we resort to higher-order rules.

We may illuminate Hayek's conception of rule-following and judgement by looking at a sharply contrasting account, the idea that *rule-following ultimately depends on judgement*. One variant of this Wittgensteinian view sees the observance of a rule as hinging on an intuitive grasp of what actions will fall under it. To obey a rule is thus seen as a practical and not as a theory-guided activity, as equivalent to the mastery of a technique or practice. When we follow a rule we do not, indeed cannot, consult some external criterion (such as another rule) confirming that we do obey the rule. According to this first variant, then, judgement—an implicit understanding or command of the rule—precedes our following it.

Another Wittgensteinian variant makes the specific content of a rule one follows dependent on the latest instance in which one has observed that rule. The basic idea is here that the continuation of a rule always involves an element of creativity and subjectivity; what particular rule one actually follows is at stake anew in each further instance. According to this version, we can only with hindsight, when looking back at the series of instances that give a rule its content, say which specific rule was followed. This second variant is diametrically opposed to Hayek's conception. While Hayekian judgement is rigidly rule-directed, this account regards judgement as unbounded to the point of arbitrariness.[11]

---

[11] I have here spoken loosely of the Wittgenstein*ian* conception that rule-following depends on judgement. What Wittgenstein's own views were remains disputed. The second of the two Wittgensteinian variants distinguished I take to underlie Kripke (1982), while I find the first variant to be at the core of McGinn (1984). McGinn also provides an extensive assessment of Kripke's Wittgensteinian account.

In an attempt to break 'the twin stranglehold of methodical rules and arbitrary subjectivism', Ronald Beiner argues for a mediating conception of judgement and rule-following. Judgement, he writes, 'is a form of mental activity that is not bound to rules, is not subject to explicit specification of its mode of operation (. . .), and comes into play beyond the confines of rule-governed intelligence. At the same time, judgment is not without rule or reason, but rather, must strive for general validity.'[12] While far from exhaustive and incontestable, Beiner's conception as well as the Wittgensteinian variants mentioned help to bring into focus the entirely passive role that Hayek attributes to the rule-follower. These alternative views further enhance the impression that the hands of the Hayekian judges are completely tied by the dictates of rules.

Within the systematic thesis the second component is Hayek's claim that some of those meta-rules guiding the interpretation and application of the first-order legal rules are observed *unknowingly*. It is not clear how this claim is to be understood. Certainly, Hayek cannot mean that those tacit meta-rules leave us no choice among rival interpretations, forcing us to select the 'correct' solution. This would amount to an untenable claim about a hidden causal influence that our sense of justice (in which those tacit meta-rules would presumably be ingrained) has on our judgement of how a particular first-order rule is to be applied.

Perhaps Hayek has recourse to the notion of tacit meta-rules in order to account for the fact that in spite of their highly abstract nature there is, with regard to many rules, usually a remarkable consensus on how they should be interpreted. Yet if his aim really is to explain why a legal public is not in chaotic disagreement about every single legal norm, he need not resort to the obscure idea that there are meta-rules observed unconsciously. It would suffice to say that the public shares certain background assumptions which nobody calls into question either because nobody is aware of them or because nobody disputes them as they do not raise problems of justice.

What else can Hayek's idea that some of the meta-rules are followed unconsciously be about? Given his insistence on the importance of preserving the rules of just conduct and the social wisdom they embody, Hayek must mean this claim to have more

---

[12] Beiner (1983: 2).

than theoretical significance. I can think of two respects in which the idea of tacit meta-rules may, in Hayek's social thought, be relevant *practically*.

First, man's sense of justice may retain certain unconscious (meta-) rules even after in a long historical process the main rules constituting that sense have been recognized and incorporated in the law. Although eluding articulation, these meta-rules may be indispensable to the application of the explicit legal rules. '[N]o system of articulated rules', Hayek says, 'can exist or be fully understood without a background of unarticulated rules' (1978: 81–2). This insight, he might argue, will be of the highest practical importance when attempts are undertaken to radically alter the legal system. Tampering with the traditional, evolved rules of just conduct might, Hayek appears to fear, endanger or even destroy the knowledge and wisdom contained in those tacit meta-rules. The practical conclusion to be drawn would be a warning against any institutional reform that wants to do away with, or substantially to modify, the (market) rules of just conduct.

If the preservation of tacit social wisdom is the thrust of Hayek's claim about the unconscious observance of meta-rules, this claim is difficult to discuss for it has a considerable self-immunizing capacity. How can something be examined if one does not know whether it exists? A critic cannot see Hayek's claim as anything other than a stratagem for declaring the market rules taboo. Surely an argument in favour of the market and its rules must be based on more robust reasoning than Hayek's extremely speculative notion of supra-conscious meta-rules.

Quite apart from this fundamental objection there is another consideration militating against the thesis that man's sense of justice contains invaluable tacit meta-rules indispensable for the application of the rules of law. The idea of such meta-rules would possess some plausibility if we found it difficult to understand the content and function of Hayek's rules of just conduct. But this is not the case. As we have seen earlier, the rationale underlying these rules is that of 'private property' or, more broadly, of 'the internalization of external effects'. Under changing social and technological circumstances the implementation of the idea of private property may pose certain problems. We may not have 'yet succeeded everywhere in so delimiting the individual domain as to constrain the owner in his decisions to take account of all those effects' (1973: 109).

Nevertheless we have well-corroborated guidelines to hand: 'In our efforts to improve the principles of demarcation we [can at least] build on an established system of rules which serves as the basis of the going order maintained by the institution of property' (1973: 109). The internalization of external effects, Hayek writes, 'is achieved on the whole by the *simple* conception of property as the exclusive right to use a particular thing' (1949: 20, emphasis added). He concedes that there are problems with regard to land or 'the control of the air or of electric power, or of inventions and of literary or artistic creations'. To solve them we must have recourse to the idea of property: 'nothing short of going back to [the] rationale of property will help us to decide what should be in the particular instance the sphere of control . . . of the individual' (1949: 20-1, emphasis omitted). Hayek himself demonstrates here that we know the core idea informing the rules of just conduct fairly well. Hence, it is not particularly plausible to assume that in order to understand and be able to apply them we are in need of higher-order rules. From this I infer that Hayek's claim about the tacit observance of meta-rules is wanting if its thrust is to warn against the loss of their social wisdom in cases of radical reform.

There is another respect in which Hayek's thesis that some of the meta-rules are followed tacitly may be practically relevant. Those unconscious meta-rules, he also appears to think, account for the limits to explicit justifiability when the rules of law are being applied. He seems to have such limits in mind when he says that the 'governing influence of a background of unarticulated rules explains why the application of general rules to particular instances will rarely take the form of a syllogism, since only articulated rules can serve as explicit premises of such a syllogism' (1978: 82; similarly in 1960: 208-9). The conclusion suggested is that we cannot expect judges to present a wholly explicit account of the reasons leading them to view a case in a particular way, that we cannot expect them to give us a fully exhaustive justification for their decision.

Hayek seems opposed here to a deductive model of rationality. This model insists not only that for a course of action to be taken a reason must be given but also that upon demand further reasons should be produced explaining why one should accept the first reason as valid at all. For Hayek, the deductive model epitomizes a fundamental error of 'Cartesian rationalism', the error that 'anything which . . . could not be fully justified on rational grounds appeared as an irrational superstition. The rejection as "mere opinion" of all that could not be demonstrated to be true by his criteria became the dominant characteristic of the movement which he [Descartes] started' (1973: 10). Obviously, behind the deductive model of rationality an infinite regress looms. If this model were to apply to legal reasoning, courts could hardly ever meet the demand for justification and could, Hayek might fear, easily be seen as deciding irrationally or arbitrarily. There can be no question that Hayek's reservations about the deductive model are well founded.[13] However, it seems that his attempt to contain the possibility of an infinite regress by declaring some of the higher-order rules tacit still betrays in itself a commitment to a deductivist view which, officially, he rejects.

When Hayek tries to exclude the possibility of an infinite regress by introducing the notion of tacit meta-rules, he makes the judges' reasoning appear arbitrary in a different way. How do Hayekian judges solve a legal problem of justice? Hayek would probably say that they would, in a state of disinterested and dispassionate reflection, consult the law, listen to what their sense of justice with its partly tacit meta-rules tells them, and then decide a case accordingly. *Vis-à-vis* the legal subjects seeking justice before the court, a judge would point to the legal rules he found to be relevant and explain what he understood them to mean. In so far as he felt himself unable to accommodate a case within the explicit body of law, he would, according to Hayek, simply inform the parties that his sense of justice had told him such and such to be the solution.

Jurisdiction of this sort may be acceptable in a society where judges possess authority by force of traditional legitimacy. In modern Western societies, however, it could easily be considered arbitrary. Modern societies are discursive societies, and their citizens expect judges to give reasons for their decisions. No judge could claim validity for his decisions merely on the grounds that they were what his sense of justice had told him. To be sure, adjudication is not an open-ended discourse analogous to that conducted in political and legal philosophy. Within a reasonable time, a final and binding decision must be taken. Yet even if the existing law does not cover a case, judges must base their decisions

---

[13] See e.g. Rescher (1988).

on reasons, whether these result from extending an existing rule, invoking a new one, or drawing an analogy. To leave the decision of hard cases entirely to the judge's sense of justice must inevitably be seen as opening the door to potential arbitrariness, for judges' sense of right and wrong is the product of their political preferences and of the social and professional climate within which they move. So Hayek's attempt to contain rationalism's potentially boundless justificatory demands by postulating supra-conscious meta-rules must fail.

The analysis presented here suggests that the notion of unconsciously observed meta-rules of law is too speculative and creates more problems than it solves. The idea of meta-rules serving the interpretation and application of the rules of law invites an infinite regress and is therefore unable to provide an account of the faculty of judgement. The claim that some of those meta-rules are followed unconsciously raises the question of how they influence the judge's reasoning and whether they do not reduce him to an automaton applying them mechanically. The fact that we know quite well that the Hayekian rules of just conduct pivot round the notion of private property calls into question the very necessity of having meta-rules guiding our understanding of those market rules. And, as we have just seen, the appeal to unknowable meta-rules harbours the risk of covert arbitrariness and bias. In view of these objections, the systematic thesis about tacit meta-rules informing the interpretation and application of law must, I believe, be abandoned.

7

Cultural Evolution

As we saw in the preceding chapter, Hayek's thesis about the tacit observance of certain rules vital for the market introduces into his social theory an element of opaqueness that contrasts sharply with the entirely transparent, though seriously flawed, idea of a spontaneous economic order. Hayek shrouds the rules of the market in still greater obscurity when he makes the further claim that they possess a social wisdom of which human reason is incapable. This claim lies at the heart of his theory of cultural evolution, and it is this theory which we shall now examine.

The self-co-ordination in the market and the institutional and social background conditions required for this process to operate do not pose intractable explanatory problems. We do not find it particularly difficult to understand how, in the market, co-operation works. Nor does Hayek. Not least, his idea of a spontaneous economic order—the idea that among people observing certain rules and continuously adjusting to local changes a complex network of economic relations develops—represents an attempt to capture the main features of the market mechanism.

There seems, then, to be nothing mysterious, nothing '*really* incomprehensible' (1988: 94), about the market process and the institutional framework within which it takes place. What Hayek calls 'rules' are constraining and enabling conditions under which people are free to pursue their interests in the way they deem best and to engage in exchange with whomever they want. To common sense it appears natural to think that certain co-ordination or allocation problems may be eased or solved by altering some of those background conditions. Such reform, one would think, does not present insurmountable intellectual obstacles as it should not be too difficult to anticipate what the overall consequences of modifying some of the rules will be. This, however, says Hayek, is a 'fatal conceit' (1988). The widespread belief in man's ability to grasp all the interdependencies between the market rules and the market process and, therefore, in the possibility of comprehensive institutional reform is, in his view, false—for two related reasons. He thinks this belief overestimates the powers of the human mind and neglects the social wisdom inherent in those rules.

Nobody, Hayek says, possessed the imagination and intelligence needed to devise the institutions which have given rise to modern Western society: 'at no moment . . . could individuals have designed, according to their purposes, the functions of the rules that gradually did form the order' (1988: 72; likewise in 1979: 164). Hayek does not only make the uncontentious claim that as a matter of historical fact modern market society has not been planned in advance. He also maintains that even today '[w]e do not really understand' how the market rules bring about economic order (1979: 166).[1] There are, he thinks, 'constitutional limitations' to man's knowledge about how those rules work, limitations which 'form a permanent barrier to the possibility of a rational construction of the whole of society' (1973: 15). Hence his insistence that any attempt at radically overhauling the institutional foundations of Western market society must fail, whatever its specific ambitions may be.

To say, as Hayek does, that '[w]e were not intelligent enough' (1979: 164, emphasis omitted) to design the institutions of the market is to imply that they are of a sophistication inaccessible to human comprehension. Indeed, Hayek does speak of the ' "intelligence" incorporated in the system of rules' (1979: 157, emphasis omitted), of 'that higher, superindividual wisdom' (1960: 110) and accumulated 'experience' that is embodied in those institutions (1960: 60). It is this conception of traditional rules as formations preserving the wisdom and the experience of many generations that provides Hayek with the second reason for his warnings against extensive institutional reform. Not only is the human mind unable to find rules superior to those already existing, but also, he fears, precious social knowledge stored in the traditional rules may in the course of sweeping reform be irretrievably lost.

Maintaining that the market rules possess a social wisdom the human mind cannot match, Hayek denies that the idea of a spontaneous economic order explains its subject sufficiently. With his claim he says, in effect, that the explanation offered by that idea is incomplete and must be coupled with an account of how

[1] Further similar passages in 1960: 62–7; 1979: 155, 167; 1983: 41, 46–7; 1987a: 40; 1988: 14.

'the accumulated stock of knowledge' (1960: 27) inhering in the rules contributes to the self-co-ordination in the market. Thus, Hayek's thesis about the wisdom embodied in the rules of the market is clearly in conflict with his own view that the idea of a spontaneous economic order furnishes a satisfactory account of the market process. Mention has to be made of this conflict at the outset because it is the source of a fundamental tension running straight through the whole of Hayek's social and political thought and surfacing also in this chapter and the next. This is the tension between the social transparency presupposed by, and the rationalism exhibited in, his idea of a spontaneous order, and the opaqueness and anti-rationalism to which his evolution-based traditionalism commits him.

We shall begin our examination of Hayek's traditionalism with an exposition of the theory of cultural evolution he invokes to underpin his conservatism. I then analyse the ambiguous scope of Hayekian evolution, his functionalism, and his adaptationism. The chapter concludes with an overall assessment of his evolutionary theory and a discussion of his instrumentalist conception of the rules of individual conduct.

HAYEK'S THEORY OF CULTURAL EVOLUTION

If the traditional market institutions embody the 'superindividual wisdom' Hayek ascribes to them, how could they come into existence, as nobody had the knowledge and foresight required to create them from scratch? In his answer, Hayek opts for an invisible-hand account or, more precisely, for a theory about the *cultural evolution* of social and economic institutions. The rules of the market are, Hayek writes, 'the product of a slow process of evolution in the course of which much more experience and knowledge has been precipitated in them than any one person can fully know' (1967: 92). More specifically, cultural evolution is a process 'in which practices which had first been adopted for other reasons, or even purely accidentally, were preserved because they enabled the group in which they had arisen to prevail over others' (1973: 9). The adoption of more efficient rules did not grow out of public discourse and rational choice. Rather, it was 'those groups who *happened to fall*' on these new rules that 'prospered and multiplied' (1983: 46, emphasis added). Hayek again stresses the evolutionary, non-intentional character of the process leading to market rules when he pointedly remarks that 'we hardly can be said to have selected them; rather, these constraints selected us: they enabled us to survive' (1988: 14).

There are two particular points in need of elaboration if this evolutionary theory is to have at least some plausibility. First, how does Hayek substantiate the idea that the rules of the market contain what he calls their superindividual wisdom? Second and even more important, what is the selection mechanism by which those rules emerged?

In which sense does Hayek think the market rules—the evolving rules he conceives as 'general purpose tools' (1976: 21)—embody collective wisdom? They are, he says, 'adaptations to certain *kinds* of environment because they help to deal with certain *kinds* of situations' (1976: 4). The market rules represent genuine ' "knowledge of the world" ' and '[act] like information about the environment'. Such knowledge differs in two respects from scientific theories. It is not given in explicit form, and it is not, generally, 'knowledge of cause and effect' (1978: 10). This means the rules do not give us a theoretical account of the innumerable causal interdependencies existing between man and the world surrounding him, interdependencies we know only minimally since their complexity mostly eludes our grasp. But (and this is crucial for an adequate understanding of Hayek's position) the rules adapt us to the world by prescribing in general form certain constraints which, given those causal complexities and mankind's past attempts to cope with them, have proved most conducive to successful individual agency. Norms, he writes, 'are thus an adaptation to a factual regularity on which we depend but which we know only partially and on which we can count only if we observe those norms' (1967: 80). The rules of the market, like all behavioural rules, confine themselves, Hayek thinks, to singling out certain general conditions to which we must conform if we are to achieve our aims; yet they do not reveal how their observance makes us act successfully. This explanatory silence on the part of the rules he calls their 'abstractness' (1973: 29–31).[2]

---

[2] The term 'abstract' has for Hayek, as we remember, other meanings as well (cf. Ch. 3 n. 2). There is a close parallel between Hayek's 'abstract', i.e. tacitly adaptive, rules of the market and his 'hypothetical physiology' (Forsyth 1988: 239–40) of the mind as propounded, above all, in Hayek 1952*b* and in a few essays

Hayek's insistence that the abstract rules of the market are the product of a *cultural* evolution is designed to dispel two misunderstandings: that those rules spring from reason, or from instinct. Hayek is emphatic that man did not arrive at abstraction 'by processes of logic from [his] perception of reality' (1973: 30); human reason lacks the ability to 'directly master all the particulars' (1973: 33) of the environment and in this way to discover suitable abstract rules. Nor does he believe that such rules are grounded in man's genetic endowment; sociobiology he dismisses because, he says, genetic evolution is far too slow to account for the rapid pace at which social and economic institutions have changed (1979: 154). Still, he concedes the existence of a 'stratification of rules of conduct' (1979: 159), acknowledging that individual agency and social life are also governed by rationally chosen rules, and genetic rules. But within the institutional framework of the market he accords paramount importance to the culturally transmitted rules.

such as 'Rules, Perception and Intelligibility' (Hayek 1967: 43–65) and 'The Primacy of the Abstract' (Hayek 1978: 35–49). In 1952b (*The Sensory Order*), whose origins go back to 1919–20 when he was strongly interested in the psychology of perception, Hayek offers a conception of the mind 'not as a passive receiver of sensations from the external world, but as an active mechanism characterized by the physiological capacity to *classify* the phenomena encountered by the sensory organs' (Kukathas 1989: 47). Hayek wants his conception of the mind to be seen as further developing Ernst Mach's analysis of perceptual organization (1952b: vi) while at the same time avoiding the (in Hayek's view) untenable idea of Mach's that 'elementary and constant sensations' are the 'ultimate constituents of the world' (1952b: 176). According to Hayek, the nervous system does not, via its sensory organs, collect raw inputs from the environment and transmit them to the mind where, then, they are sorted out and included as bits in an ever more detailed picture of the world. Rather, the neural order itself already classifies the flow of stimuli offered by the physical world, bestowing upon them their distinctly mental qualities (1952b: 53). This means the categories helping us to orient ourselves in the world and to acquire an understanding of it are already built into the nervous system; the neural 'apparatus of classification provides . . . a theory of how the world works' (1952b: 130–1). In addition, the classificatory categories operating within the nervous system do not merely store a purely descriptive account of the world but contain a 'reproduction of the environmental order' such that they enable the organism 'to behave appropriately towards its surroundings' (1952b: 16 *passim*). Thus, mental categories as well as market rules are evolutionary devices allowing people to cope with their environment without their knowing exactly how this environment operates. Other parallels are briefly explored in Kukathas (1989: 47–54) who, moreover, examines how far Hayek's epistemology may be called Kantian. *The Sensory Order* is presented extensively in Forsyth (1988: 238–44) who also pays particular attention to Mach's influence on Hayek. Bouillon (1991) is an attempt to expound the links in Hayek between his epistemology and social theory.

Now let us turn to the mechanism by which Hayek claims the rules of the market evolved. He believes those rules developed 'because the groups who practised them were more successful and displaced others' (1973: 18); because they 'prospered more than others and grew' (1979: 161, footnote omitted); and, again, 'because they enabled th[e] groups practising them to procreate more successfully and to include outsiders' (1988: 16). To paraphrase: it is because adherence to market rules led to group success that those groups have emerged, and persist. Yet how can what causally followed from the observance of the market rules, and was not foreseeable, account for the existence of those rules? If Hayek wants this functionalist explanation to make sense, he must point out a continuous causal mechanism by which the consequence (group success) feeds back on the explanandum (the adherence to the market rules).[3]

Hayek does outline such a feedback mechanism—his *group selection process*. Imagine, he suggests, an initial equilibrium situation. There are various groups each with its own rules of social and economic co-ordination. Now within one of the groups' systems of rules a chance mutation occurs; the ways in which the members of that particular group co-operate, and co-ordinate their activities, change. Three outcomes are possible.

First, nothing in the group's overall performance changes. The mutation in the system of rules does not affect the group's efficiency, wealth, and size; it is neutral. And the equilibrium among the various groups persists. Or secondly, the group shows signs of decline. Inefficiency and poverty spread, and the population shrinks. The mutation is harmful. If the group does not return to the old ways, it will dissolve and its members will join other groups. Or thirdly, the group begins to use its resources more efficiently, to prosper more than other groups, and to grow. The mutation is beneficial. If those other groups do not themselves adopt the new rules, they will fall behind, will be marginalized, and may eventually disintegrate.[4] It was such random variation and natural

---

[3] For a particularly helpful account of functionalist explanation, see Elster (1985a: 27–9; and 1979: 28–35).

[4] Passages where Hayek sketches, or at least mentions, the group selection process abound though none of them gives a reasonably comprehensive account: 1967: 67, 71–2, 78–9, 163–4, 168, 243; 1973: 9, 17–19; 1976: 4–5; 1978: 7, 61–2; 1979: 155, 161, 204 n. 48; 1983: 32, 39, 47; 1987a: 40–3; 1987b: 233–4; 1988: 6, 16, 20, 70, 136.

selection of rules, Hayek believes, which propelled the evolution
of social and economic life, transforming first the small band of
gatherers and hunters into a tribal society from which, more recently, modern market society has arisen.[5]

In what respect do mutant rules enhance, or weaken, a group's
position? In his answer, Hayek is not consistent, often suggesting
vaguely that new rules are selected because they confer on the
group comparative advantages of efficiency, power, and wealth.
Yet in the end it seems he regards the population size as the
crucial variable: 'Any human group which practises a system of
moral conduct which enables it to maintain a much larger
population is bound gradually to displace the others' (1987a: 43).

In the exposition so far, Hayek's evolutionary story has been
told in *collectivist* terms, and I think it is this version to which he
actually subscribes. But in his writings, sometimes alongside the
collectivist version, we also find indications for an *individualist*
variant of his tale (e.g. 1973: 18; 1979: 161, 167, 204 n. 48;
1983: 32) which runs as follows. Individuals experiment with
established patterns of conduct. If somebody's new practices turn
out to be more efficacious, he will be imitated by others. In this
way, more beneficial rules will spread throughout the population
until finally they are observed across the whole group. Such a
group will have competing advantages over other groups and will
displace them should they fail to adopt the new rules.

Both the collectivist and the individualist versions rely on 'group
success', but they conceive of it differently. The collectivist notion
of group success lacks any distributive dimension. It does not
warrant the conclusion that, since the group is more successful
than others, each of its members is better off too; the operation of
its system of rules may well worsen the prospects of some group
members. In the individualist variant of the story, group success
is the aggregate of the successes of each of the individual group
members.

Among the problems the individualist story harbours we may
briefly mention three. The first has to do with the conception of

[5] Hayek does not tell us much about the three stages of cultural evolution. In
particular, he only rarely distinguishes the tribal society as a phase of its own (he
does so in e.g. 1978: 61) and usually confines himself to contrasting the small band
with the Great or Open Society, i.e. with the market society (e.g. 1976: 88–91).
For a few remarks on the difficulties of dividing the process of cultural evolution
into a sequence of distinct periods, see 1988: 29–31.

group success just outlined. Individual successes need not add up to group success; the successes of some individuals may be due to parasitic behaviour which, if followed generally, would be self-defeating. The second problem concerns the compatibility of an individualist account with the type of rules whose evolution Hayek wants to explain. The individualist story would make more sense if the rules in question were, say, maxims and recipes for the successful entrepreneur. But that is not what they are. They are rules of (just) conduct, meant to govern not private individual action but social interaction. Thus it is hard to believe that they could be introduced by individual experimentation or in any way other than by collective action such as legislation. This Hayek himself faintly recognizes at least once when he remarks that even if an 'individual would succeed in rationally constructing rules which would be more effective for their purpose than those which have been gradually evolved . . . , they could not really serve their purpose unless they were observed by all' (1960: 66). The third problem is this. If Hayek tells his evolutionary tale in individualist terms, there is, as V. Vanberg[6] has observed, no need for him to put any special emphasis on a process of group selection. The diffusion across the groups of new and more efficient rules is, then, entirely the consequence of individual experimentation and individual imitation, and groups have no special explanatory role of their own.[7]

To complicate things further, Hayek also occasionally implies that selection may work both at individual and group levels, for example when he says that 'cultural evolution operates *largely* through group selection' (1988: 25, emphasis added) and 'through the success of individuals *and* groups' (1960: 59, emphasis added). But nowhere does he work out this two-tiered approach.[8]

As indicated already, I believe that ultimately Hayek has in mind a collectivist version of cultural evolution. Not only is the textual evidence overwhelming, but there is also his social theoretic functionalism (to which we shall come later) committing him to a group theory of cultural evolution. Further, Hayek himself

[6] Vanberg (1986: 85 n. 12).
[7] For a detailed exposition and excellent discussion of the two versions of Hayek's theory of cultural evolution, see Vanberg (1986).
[8] In his comment on Vanberg (1986), Hodgson (1991) considers another type of hierarchically structured evolutionary process, that of selection simultaneously working at several *group* levels.

stresses the contrast between the selection of individual organisms in biological evolution and the selection of social groups in cultural evolution (1967: 67; 1987*b*: 229–30; 1988: 25).

The comparison with biological evolution may indeed serve to highlight, and summarize, what is distinctive about Hayek's theory of cultural evolution. Biological evolution occurs when mutations, random variations in the genetic endowment, so modify an organism's characteristics that it leaves more offspring than other organisms of the same species. The fact that over several generations mutant organisms survive and breed more readily than non-mutants is taken to be the work of 'natural selection' and to indicate differential adaptation to the environment. It is in this sense that certain genetic combinations are said to be selected. Note that the concept of (improved) 'adaptation' is linked here to the idea of (higher) reproductive capacity. 'Adaptation' does not mean that evolutionary selection improves the individual organism's adjustment to its environment by, say, enabling it to extend its life span. If adaptation were to consist in longevity, the optimal solution would be to have no offspring at all since breeding compels parents to divert energies which they could have used for themselves.[9] In other words, the focus of adaptation is not on how an organism fares as an individual but on its genetically grounded capacity to replicate.[10]

Now what are the analogies and differences with cultural evolution? Biological evolution works on the individual organism,[11] Hayekian cultural evolution on groups and societies. The characteristics enhancing the organism's reproductive capacity are based genetically while the competitive advantages of groups and societies derive (Hayek thinks) from the traditions, practices, and behavioural rules observed. Mutations both in the genetic material and in those cultural rules are governed entirely by chance. Finally, what is selected are certain genetic combinations on the one side and systems of rules on the other. Still, whatever the resemblances are, Hayek's theory of cultural evolution must, as he is aware, be

[9] Elster (1979: 8–9).

[10] I have greatly benefited here from the account given in Bateson (1988), and the discussions in Elster (1979: 4–9; and 1989*b*: 71–81).

[11] That, at least, is the Neo-Darwinian orthodoxy. There is in evolutionary biology a controversy about the likelihood of group characteristics changing in Darwinian fashion. See Bateson (1988: 19–21), and the literature mentioned in Hayek (1988: 25), and Hodgson (1991).

sound in itself and can borrow none of its plausibility from the successes of evolutionary explanations in biology or ethology. So let us look more closely at some of the aspects peculiar to it.

THE SCOPE OF CULTURAL EVOLUTION

Any assessment of Hayek's theory of cultural evolution is hampered from the beginning by his ambiguity about the scope of that evolutionary process. He is never clear about what exactly, in the course of cultural evolution, mutates and is (or is not) selected. Almost everything cultural, we are led to believe, has developed through evolution: 'Our habits and skills, our emotional attitudes, our tools, and our institutions—all are . . . adaptations to past experience which have grown up by selective elimination of less suitable conduct' (1960: 26). We find in Hayek's writings numerous other circumscriptions of the material on which cultural evolution operates. He thus talks of conventions, customs, rules, practices, traditions, morals, language, law, money, and values as all being the result of evolutionary selection (see e.g. 1979: 153–76).

Plainly, such latitude harbours difficulties. It is not only that certain terms are potentially misleading. The fact that a particular practice is regarded as a 'tradition' does not warrant the conclusion that it is a long-standing evolutionary growth. Traditions invented and established recently are not as unusual a phenomenon as one might think.[12] By far the most serious problem concerns the lack of guidance as to *which* of all those evolved rules, institutions, and so forth do store the tacit social wisdom Hayek is anxious to safeguard. Such guidance is indispensable if reform is not inadvertently to extinguish that wisdom.[13] Hayek shows an awareness of this problem when he remarks that '[t]he important question of which of these rules of individual action can be deliberately and profitably altered, and which are likely to evolve gradually with or without such deliberate collective decisions as legislation involves, is rarely systematically considered' (1967: 72). Regrettably, Hayek himself does not systematically consider this question either. Contrary to what he frequently suggests, the answer cannot simply be

[12] For illustration, see the collection of essays in Hobsbawm and Ranger (1983).
[13] This problem is also diagnosed and discussed in Rowland (1988).

that *all* rules and institutions not set up intentionally to serve some specific purpose are evolutionary creations and must, therefore, be presumed to contain such wisdom.

Now the problem would largely disappear if one knew that cultural evolution by natural selection, though not unfailingly beneficial across the whole range of human institutions, does preserve social wisdom provided that one restricts the evolutionary process to certain types of rules and practices. More specifically, one would have to know that cultural evolution conduces to the further refinement of that wisdom if it occurs *within an institutional framework* we are able to arrange. Various passages in Hayek's writings do suggest such a view. On several occasions he seems to say that as long as the familiar legal rules defining the spheres of legitimate individual choice are enforced, the adjustment of customs and morals can be left to evolutionary experimentation. It is, Hayek writes, 'this flexibility of voluntary rules which in the field of morals makes gradual evolution . . . possible' (1960: 63; likewise in 1960: 67; 1973: 46; 1976: 57).

Several commentators[14] think that when talking of cultural evolution Hayek has in mind such bounded natural change. Apart from the literal evidence this interpretation can muster, it also appears able to accommodate Hayek's attitude towards political and legal reform. To argue that evolutionary change is infallibly beneficial if it is limited to rules and practices not forming part of the legal system presupposes that the law itself, and its development, require monitoring and that legal reform (should such become necessary) must be backed by theoretical understanding and be brought about by collective action. Hayek does subscribe to controlled legal change. He says it is the rules of law 'which, because we can deliberately alter them, become the chief instrument whereby we can affect the resulting order' (1973: 45). Though in principle endorsing a reformist attitude Hayek thinks deliberate change must be kept within narrow confines if political totalitarianism and economic impoverishment are to be avoided. While arguing for continuous local refinements that increase internal coherence and consistency (1973: 88–9, 94–123; 1976: 24–30, 38–44; 1978: 11, 18–20), he opposes any attempt to replace or radically alter the existing legal system as a whole: 'There

---

[14] Vanberg (1986: 90); Crowley (1987: 79); Heath (1989: 108–9).

is ... certainly room for improvement, but we cannot redesign but only further evolve what we do not fully comprehend' (1979: 167). It merely confuses rather than clarifies things when in this context Hayek talks of the 'evolution of law' (1973: 85) and of judges and legislators as agents of 'political evolution' (1973: 65). Still, we can recognize here a conception of cultural evolution as variation and selection within a stable legal framework. This conception locates tacit social wisdom in society's moral rules, thereby designating the areas where uncurbed change should take its course, and at the same time identifying the human institutions that may be modified without the risk of destroying embodied wisdom.

But does—indeed can—Hayek really conceive of cultural evolution as moral change under legal constraints? This must be doubted. Obviously, a conception of bounded cultural evolution presumes that an unambiguous distinction can be made between moral rules and legal rules. Otherwise, legislation may adulterate rules whose development would better be left to itself; or, conversely, fearing to forfeit embodied knowledge, legislation may not alter recognizably dysfunctional rules which, to general benefit, it could. Now Hayek, it seems, is unable to draw a clear distinction, for two reasons.

First, a conception of bounded cultural evolution assumes that only the rules of morality, but not the legal rules, are evolutionary growths and, therefore, contain experience accumulated over many generations. Yet, according to Hayek, the two types of rules do not substantially differ in their origins.

The main point ... which ... should be stressed once more, is that the difference between moral and legal rules is not one between rules which have spontaneously grown and rules which have been deliberately made; for most of the rules of law also have not been deliberately made in the first instance. (1976: 58; likewise in 1967: 88, 92, 101–2; 1973: 46, 100)

If law too has developed in an evolutionary process, the presumption that its products embody the wisdom of mankind must hold for the legal rules as well. That means a distinction, on which the bounded conception of cultural evolution is based between moral rules and legal rules, cannot be drawn and any division of labour between evolutionary moral mutation and engineered legal adjustment lacks justification. If legal rules are evolutionary growths as well, they also contain tacit wisdom which any legal reform may impair. Cultural evolution must, we are forced to conclude, reign across the board.

There is a second reason why Hayek cannot possess a criterion that would allow him to distinguish between moral and legal rules and, on that basis, to defend a bounded conception of cultural evolution. This reason has again to do with the common origins of moral and legal rules and, importantly, with their function. Hayek does not revere evolved rules (of whichever category) merely for some profound general wisdom they may enclose. He thinks those evolved rules, or at least some of them, have a specific function which they received, and could only receive, in the course of cultural evolution, and he believes this function reflects, and makes use of, experience which as individuals we cannot have and cannot reconstruct. This function is, of course, that of enabling the formation of a spontaneous economic order. As we have seen earlier, Hayek claims that, since we have never been intelligent enough to design rules capable of generating and maintaining such order, the market rules owe this ability to their evolutionary origin. A spontaneous economic order forms, he explains,

because in the course of millennia men developed rules of conduct which lead to the formation of such an order out of the separate spontaneous activities of individuals. The interesting point about this is that men developed these rules without really understanding their functions. (1978: 10)[15]

If, as Hayek says, the rules of the market are evolutionary growths and enshrine experience which we cannot know, it is only consistent to think that their further development too must be left to cultural evolution. Hayek is ambiguous about which rules are required if a spontaneous economic order is to unfold. Yet at any rate he unmistakably believes that the rules of private property, contract, and tort are indispensable (e.g. 1976: 109). Since these are legal rules, their further development, it must be assumed, would have to happen by the same type of evolution that brought them forth. So Hayek cannot sustain a conception of cultural evolution as change within a legal framework that is not itself

---

[15] Hayek's claim about the evolutionary origin of the rules conducive to spontaneous economic order is also to be found in e.g. 1967: 66–81, 88, 101; 1979: 158, 164; 1988: 16.

subject to selective pressures—if he takes seriously his own claims about the evolutionary origin of the market rules, and of their function.[16]

The discussion so far has shown that Hayek cannot be interpreted as consistently espousing a bounded conception of moral but not legal evolution. Nor can he be seen as favouring wholesale evolutionary change either, for he endorses controlled legal modification and gives judges and legislators a role. So what conclusion is to be drawn? I think Hayek has simply failed to sort out this inconsistency, and I do not believe that his writings yield a mediating position capable of resolving it. This contradiction reflects a deep tension, registered by numerous scholars,[17] in Hayek's work between a conservatism advised by an unqualified reverence for the traditional and an institutional reformism inspired by the idea of a spontaneous order.[18] So the question of whether it is only moral rules, or moral *and* legal rules, that Hayekian cultural evolution randomly varies and chooses by natural selection, and the question of which rules acquire 'evolutionary wisdom', must remain unanswered. Yet even if they could be settled, there are other problems no less troubling for Hayek's evolutionary theory.

PROBLEMS WITH HAYEK'S FUNCTIONALISM

In his claim that certain rules have developed because they enable the group or society to be efficient, to prosper, and grow Hayek betrays a functionalist view of those rules and of the institutions they form. Occasionally, he appears to confine this perspective to only a few rules and institutions. He says, for example, that 'the

[16] It is hard to imagine how under the conditions of the modern state legal evolution could operate. The development of common law is not an evolutionary process since it is not based on random variation and natural selection. Legal evolution must also differ from gradual change by legislative measures; legislation presupposes foresight, rational assessment of alternatives, and collective action—all things alien to evolution properly understood. Still, occasionally Hayek does seem to hold fast to a sort of legal evolution, for example, when he remarks that '[c]ultural and moral evolution do require further steps if the institution of several property is in fact to be as beneficial as it can be.' (1988: 35, 74)

[17] See e.g. Gray (1980), but cf. also Gray (1986: 129–30); Paul (1988: 258–9); Rowland (1988); Kukathas (1989: 206–15); Tomlinson (1990: 64–5).

[18] Thus Hayek's (1960: PS) 'Why I am not a Conservative' must not be taken at face value as it only tells part of the story. Cliteur (1990) even claims that Hayek *is* a downright conservative.

institution of private property serve[s] a function necessary for the maintenance of the spontaneous order of society' (1973: 29). Here, Hayek seems committed to a *limited functionalism*, asserting that there are some clearly discernible rules or institutions (such as private property) each with its own distinct 'purpose' (such as that of maintaining spontaneous economic order). The institution of the family might be another example; its function is, Hayek implies, the domestication of male sexuality (1987a: 37–8). Such limited functionalism would admit of other social institutions to which no such specific roles can be attributed.

However, strong evidence suggests that Hayek embraces a *holist functionalism*. There cannot be much doubt that he believes any rule (or institution, or other more permanent social structure) must be seen as being integrated into a complex body of rules which *as a whole* serves the group's existence and determines its survival chances. Hayek thus talks of the 'presumption that *any* established social standard contributes in some manner to the preservation of civilization' (1960: 36, emphasis added). He has the same idea in mind when, approvingly, he quotes Macbeath (1952) who writes of 'the principle laid down by Frazer . . . and endorsed by Malinowski and other anthropologists, that *no* institution will continue to survive *unless* it performs some useful function' (1960: 433 n. 21, emphasis added). Hayek's holist functionalism manifests itself again in his insistence that rules 'have a function within an operating system . . . —a function which [can] be derived . . . only from an understanding of the whole structure' (1976: 23). This means the function a rule has is entirely subservient to the overall purpose of the body of rules as a whole. At an advanced evolutionary stage this purpose consists, as we know, in 'the maintenance or restoration of an order of actions which the rules tend to bring about more or less successfully' (1976: 25).

It appears then that Hayek cannot really subscribe merely to the limited functionalism mentioned above. For he not only believes that the function a particular rule performs is completely dependent on the overall purpose of the system of rules as a whole. He also thinks that from society to society that system, though serving the same purpose, may so vary that a particular rule is highly functional in one society and less so, or even dysfunctional, in another: 'the rule one ought to follow in a given society . . . in order to produce the best consequences, may not be the best rule in another

society where the system of generally adopted rules is different'
(1976: 26). Nevertheless, though depicting a society's institutional
framework as a highly integrated system of rules, he does not
conceive of it as a clock in which every single component fits
perfectly into the mechanism. The system of rules will always
function only 'more or less adequately' (1976: 23), always admitting
of still more efficient rules (1960: 158; 1979: 167) and thus leaving room for cultural evolution.

Hayek's holist functionalism neatly dovetails with his claim that
cultural evolution works on the body of rules in its entirety. He
wants it to be clear

that systems of rules of conduct will develop as wholes, or that the
selection process of evolution will operate on the order as a whole; and
that, whether a new rule will, in combination with all the other rules of
the group, and in the particular environment in which it exists, increase
or decrease the efficiency of the group as a whole, will depend on the
order to which [the general observance of all the rules] leads. (1967: 71)

What Hayek says here may be spelled out as follows. A group's
or society's system of economic co-operation and co-ordination
finds its institutional expression in the system of rules to which
that society adheres. Any such integrated body of rules has a
specific *character*, and it is this character which determines how a
society fares. Non-neutral mutations, even if they are confined to
a single rule, modify the character of the entire system and, hence,
directly affect society as a whole. Indeed, if Hayek's theory of
cultural evolution is to hold at all, he must crucially assume that
there exists an unmediated and exclusive causal link between the
specific character a society's institutional framework possesses and
the survival chances of that society. To put this assumption as
curtly as possible: it is the character of a society's system of rules
alone which causally *determines* its efficiency, prosperity, and
population size, and—thereby—its chances to prevail in the evolutionary competition with other societies.

This assumption is highly problematic in various respects. To
begin with, it is unclear which rules and institutions belong to
the system of rules that determines a society's chances of survival.
We encounter here the same vagueness we experienced when we
tried to reconstruct the scope of Hayekian cultural evolution. Does
Hayek mean 'the system of rules' to comprise only such economic

institutions as private property, contract, and tort? Or does he think, what various passages suggest, that institutions like the family (e.g. 1987*b*: 230–1) and religion (e.g. 1988: 136–7) belong to the system as well and affect a society's chances too? Hayek's social thought provides no systematic clue as to how this question is to be resolved. Any more inclusive account presupposes a measure of functional harmony among all the institutions, traditions, and practices that belies the structural tensions and conflicts existing in actual societies. Yet even if the ambiguity could be removed, the assumption would not thereby become plausible, as other problems plague it too.

One of these further problems concerns the monocausal nature of Hayek's explanation of why in evolutionary competition societies prevail, or go down. In his view, it is solely a society's system of rules that determines its survival chances. Hayek does not allow for rival causes. Such monocausality is hardly tenable.

Sweden's power in seventeenth-century Europe was due not to the superiority and efficiency of its institutions but to its rich mineral deposits which 'not only . . . furnish[ed] the material for a successful domestic arms industry' but also provided the revenue to hire military might and political influence.[19] Similarly, the oil-producing Arab countries cannot be said to owe their wealth and influence to their peculiar economic and political order. Of course, when pointing to the importance of a society's material resources we should not suggest—as Paul M. Kennedy does[20]—that in the end only resources matter. The examples given are merely intended to serve as a reminder that there are factors other than its institutional system that explain why a country becomes dominant. Now the problem is not only that Hayek has a monocausal perspective while there are usually several factors to be taken into account. Rather, the difficulty is that ultimately those causes are too many and too diverse to be disentangled and accommodated in a comprehensive explanatory theory. The standing of a society always depends on so many, and so many particular, factors that a comparison among various societies must almost necessarily fail to yield any substantive and generally valid theoretical insights. As Anthony de Jasay succinctly puts it:

---

[19] Runciman (1989: 44 n.).   [20] Kennedy (1988).

Genetic mutation may equip a subject with a competitive advantage over a multitude of others of its kind, all other things being equal between them. But a society that happens upon 'suitable' rules and institutions is one of a kind, no other thing is equal between it and its handful of competitors, and whether it prevails or not cannot be imputed to the set of institutions it is using.[21]

There is a further problem. As we saw, Hayek must take it for granted that a society's institutions are functionally so tightly knit that the inefficiency of any one institution inevitably affects the overall efficiency of that society as a whole, thereby decisively impairing its position and eventually dooming it to disintegration. In addition, he must also assume that people live in a finite world, permanently competing for resources and space. Only if there is competition fierce enough to crowd out societies with an inefficient set of institutions do the selective pressures necessary for evolution exist; in a non-competitive world, efficient and inefficient societies may persist side by side.[22] Now both assumptions may hold, but not to the degree required for evolutionary selection to take place. The institutional framework may be as loose, and competition as lame, as easily to permit institutions to proliferate parasitically. We have to think here only of the trend to bureaucratization in the public and the private sectors of advanced societies. As again de Jasay sums up: 'For a variety of reasons, we should expect survival of the fittest to survive to produce a population of institutions with many monsters and with no bias towards the benign and the instrumentally efficient.'[23] Even if we concede that over long periods of time some trend to more efficient societal organization may be observed, there is no warrant to sit back and hope that natural selection, instead of active reform, will in time dispose of dead weight and enhance the efficiency of existing institutional structures, turning them into those, say, of a slender market society.

Finally, the tightness, indeed monolithic nature, which Hayek is forced to ascribe to a society's institutional system is still problematic in a different way. We noticed that such a system may

[21] de Jasay (1989: 79).
[22] For critical remarks on this additional assumption as it is employed in theories of social evolution generally, see Hallpike (1986: 73-6).
[23] de Jasay (1989: 78).

contain loose joints allowing single inefficient institutions to exist without terminally weakening a society's overall performance. Hayek must also presume that an institutional mutation, a new rule, will always confer its new advantage, or disadvantage, on society as a whole and change its competitive position *vis-à-vis* its neighbouring societies. Yet there exists another possibility too. Institutional mutations may be beneficial, or harmful, to one class, interest-group, or estate in relation to other classes, interest-groups, or estates within the *same* society, leaving the society's external position unchanged. This suggests a more differentiated evolutionary social theory of the type recently advocated by Walter G. Runciman.[24] According to Runciman, the units of variation and selection are not, as in Hayek, entire institutional systems but practices, and (re-)combinations of practices, which give certain social roles advantages in the competition for power. As Runciman explains:

What matters is whether the practices involved in such innovations confer a competitive advantage on their carriers such that their novel roles come to modify the structure and culture of the society in which they occur to the point that it evolves into a different mode or sub-type of the distribution of power.[25]

Runciman implies that his approach may also help to explain changes in the relative positions of different societies. Still, its focus is primarily on intra-societal evolutionary change. We need not enter upon a detailed exposition and discussion of Runciman's ambitious project in order to be able to see serious shortcomings in Hayek's theory of cultural evolution. Hayek's monolithic conception of society, his exclusive concentration on entire systems of rules, blinds him to the possibility that a society's changing efficiency, wealth, and size may spring from internal evolutionary pressures. Moreover the contrast with Runciman's approach highlights the almost complete absence of 'power', a notion featuring prominently in almost any modern social theory other than Hayek's.

We have identified serious problems besetting Hayek's holist functionalism. These problems are acute enough to render untenable the claim comprised in his theory of cultural evolution that natural selection works on the whole institutional system. Still, Hayek's evolutionary theory offers, perhaps, other insights worth

---

[24] Runciman (1986; 1989).   [25] Runciman (1989: 45).

retaining. One of them may be the idea, to which he attaches great significance, that the market rules are adaptations.

PROBLEMS WITH HAYEK'S ADAPTATIONISM

According to Hayek's theory of cultural evolution, the higher adaptiveness of an institutional system shows in the fact that its carrier, its host society, will be more efficient and more prosperous and will, through its growing population, displace rival societies. An adaptive system of rules enables the society to survive, a maladaptive system spells its decline and eventual disintegration. As has been expounded earlier, it is not single specific rules but the overall character of the system of rules and institutions as a whole which determines the degree of a society's adaptiveness (e.g. 1967: 67, 71).[26]

Hayek's adaptationism does not strike us as immediately plausible. The most obvious point in need of clarification is this: *what* does a system of rules adapt its host society *to*? In his answer, Hayek is once more lamentably vague, offering at least three alternative accounts. Rules, he says, are an adaptation, first, to man's environment; second, to the nature of man; and third, to man's constitutional ignorance about the consequences of his actions. Let us examine these three versions in turn.

Mostly Hayek says the rules are 'an adaptation to our environment' (1976: 5).[27] Though he does not specify what kind of surroundings he has in mind, by likening the rules to tools (e.g. 1960: 27; 1976: 5, 21) he implies environment to mean 'nature'. This also follows from his remark that new institutions may 'constitute a better adaptation . . . to some permanent feature of our environment' and may, thus, embody 'a perception of the general laws that govern nature' (1960: 33). What, in this context, adaptation stands for, Hayek elaborates in passages such as this:

our adaptation to our environment does not consist only, and perhaps not even chiefly, in an insight into the relations between cause and effect, but also in our actions being governed by rules adapted to the kind of world

---

[26] For a few observations on the difficulty unambiguously to distinguish between the functionality and the adaptiveness of institutions, see Hallpike (1986: 86).

[27] Similar passages in 1960: 27, 33, 157; 1967: 71; 1973: 12, 18; 1976: 4, 21; 1978: 10; 1987b: 229.

in which we live, that is, to circumstances which we are not aware of and which yet determine the pattern of our successful actions. (1973: 12)

It is not difficult to recognize that once more Hayek is talking here about the 'abstractness' (1973: 29–31) of rules, that is, about their capacity to guide us in our conduct without revealing how they enlist the causal regularities of the natural world to our benefit.

An example of a rule fitting this description may be helpful. I borrow it from Samuel Coleman who uses it in a related context, though not with regard to Hayek:

Turkish farmers leave the stones on their cultivated fields. When asked why, they say that is the way it has always been done and that it is better that way. In point of fact, it is. When U.N. agronomists, after consider-able exhortation, persuaded some young Turks to remove the stones from their fields, their crops suffered. Apparently the stones help condense and retain the dew in the arid climate, but this was unknown.[28]

Ostensibly, rules do exist that adapt man to his natural environ-ment even if he does not know or notice in detail how they serve him. The problem, however, is that, even though there are such rules, they are not the type of rules that Hayek's theory of cultural evolution is about.

The rules whose wisdom Hayek's theory of cultural evolution is meant to explain are the rules which together form a society's institutions of social and economic co-ordination. They are rules intended to govern social interaction and economic co-operation, and they do so by, for example, demarcating for everybody a protected private sphere. As such they cannot include rules giving those who observe them increased mastery over the forces of nature. Hayek cannot, therefore, plausibly claim that a system of rules adapts its carrier, society, to its environment.[29]

[28] S. Coleman (1968: 242).

[29] Hayek might still hold fast to his claim and argue that certain institutional systems improve societal adaptation to nature because they are more conducive to scientific and technological progress. The idea would be that in the course of cultural evolution liberal institutions are selected for their hospitality to science and technology. There is, in Hayek's work, one passage faintly suggestive of such a view (1960: 33). However, he does not pursue this idea anywhere. Moreover, it would be at variance with his repeated assertion that the rules and institutions *themselves* represent a (direct) adaptation to the environment. Also, science may flourish under greatly varying institutional conditions; thus, no particular type of institutional system would enjoy a competitive advantage and would, consequently, be selected.

At least once Hayek says the rules adapt society 'to the general characteristics of its members' (1960: 157). This suggests rules are an adaptation to human nature. Unfortunately, nowhere does Hayek give an account of human nature that could render such a reading plausible. He does not deny that we partly behave as we do because this is what human beings always did. So he thinks that our longing for solidarity and shared purposes springs from 'deeply ingrained instincts' (e.g. 1976: 146) constituting a genetically founded morality. This morality he traces back to our ancestors who acquired it while living for 50,000 generations in small groups (1979: 159–60). The difficulty now is that the rules emerging from cultural evolution cannot, on Hayek's own account, be an adaptation to this 'natural' morality. The innate morality, though 'adapted to the hunting and gathering life of the small bands' (1979: 160), has under the conditions of modern society become maladaptive. For the rationale of a modern (market) society, Hayek says, is that of a spontaneous order, and it requires moral rules incompatible with those of that old ethic. Civilization, he explains, 'has largely been made possible by subjugating the innate animal instincts' (1979: 155) and replacing them with the market morality. Such repression does not constitute an adaptation.

So, if not to man's innate morality, to what else in human nature could an institutional system be seen as adapting society? Hayek does not identify further behavioural traits which he would attribute to our nature as human beings.[30] This is not very surprising, given the great emphasis he puts on the role cultural evolution played in shaping our habits, emotions, attitudes, and so on. Thus, if indeed man is chiefly a cultural being, it is hard to avoid a vicious circle and make good the claim that cultural rules adapt society to the—largely cultural—nature of its members.

We find Hayek offering a third version of his adaptationism when he presents rules as an adaptation to man's ignorance about the consequences of his actions. A system of rules of conduct, he writes, is 'an adaptation to th[e] inescapable ignorance of most of the particular circumstances which determine the effects of our

---

[30] In particular, Hayek does not declare individual self-interest to be part of human nature and, hence, does not claim (as, perhaps, one might expect him to do) that the rules of the market are an adaptation to man's self-love because they are morally less demanding than a more 'altruistic' morality.

actions' (1976: 20).[31] Hayek's sweeping formulation evokes the idea of an ignorance pervading all social life while in fact he has in mind (but rarely says so) only a very specific type of economic ignorance. This is the individual's ignorance of 'what will be the effects of his actions on those unknown persons who do consume his products or products to which he has contributed' (1988: 81). Hayek depicts such opaqueness as part of the human predicament and the rules of the market as 'a device for coping with our constitutional ignorance' (1976: 8), 'a device we have learned to use' (1960: 66) in the course of cultural evolution.

But Hayek contradicts his own claim; further, this ignorance is not really a feature of the human condition; and finally, those rules cannot convincingly be seen as an adaptation to it. He undermines his own position when, elsewhere, he argues that the ignorance of the consequences of one's actions greatly facilitates, rather than hinders, the co-operation in the market (1976: 3). Moreover such ignorance may at best be regarded as a circumstance of mass society. We see this when we go back to the small prehistoric band from which, according to Hayek, cultural evolution started. He describes co-operation among its members as follows:

at any one moment they will know more or less the same particular circumstances.... [T]he concrete events which the individuals encounter in their daily pursuits will be very much the same for all, and they will act together because the events they know and the objectives at which they aim are more or less the same. (1973: 13–14; similarly in 1983: 45)

In a small group, then, the members shared the same goals and the same knowledge. Yet if that was the case, we must wonder how the process of cultural evolution could have taken off at all. Since everybody knew what everybody else also knew, the members were not subject to the kind of ignorance to which (in Hayek's view) new and more market-oriented rules would have adapted them better. Hence, cultural evolution would never have started.

We have examined the three versions of Hayek's adaptationism and found them all wanting. The rules which make up the institutional system of social and economic co-ordination can be regarded as adaptation neither to the environment, nor to the nature of man, nor to his ignorance about the consequences of his actions.

[31] Similar passages in 1960: 30, 66; 1973: 13; 1976: 8–11, 29; 1978: 72; 1983: 45–6; 1988: 76.

So what is it that leads Hayek to embrace adaptationism in the first place? The answer to this question will provide the starting-point for a few more, and more general, observations on his theory of cultural evolution.

MORE PROBLEMS

It is an often recurring theme in Hayek's writings that even today we still do not understand, or understand only partly, the rules and institutions of our society (e.g. 1979: 155; 1983: 40, 46, 55). Given the fact that most of those rules have been in existence for a long time, it does not appear unnatural to presume (as Hayek does) that they do serve some as yet unrecognized purpose, helping society to persist by adapting it to certain exigencies to which it is subject (e.g. 1960: 36). This adaptationist presumption, and the way by which he arrives at it, are not unique to Hayek. Christopher R. Hallpike diagnoses the same line of thought among many anthropologists and sociologists.

In view of the frequent inability of individuals to explain their customs and institutions, many theorists have therefore supposed that societies must be treated as natural, adaptive systems comparable to organisms, each of whose parts has some function in relation to the necessary conditions of existence of the society and its members.[32]

Now what would Hayek have to do in order to substantiate the particular adaptationism to which he subscribes?

Hayek must give an account explaining in which respects a society's institutional system can be seen as adaptive. This account must satisfy at least the following two requirements. First, it must specify precisely how the character of the institutional system constitutes for its carrier, society, an adaptation. And second, it must establish that it is the adaptive aspect (specified in step one) of the character that explains the survival, and diffusion across societies, of the particular type of institutional system. This would be 'most effectively demonstrated by showing that there is a high level of competition and that success or failure in adaptation will have a significant effect'[33] on the societies' survival.

On his own admission, Hayek is unable to offer any such

---

[32] Hallpike (1986: 94).　　[33] Hallpike (1986: 97).

account, apparently for two reasons. First, he says one does not generally know enough about the early stages of cultural evolution when social and economic life took place in the small band:

The facts about which we know almost nothing are the evolution of those rules of conduct which governed the structure and functioning of the various small groups of men in which the race developed. On this the study of still surviving primitive people can tell us little. (1979: 156)

The further reason is that one does not have sufficient information, even about humanity's more recent history, to be able to tell what the rules are an adaptation to:

To put it crudely: while we know that all those values [a term Hayek uses synonymously with rules] are relative to something, we do not know to what they are relative. (1967: 38)

In similar fashion, he goes on to remark that

[w]e may be able to indicate the general class of circumstances which have made them what they are, but we do not know the particular conditions to which the values we hold [the rules we observe] are due, or what our values [rules] would be if those circumstances had been different. (1967: 38)

So what Hayek is saying is, in effect, this. Although we know next to nothing about the early forms of social and economic life and even though we do not know exactly what the rules of the market adapt a group or society to, we can still safely assume that they are the product of cultural evolution by natural selection. In Hayek's own words: 'the basic conclusion that the whole of our civilization and all human values are the result of a long process of evolution . . . seems inescapable in the light of our present knowledge' (1967: 38).

Given Hayek's admission about the lack of information concerning, especially, the history of the early societal formations, this conclusion is anything but inescapable; it is entirely unwarranted. Unless Hayek presents an evolutionary story that satisfies the two conditions stated above, his evolutionist view of rules as adaptations with great survival value is no more than a piece of unfounded speculation. Hayek's failure to recognize that the plausibility of any such evolutionist claim wholly depends on a detailed adaptationist account is all the more puzzling since elsewhere he expressly acknowledges that the 'grandiose success' of Darwin's application of the idea of evolution was *'due to a careful docu-mentation* we cannot admire enough' (1987*b*: 228, emphasis added).

Hayek believes not only that in spite of our ignorance about the 'concrete facts' we are able to tell the institutional development of modern market society as an evolutionary tale, but also that it is exactly

the insight into the impossibility of such full knowledge [which] induces an attitude of humility and reverence towards that experience of mankind as a whole that has been precipitated in the values and institutions of existing society. (1967: 39)

So Hayek turns what is a fatal flaw of his theory of cultural evolution (its lack of empirical evidence) into a source of profound insight and political conservatism. His unsupported belief that the persistence of institutions attests to their adaptive value becomes the basis of an ideological defence of the status quo—which, for Hayek, is that of a classically liberal market society. At the same time, this belief causes him great trouble since he must—but his evolutionary theory cannot—explain why the planning and inter-ventionist state of the twentieth century is a mischievous political aberration rather than a more recent efficiency-enhancing societal mutation.[34] His insistence that cultural and legal evolution must go on (e.g. 1988: 35–6, 74) only exacerbates this problem.

Where do my criticisms leave Hayek's theory of cultural evo-lution? Hayek, as we remember, invokes his theory in order to give credence to his claim that the rules of the market—the rules of just conduct—possess a social wisdom of which human reason is incapable and unaware. The scope of cultural evolution, I said, is unclear, not allowing us to know which rules do, and which do not, embody tacit social wisdom. The holist functionalism on which his group-selection mechanism rests is, I claimed, untenable and his adaptationism plainly implausible. And, I argued, he effectively denies the availability of the very knowledge required if the emer-gence of the market institutions is to be explained in evolutionist terms. So nothing Hayek offers warrants the idea that, as we do not fully understand our institutions, they must contain tacit wisdom.

[34] See Buchanan (1977: 31); Barry (1982: 46); Gray (1987: 242); Sicard (1989: 182–8).

Hayek's cardinal error lies, I think, in his curious instrumental conception of the rules of just conduct. His adaptationism portrays them as guidelines enabling us to cope with the causal complexities of the world while being silent about how the observance of rules turns those causalities to our advantage. Since the rules he is primarily talking about are rules of social interaction structuring human co-operation and co-ordination, we may, most plausibly, take him to mean that those rules adapt us to the *social* world. Yet unlike nature, the social world is not a field of invariable causal regularities generating and maintaining economic order if only they are manipulated adroitly. So rules of conduct cannot really be seen as means of dealing with independently existing social processes and energies. *This* instrumental perspective must be rejected.

Still, the rules of just conduct do have an instrumental side. It is certainly true that they serve to organize social and economic life, and to do so efficiently. The market rests on a system of rules that allow foresight and enable people to interact smoothly. By delimiting spheres of legitimate individual choice they reduce the risk of conflict and, where conflict has occurred, guide its resolution.

While then, in a very abstract sense, the rules of just conduct *are* instrumental, they are also at the same time, as Hayek completely fails to realize, always *constitutive*. They reflect what kind of beings we strive to be and how, committed to moral conceptions of the person and of society, we want conflict to be resolved and the distribution of the benefits and burdens of socio-economic co-operation to be regulated. In other words, to establish social order and to structure economic life are not merely technological problems. Rules cannot just be seen as accommodating us, in some optimal way, to the unchanging causalities of the social world, thereby making possible a functioning society and economy. They are not tools helping us to solve some problem given independently of how we want to conceive of ourselves. Even though they are a means to ordering social and economic life, we want them to express the kind of moral beings, and the type of society, we believe we should be.[35]

---

[35] For a subtle account of the non-instrumental, constitutive nature of the rules grounding political order, see Michael Oakeshott's (1975: 108–84) essay 'On the Civil Condition'. The consequences for social theory of viewing rules and rule-based conduct as constitutive are explored e.g. in Taylor (1985: 91–115).

We can now recognize the source from which Hayek's contention that we do not 'understand' the rules, and are unable to grasp their tacit social 'wisdom', derives its superficial plausibility. As constitutive rules, the rules of just conduct, while regulating social life, presuppose and mirror specific normative conceptions of the person and of society. To observe those rules is to act in ways that constitute the rule-followers as a certain type of moral person and their society as a distinct kind of moral association. Hayek's purely instrumental view of rules, excluding from consideration any aspect other than the adaptive one, must fail to 'understand' rules of just conduct because it cannot comprehend their constitutive character. Dimly aware that there is more to the rules of conduct than their instrumental value, Hayek is led vaguely to talk of their 'social wisdom'.

An instrumental view of rules and social institutions permeates not only Hayek's theory of cultural evolution and, indeed, the whole of his social theory; it also dominates his liberal political philosophy and, in particular, his conception of the grounds on which liberal political, social, and economic institutions should and can be defended. Having analysed Hayek's social theory, we are now ready to examine the force of his instrumental justification of a liberal market regime. This will be the task of the next chapter.

8

Hayek's Project: The Instrumental Justification of the Liberal Market Society

Hayek believes that a correct understanding of how the social world operates and, concomitantly, a clear awareness of the limitations to purposeful intervention in social and economic life are crucial if in public affairs political philosophy is to provide practical orientation and to avoid sheer wishful thinking. Now he considers social theory essential not merely in the sense that it is one of several disciplines whose findings philosophical reflection must attend to when it addresses the fundamental problems of social and economic order and of the role the state may play. Hayek goes much further and, in effect, assigns to social theoretic arguments unreserved primacy over any other sort of reasons. Thus, he thinks liberalism is the right political doctrine because, unlike socialism and other collectivist creeds, it is committed to institutions that do take account of the social world as it is. He even deems the liberal market society the only feasible alternative because it alone admits of those self-co-ordinating mechanisms, such as the market, on which modern society vitally depends. Similarly, he portrays the institutions of the liberal market society as the work of a singular evolutionary development in the course of which they have proved their value and wisdom. So it is concerns of viability that are decisive when, in his political philosophy, Hayek endeavours to justify the institutions of the liberal market society. Feasibility considerations are characteristic of instrumental reasoning.

As I have explained in my Introduction, we only understand this conception of political philosophy, and the pivotal role assigned to social theory, when we read Hayek as pursuing an instrumental justification of liberalism. Basically, this justification seeks to demonstrate that the liberal market society has the only institutional framework suitable to realize the given values and ends of politics. Such demonstration is the domain of social theory.

Having, in the preceding chapters, expounded and critically analysed Hayek's social theory we are now in a position to examine his instrumental liberalism. The key notions of that social theory are the idea of a spontaneous order and the theory of cultural evolution. Correspondingly, we find in Hayek's writings two different arguments designed to justify liberal institutions. The first, relying on the idea of a spontaneous order and recognizably liberal in spirit, I shall call the *proceduralist* argument. It defends the institutional framework of the liberal market society, and self-co-ordination in the market, on the ground that they alone are capable of dealing with certain circumstances of modern social life in a way that secures general prosperity and social peace. The second, turning on the theory of cultural evolution and of an unmistakably conservative tendency, I shall label the *traditionalist* argument. It seeks to establish that the institutions of the liberal market society—being long-standing traditions of evolutionary origin—are indispensable for the survival of mankind even though a rational justification explaining what precisely their contribution consists in cannot be given. Hayek does not himself distinguish the two arguments. Perhaps, he would even have insisted that they form a coherent though complex whole. Nevertheless, I shall treat them as largely separate justifications, not primarily for expository convenience but, more importantly, because they differ in their practical recommendations.

Below I begin with the second, traditionalist argument. Its flaws are more obvious and, from a liberal viewpoint, it is manifestly less attractive. We shall then examine in much greater detail the proceduralist argument. The chapter concludes with an analysis of how the various liberal (and conservative) arguments of a moral philosophical nature which Hayek also seems to advance relate to his instrumental perspective.

THE TRADITIONALIST ARGUMENT

The traditionalist argument Hayek advances to defend a liberal regime draws its inspiration from his theory of cultural evolution.

This theory, as we recall, explains liberal market institutions as traditions stemming from cultural evolution by natural selection. Unable to reconstruct that process and to reproduce the human experience which shaped those institutions, we must, Hayek insists, hold fast to them and treat them as a repository of precious social wisdom.

Hayek does not want the theory of cultural evolution to be seen just as edifying philosophic history. It does not, in his view, merely establish a vague presumption in favour of existing institutional arrangements, cautioning against over-zealous political reform. Rather, he thinks the theory irrefutably demonstrates that we must stick to the traditional market institutions if we want to secure the survival of humanity. He thus feels entitled to write that '[v]irtually all the benefits of civilisation, and indeed our very existence, rest ... on our continuing willingness to shoulder the burden of tradition' and that 'the alternative is poverty and famine' (1988: 63; similarly 1987*b*: 227; 1983: 53).

Now the contours of Hayek's instrumental justification of the traditional rules and institutions of the market are not difficult to recognize. His strategy is to identify an end shared also by the adversaries of the market and to show that only market traditions, but no alternative institutional arrangements, are capable of achieving it.[1] The end, he thinks, on which all—both advocates and opponents of the market—are in agreement is the preservation of mankind and the elimination of famine and poverty. He then invokes the claim (which he believes is a sound scientific thesis derived from the theory of cultural evolution) about the market traditions being 'an indispensable condition of the very existence of present mankind' (1987*b*: 227) and concludes that, since everybody endorses the end, everybody must also endorse the only effective means to that end: the rules and institutions of the market. Hayek's argument is directed against socialism and related intellectualist ideologies which, with their contempt for tradition and their preference for 'new and better "social" morals' (1988: 75), he depicts as self-defeating doctrines spelling economic disaster and dooming the world to misery and starvation.

Hayek explains socialism's hostility to traditional institutions (1967: 85; 1988: 54) as the result of its adherence to *constructivist*

---

[1] Hayek outlines this strategy in 1973: 78–81.

rationalism, a theory about the role and range of reason in public affairs and, importantly, about the conditions of rational justification.[2] He discovers constructivist rationalism not only in collectivist ideologies, but also in certain strands of (Continental, especially French) liberalism (e.g. 1960: 54–8; 1967: 160–1; 1978: 119–21, 126–8), and he traces it back, ultimately, to the French philosophy of the Enlightenment and identifies René Descartes as its founding father (1960: 65; 1967: 84–5; 1978: 5; 1988: 48).

Constructivist rationalism comprises three major tenets.[3] It assumes, first, that 'all social institutions are, and ought to be, the product of deliberate design' (1973: 5). It presupposes, secondly, that reason is sufficiently powerful to know, and simultaneously to take into account, all the details of the human condition necessary to shape the institutions of society according to the preferences of its members (e.g. 1973: 29–33; 1988: 48–9). Together these two constructivist assumptions represent the very position which Hayek's theory of cultural evolution seeks to subvert. Yet, however misguided they may be, Hayek's own theory suffers, as Chapter 7 showed, from too many defects to be plausible itself.

Our interest is in the third constructivist tenet, which is about justification. Constructivism, according to Hayek, sets excessively astringent conditions for a justification of institutional arrangements to be valid. Constructivism, he says, insists that all institutions 'not visibly serving approved ends . . . should be discarded' (1978: 13). It is in this demand, especially, that he discerns the pernicious influence of Descartes. Descartes, Hayek writes, 'had taught that we should only believe what we can prove. Applied to the field of morals . . . , his doctrine meant that we should only accept as binding what we could recognise as a rational design for a recognisable purpose' (1978: 5).[4] In this and other similar passages

---

[2] Constructivist rationalism is a subject to which Hayek returns frequently. For extensive expositions and discussions, see 1967: 82–95, 243–4; 1973: 1–34; 1976: 17–23; 1978: 3–22; 1988: 48–88.

[3] In what follows, I shall concentrate on the contents of constructivism (as Hayek expounds them) and skip the problem of who, in the history of political ideas and among the thinkers he takes aim at, can or cannot indisputably be identified as a 'constructivist rationalist'. As Kukathas (1989: 207–13) demonstrates, the discriminatory force of this notion is dubious, and not least Hayek himself turns out to be a constructivist of sorts.

[4] Whether Descartes really held this view must be doubted. As Williams (1978: 46–7, 34) observes, Descartes 'stresses repeatedly . . . that his 'Doubt', his instrument of reflective enquiry, is not to be brought into practical matters', and, from

Hayek appears to reject the idea that the acceptance of, and submission to, an institution should depend entirely on its being the rational means to some end. So he seems to repudiate the very instrumental perspective I attribute to him. However, I believe such a reading overlooks what Hayek really finds so false about the constructivist conception of justification.

What Hayek actually rejects is the *explanatory explicitness* on which the constructivists insist. Hayek unreservedly shares the view that institutions have means-character. After all, it is one of his major claims that institutions are evolutionary achievements adapting us to the world. He merely opposes the constructivist demand that the instrumental nature of institutions must be fully explained if they are to be legitimate. This comes out, for example, when he criticizes constructivism for accepting only what is '*visibly* serving approved ends' (1978: 13, emphasis added) and 'is rationally *recognized* as serving specific purposes' (1979: 162, emphasis added). His hostility to explanatory explicitness is most noticeable also in the 'litany of errors' of which he accuses constructivism (1988: 60–2).

Hayek feels that this constructivist requirement, if adopted, disables him from presenting a valid justification of market institutions. Therefore, he rejects it (e.g. 1988: 71). The constructivist insistence on explanatory explicitness is at odds with at least two claims to which Hayek attaches great importance: the thesis that market institutions are traditions tacitly embodying the accumulated experience of innumerable generations—experience which cannot be known as it is not accessible to explicit statement and scientific reconstruction—and the thesis about the human ignorance of how each single market rule and institution contributes to the generation of spontaneous economic order. Thus, in so far as Hayek relies on his theory of cultural evolution, he seems to make the acceptance of the market institutions a matter of faith and not of argument. He suggests that these institutions are justified because they are the only 'instrument' available and capable of securing the survival and well-being of mankind and, at the

the *Discourse on the Method*, he quotes Descartes as saying 'that so far as practical life is concerned, it is sometimes necessary to follow opinions which one knows to be very uncertain, just as though they were indubitable . . .'. Hayek, it seems, reads Descartes entirely through Hume's eyes, and Hume is notoriously hostile to Cartesianism. For an exposition of Hume's view on Descartes and Cartesianism in politics, see Livingston (1984: 272–84).

same time, he repudiates any call for an account of *why* this should be so, declaring that such an explanation is beyond the reach of human knowledge. He goes even further and, prompted by his explanatory scepticism, rules out as impossible *any* justification of legal and moral rules and institutions. '[W]hile it is true', he asserts,

> that traditional morals, etc., are not rationally justifiable, this is also true of any possible moral code, including any that socialists might ever be able to come up with. Hence no matter what rules we follow, we will not be able to justify them as demanded; so no argument about morals— ... or law ... —can legitimately turn on the issue of justification ... (1988: 68, emphasis omitted)

Not argument, but quietism and blind 'submission' (1960: 63), it seems, should guide our attitude to the moral and legal institutions of the market. Indeed, one of the fundamental errors, Hayek says, of constructivists and socialists is their belief 'that *some* justification is necessary' (1988: 67, Hayek's emphasis).

Now can Hayek's justification of the moral rules and institutions of the market, deduced from his evolutionary theory and stressing their indispensability for mankind, succeed? That what he presents is, or is at least meant to be, such a justification cannot be doubted. To be sure, he rejects any demand for a justification. Also, he seems flatly to deny that he himself is offering anything of the kind, saying that 'this morality is not "justified" by the fact that it enables us ... to survive'. But then, sensing that he still ought to come up with some argument in favour of market morality, he adds that nevertheless 'it does enable us to survive, and there is something perhaps to be said for that' (1988: 70, emphasis omitted). To say what 'is to be said for' market morality amounts, of course, to a justification of this moral code. If Hayek did not submit some such reasoning and, instead, really believed that there was none available, a defence of the market system, indeed of any moral and legal system, would be a truly irrational undertaking and a pointless endeavour.

So what should we think of Hayek's attempt to justify the rules and institutions of the market in this way? As it is his theory of cultural evolution that inspires this justification, the faults besetting the former inevitably also vitiate the latter. I have discussed that theory extensively in the preceding chapter. What remains to be shown, therefore, is how those faults afflict, and eventually abort, Hayek's justificatory strategy.

First, something must be said about the demand for explanatory explicitness Hayek ascribes to constructivism. To reiterate: constructivists believe, *inter alia*, 'that it is unreasonable to follow what one cannot justify scientifically or prove observationally' or 'what one does not understand' (1988: 61). Hayek is quite right to reject this demand—but for the wrong reason. Also, he draws an unwarranted conclusion.

Hayek rejects the constructivists' explicatory demands because, he claims, we do not know enough about the evolutionary process to grasp the accumulated wisdom contained in the rules and institutions of the market and to recognize the functional contribution each rule makes to the formation of spontaneous economic order. However, he should, but does not and cannot, repudiate the constructivist demand because it presupposes the same mistaken functionalist view of moral rules and institutions to which he himself subscribes. To maintain, against the constructivist maxim of accepting only what one 'understands', that we have never been able to comprehend moral rules 'in the sense in which we understand how the things that we manufacture function' (1988: 14) is to share with constructivism the idea that in principle, if one had the knowledge, moral rules *could* be understood analogously to how manufactured things work. However, the holist functionalism, adaptationism, and the instrumental conception of moral rules, which all underlie this idea, are unsustainable. Thus constructivism (as Hayek describes it) goes astray if it presumes that the justification of a moral code and a system of institutions could be based on an explicit *functionalist* account.

But the more basic constructivist call for justificatory explicitness is sound even though Hayek fails to appreciate that. Realizing that an explicit functionalist account of market morality and institutions is not attainable, he wrongly concludes that *all* justification is impossible. If that conclusion were true, all reflection upon why we should endorse one particular set of rules and institutions rather than another would end. If we could not be given a (good) reason for following one code of rules rather than another, the acceptance of any code would be purely arbitrary. Hayek cannot in earnest subscribe to such a position since it would render irrelevant, even meaningless, the whole of his efforts to defend the market against socialism and other types of collectivism. While constructivism and Hayek are wrong in their functionalism, the former is right in its demand that the justificatory reasoning must be as explicit as possible. The whole human practice of rational argument in public discourse depends on that. Actually, Hayek does not heed his own conclusion and does offer a justification of the market in terms of its instrumental indispensability. This brings us back to the question of how plausible a justification that is, given the flaws of his evolutionary theory.

This theory not only fails to render plausible the general thesis that traditional institutions do contain tacit social wisdom and must for this reason be kept out of the reach of constructivist reformers, but also offers nothing to support the more specific assumption underlying Hayek's justification that the surviving evolutionary institutions and traditions are always compellingly those of a *liberal market society*. Nothing in the group selection process which Hayek sees at work guarantees that cultural evolution has an irrevocable trend towards ever more liberal societies; nothing ensures that, once liberal, they remain so. Therefore, even if one did accept some thesis that long-standing institutions preserve tacit wisdom, it would lend itself to a defence at best of the legal and political *status quo* but not to a justification of *liberal* institutions. Such justification cannot do without certain principles or criteria spelling out the requirements institutions have to meet if they are to be liberal ones. These principles must be backed by ethical argument explaining why the morally right institutions are of a liberal character. In short: only a normative, moral orientation can give us a critical purchase and free us from blindly accepting any institutional beast that 'cultural evolution' may bring forth.

The same lack of normative orientation shows elsewhere in Hayek's traditionalist justification of existing institutions. Hayek clearly believes that we must faithfully maintain existing traditions if we are to benefit from their wisdom in the future. He presupposes that the mere fact that a certain practice is acknowledged to be a tradition already suffices to guide those who want to carry it on. While perhaps not entirely unwarranted in highly static societies, this assumption is certainly mistaken under modern conditions, where dynamic change requires regular reflection on how existing rules should be applied to new cases in new situations. Even sincere people may easily disagree about which particular interpretation of a rule is truest to the tradition in question. Therefore, even if a practice is generally regarded as a prized tradition, this does not in itself furnish any instruction as to which interpretation must be chosen in order to preserve the tradition's latent wisdom. A non-arbitrary decision about which interpretation continues a particular tradition most closely must be based on an account of what the rationale of this tradition is. One must know what it is that makes it a beneficial practice worth continuing. Again, a normative orientation is required specifying what is 'beneficial' (or 'right' or 'liberal', for that matter) about it. Thus the Hayekian idea of our carrying on inherited traditions without comprehending their wisdom is incoherent. Even a traditionalist defence of existing institutions must come up with a justification explaining their point and arguing for their value.

Hayek cannot gain a secure normative standpoint of the kind required for a justification of liberal institutions as long as he argues only within his evolutionary theory. For this theory seems far too strong to admit of genuinely normative considerations. It describes evolutionary progress as 'a process of adaptation and learning in which not only the possibilities known to us but also our *values . . . continually change*' (1960: 40, emphasis added). Elsewhere, Hayek criticizes the 'belief in the immutability and permanence of our moral rules' (1979: 166). Values, normative standards, moral prescriptions: in his theory of cultural evolution they are all seen only as adaptive devices enabling a society to survive and grow. Such a view has implications which, one would expect, the liberal political philosopher Hayek cannot accept. It forces him to regard the values of liberalism, and liberal institutions, as merely temporary adaptations too—and not as intrinsically precious cultural achievements which a liberal should want to preserve because they allow individual autonomy and encourage human flourishing. Whatever direction institutional change takes, that theory can only note it and explain its occurrence as an increase in societal adaptiveness. It must trace liberal values and institutions back to a certain momentary environmental constellation which, if it changes, gives way to new values and institutions (e.g. 1967: 38). From an evolutionist viewpoint, there is nothing special about liberalism.

The practical attitude the theory of cultural evolution implies appears inescapably to be one of acquiescence in the status quo—whatever it is. By declaring all values equally to be adaptations subject to evolutionary change Hayek deprives himself of any secure normative standpoint from which to mount a defence of liberal institutions and critically to assess existing institutional arrangements. Thus we cannot avoid the impression that, his strenuous denial notwithstanding (1988: 27), he does in the end commit a naturalist fallacy. This impression is further confirmed when Hayek vehemently insists that the 'process of evolution towards what was previously unknown . . . [cannot] . . . appear just in the sense of conforming to preconceptions of rightness and wrongness' (1988: 74). He writes that an understandable though misplaced 'aversion to such morally blind results . . . leads men to want to achieve a contradiction in terms: namely, to wrest control of evolution . . . and to shape it to their present wishes' (1988: 74). And, removing any doubt still lingering as to what we should think morally of the institutions cultural evolution produces, Hayek concludes:

demands for justice are simply inappropriate to a naturalistic evolutionary process—inappropriate not just to what has happened in the past, but to what is going on at present. . . . *Evolution cannot be just.* (1988: 74, Hayek's emphasis)

It is no surprise when Hayek eventually characterizes cultural evolution as being geared to nothing other than the bare proliferation of human life.

[A]s with every other organism, the main 'purpose' to which man's physical make-up as well as his traditions are adapted is to produce other human beings. In this he has succeeded amazingly . . . Life has no purpose but itself. (1988: 133)

In this way, Hayek's traditionalist argument, his evolutionist defence of liberal institutions, and indeed the whole of his political philosophy collapse into a crude naturalism, ending in the 'practical' conclusion that we resign ourselves to the maelstrom of history.

Once on evolutionary terrain, any justification of political values and social institutions easily comes adrift. If Hayek's defence of liberal institutions is to succeed at all, it must be grounded in the idea of a spontaneous order, the second of the two basic notions constituting his social theory. Whether it can succeed, we have to find out now.

THE PROCEDURALIST ARGUMENT

Besides the traditionalist argument Hayek offers another, more straightforward justification of liberal market institutions and rules. This is the proceduralist argument, which ultimately turns on the idea of a spontaneous social order.

As before, Hayek seeks to justify liberal market institutions on instrumental grounds. And, retaining his Manichean perspective, he thinks a defence of liberalism must take the form of an attack on socialism. The argument is not now about the wisdom and survival-value of inherited, supposedly liberal traditions but about the unique suitability of liberalism's method of ordering and co-ordinating social and economic life. This method finds institutional expression in a liberal legal framework and in the market. Again, Hayek wants to base his argument on (what he thinks is) irrefutable social theoretic and economic evidence rather than on endlessly contestable moral reasoning. Social theory, he believes, can assess and adjudge the instrumental adequacy of the liberal and socialist methods respectively.

Hayek's argument, as I understand it, comprises four elements. First, liberalism and socialism are seen as pursuing certain political and economic *ends* which they largely share. Second, Hayek ascribes to liberalism and socialism each a specific *method* of social and economic co-ordination and interprets these methods as their means to those ends. Third, he identifies three *circumstances* of life in modern society which these co-ordination mechanisms must take into account if they are to achieve their ends. And fourth, there are the *conclusions* Hayek draws about the instrumental adequacy of the liberal and socialist methods, given their ends and given those circumstances. These four elements will now be presented in greater detail.

A justification on instrumental grounds of a certain co-ordination mechanism must say something about the ultimate political and economic ends which this mechanism is to serve. Surprisingly, Hayek is here rather reticent, perhaps because he regards these ends as self-evident. Yet from various passages we can glean what, for him, they must be. The rules and institutions of a co-ordination mechanism, he implies, should secure 'general welfare' (1976: 2, 5, 6), 'agreement and peace' (1976: 3), 'an order of peace' (1967: 165; 1976: 3), 'an order of peace and mutually adjusted efforts'

(1978: 299), and a 'peaceful co-existence of men for their mutual benefit' (1967: 163; likewise in 1976: 136). Formulated in such generality, these ends—peace and welfare through mutually advantageous co-operation—may encapsulate, indeed, 'what practically everybody wants' (1983: 30). They are the ends which, Hayek suggests, both liberalism and socialism share.[5]

However, there is one political end about which, Hayek says, liberalism and socialism radically disagree: only socialism, but not liberalism, subscribes to an ideal of social justice (e.g. 1976: 65). By social justice Hayek usually means the distribution of incomes according to moral merit or desert (e.g. 1967: 244; 1973: 85). He does not deem liberalism merely indifferent to the socialist calls for distributive justice, but rather believes that, because of their inevitable totalitarian consequences, liberalism must actively oppose them. Hayek is convinced that the attempt 'to secure that each gets what some authority thinks he deserves, must produce a society in which each must also do what the same authority prescribes' (1978: 140–1). He fears social justice entails an unfree society forcing upon its members a unitary scale of concrete ends (1967: 164–5, 171; 1976: 75–6, 136).

While, with one exception, sharing the same ultimate ends, liberalism and socialism favour fundamentally different co-ordination methods to realize those ends. In Hayek's analysis, the commitment to distributive justice leads socialists to assume that society must be structured as a hierarchical organization; else it could not bring about the required distribution (1960: 100; 1967: 170–1; 1976: 69, 85; 1978: 140). The socialist method is, therefore, that of the planned or command economy. In contrast, liberalism 'derives from the discovery of a self-generating or spontaneous order in social affairs' (1967: 162), the discovery that, once certain rules of individual conduct are established, a self-co-ordinating process will be set in motion and a web of economic relations will unfold that creates general welfare and ensures social peace: liberalism's procedure is that of the market economy.

The liberal and socialist co-ordination mechanisms will only be capable of achieving their ends if they take into consideration the social conditions under which they are to operate. Among the

---

[5] Note the absence of 'liberty'. This cannot really come as a surprise given the largely instrumental value Hayek attaches to it (e.g. 1960: 22–38, 81; 1973: 55–6).

features characteristic of modern mass society, Hayek identifies three circumstances to which the two approaches must respond appropriately if they are to succeed.

1. In modern society, people have individual ends[6] which they cannot fully realize all at the same time; ends may be incompatible, or resources scarce, or others may not be willing to make the personal contribution somebody considers indispensable for the fulfilment of his ends (e.g. 1976: 3). Moreover the members' views about the relative importance of these ends differ. This pluralism is a source of vast potential conflict. Hayek thinks reason is unable to solve such conflict as it can only assess the instrumental effectiveness of alternative means to given ends. The ends themselves elude rational evaluation; on ends 'no rational argument can produce agreement if it is not already present at the outset' (1973: 34). In consequence, no political or other authority can itself settle the clash of individual ends rationally; any ranking of ends it prescribes in order to solve such conflict is equally irrational and equally unable to command assent.

2. In modern society, a universally accepted conception of social justice does not exist. People disagree about how the benefits of economic co-operation are to be distributed. There are, Hayek writes, 'no recognized or discoverable general principles of distributive justice' (1978: 140; likewise in 1944: 82–3; 1967: 172, 244–5; 1978: 18). Again, he does not regard such disagreement merely as a, perhaps temporary, factual phenomenon that reason could overcome. Rather, he thinks such moral conflict is an elemental circumstance and permanent feature of the modern human condition. In Hayek's view, there is no philosophical argument available and capable of designating a distributive principle that rational persons would have to accept as just.

3. Modern society faces a 'division of knowledge'. No individual and no governmental agency can know in detail, Hayek

---

[6] To clarify: Hayek uses the term 'end' to denote two different things. As we have seen, he talks of the ultimate political 'ends' of survival, general welfare, and social peace, holding that alternative socio-economic systems must be assessed according to how far they achieve them. Hayek presupposes there exists a society-wide consensus on these systemic 'ends', regardless of the members' political affiliations. In the present context, however, he has in mind the individual 'ends' forming part of a person's own ambitions and projects. Hayek assumes that often they differ from individual to individual and that frequently there exists considerable disagreement about what constitutes an individual 'end' worth pursuing.

maintains, what all the members' preferences are. Nor can anyone know who of the population living, and which of the myriad things existing, in a particular society could be employed as production factors, and how they would have to be combined in order to secure efficient production and to guarantee the optimal satisfaction of individual preferences. Nor can any mind or information system cope with the speed at which economic knowledge changes. In short: the dispersion, latency, and fugacity of economic information rule out the possibility of running an economy efficiently from one central co-ordinating agency.[7]

Now given those circumstances of modern social life: which of the two co-ordination mechanisms, liberal market or socialist plan, can achieve its ends? In other words, what are—in our reconstruction of Hayek's proceduralist argument—the eventual conclusions he draws? For Hayek, there can be no doubt about the answer. The socialist method fails, he claims, because it addresses none of the three circumstances in an acceptable way.

By prescribing people's productive roles, a planned economy usurps the authority to determine which individual strivings and ends are valuable and which are not. Since reason cannot decide such questions, all directives the central planning board issues are rationally and morally equally arbitrary. The planned economy settles people's differences over the individual ends worth pursuing simply by imposing the board's own preferred ranking of ends. Such a solution cannot serve as a basis for enduring social peace (e.g. 1944: 57).

By endorsing a specific conception of distributive justice, a planned economy again arrogates to itself a moral authority it does not possess, and subjects the members of society to normative views which they may not share and for which a good reason cannot be given. Moreover the implementation of distributive justice smothers any efficient use of resources and 'would be tantamount to condoning the death of billions and the impoverishment of the rest' (1988: 120, and similarly elsewhere).

Finally, by co-ordinating production and distribution centrally, a planned economy prevents the utilization of local, latent, and momentary knowledge. 'This dispersed knowledge', Hayek writes, 'is *essentially* dispersed, and cannot possibly be gathered together

[7] For more on Hayek's notion of a 'division of knowledge', see Ch. 2.

and conveyed to an authority charged with the task of deliberately creating order' (1988: 77, Hayek's emphasis; similarly elsewhere).

Hayek's overall verdict is, inevitably, that socialism fails to attain its ends: it achieves neither peace nor general welfare—and a specific distribution only at the cost of stagnation and poverty. But what about liberalism? Its method, inspired by the idea of a spontaneous order, is that of the market economy. The liberal method restricts itself to establishing a framework of rules within which economic and social self-co-ordination can then take place. Liberalism's method succeeds, Hayek maintains, because it successfully answers the problems posed by the three circumstances of modern society. Being emphatically *procedural*, it avoids any commitment to substantive principles of how social and economic life should be co-ordinated. It does not entrust any person or agency with the task of deciding which individual ends should be given priority and still manages to reconcile the members' conflicting strivings. It does not specify and enforce some principle of distributive justice and still generates a distribution against which nobody can have a legitimate complaint. And it leaves the utilization of local, latent, and momentary economic information to those on the spot and still brings about a web of productive relations more complex and differentiated than anything central co-ordination could accomplish. In this way, Hayek concludes, the liberal procedure achieves what can be achieved at all: social peace and general prosperity.

Having reconstructed Hayek's proceduralist argument, I am going to examine it in the next two sections. My analysis will be limited in various ways. I shall not address the question of how far that argument refutes socialism. Instead, I want to ask whether it can really serve as an instrumental, 'value-neutral', scientific defence of liberalism. Moreover my critical focus will not primarily be on the degree to which the liberal method does, or does not, achieve its ends but on how it copes with the three circumstances Hayek mentions. My attention to circumstances rather than ends is a matter of emphasis only since they cannot be looked at separately: whether or not the liberal procedure attains or misses its ends depends on the extent to which it is a fitting answer to those circumstances.

I shall not consider the third of the three circumstances pointed out by Hayek, conceding that he offers powerful arguments which show why markets have an indispensable epistemological role in a modern society coming to terms with the fragmentation of economic knowledge. It is, I think, an original contribution of Hayek's to have demonstrated that only in markets and in a market price-system do the relative scarcities of resources and goods find expression accurately and promptly enough to make efficient production and allocation possible, thereby advancing general welfare. However, this epistemological argument in no way goes sufficiently far to justify *liberal* institutions. It merely shows that in a modern society markets must play an important part, but it does not address a number of questions which liberals certainly wish to see answered. It is unable even to indicate what personal and political liberties citizens should enjoy; it does not and cannot say where the line should be drawn between the private and public sectors; it does not specify what role (if any) government may have in overseeing the economy; and, on its own, it is not even capable of outlining what property rights there should be. It seems that other, non-instrumental, genuinely moral considerations are required to justify liberties, rights, and further institutions of a distinctly liberal complexion.

MARKET PROCEDURALISM AND THE DISAGREEMENT ON SOCIAL JUSTICE

The two remaining circumstances Hayek regards as characteristic of modern society are the absence of a consensus about principles of social justice and the pluralism of individual conceptions of what is worth pursuing in life. Both these circumstances bear on the end of social peace as they both harbour a potential for conflict. In this section, we shall turn to the differences people are said to have over the demands of distributive justice. I want to examine Hayek's claim that only the liberal distribution method—the market economy—manages to overcome those differences and to achieve social peace. The thesis to be probed is, more specifically, this: the market economy can settle the existing moral disagreement about social justice because its distribution method follows from reasons which, being of an extra-moral nature and therefore unimpaired by that disagreement, must be accepted by everybody. What these extra-moral reasons are we shall see in a moment. It should be noted that the justification on instrumental grounds of this

distribution method and the institutional rules underpinning it
does not require these rules to be value-neutral or morally indifferent. This they cannot be since they necessarily embody or further
certain values and ideals. But they must not be vulnerable to the
same sort of complaint which can, in Hayek's view, be levelled
against principles of distributive justice, namely that they have no
'objective' basis and are, therefore, morally arbitrary. Obviously,
if the market and its rules were similarly assailable, they could not
serve as a means of sidestepping people's moral disagreement and
could not secure social peace.

How do the liberal distribution method, and the system of rules
on which it relies, eschew people's differences over distributive
justice? Hayek starts from the diagnosis that the members of society
not only factually disagree about what social justice demands but
also that there exists no 'test' (1976: 78) or 'objective measure'
(1967: 172), and that there are no 'practicable standards' (1976:
91) or 'recognized or discoverable general principles of distributive justice' (1978: 140) permitting a rational solution. This lack
of an objective basis is, in his view, one of the reasons why socialism founders. Committed to distributive justice, socialism is
left to choose among equally arbitrary and contestable principles.
Social justice, however interpreted, 'becomes a disruptive force'
(1976: 137). But if socialism fails, why does liberalism succeed?
Hayek offers two main reasons.

The distribution in the market, Hayek says, is the result of an
impersonal process and an accumulation of unintended consequences. There is no single agent or agency deciding what everybody's share should be. No individual, Hayek argues, can therefore complain legitimately about his position in the distribution of
incomes; there is in the market nobody whom one could accuse of
unjust behaviour. People can be blamed only for the intended
consequences of their actions (e.g. 1967: 167, 170–1; 1976: 31–
3, 64–5, 70, 80–1).

The second reason given by Hayek is this. The operation of the
market, he implies, does not presuppose a knowledge of what
social justice enjoins. Justice, he intimates, even requires us *to
suspend judgement* if we do not know its specific demands. As he
puts it: 'To be impartial means to have no answer to certain
questions...' (1944: 57). Hayek also seems to entertain largely
the same thought elsewhere, and we may paraphrase it as follows.

Ignorant of what the demands of distributive justice are and, in addition, unable ever to gather and consider all the particular facts needed in order to achieve such justice, one must confine oneself to insist on justice where justice can be done. In a complex society it is impossible to reconstruct how all the manifold, remote, and often unintended consequences of individuals' economic activities determine the eventual distribution of incomes. The distributive implications of individual economic action cannot therefore be assessed morally. Justice can be demanded, however, of the actions themselves. Individual behaviour can be just or unjust, and rules of just conduct can specify what the just individual must not do. It seems to be in this sense that Hayek characterizes justice as 'an adaptation to our ignorance' (1976: 39, likewise on 127; and elsewhere).

Hayek's reasoning converges on, and culminates in, the curious idea that the distribution of incomes in the market is exempt from moral appraisal because such distribution springs from a process that is not only impersonal but also *natural*. He asserts, for example, that as long as society 'remains a spontaneous order, the particular results . . . cannot be just or unjust' (1976: 32). He expands the same idea when he writes:

[i]f market coordination . . . results from natural, spontaneous, and self-ordering processes of adaptation . . . , it is evident that demands that these processes be just . . . derive from a naive anthropomorphism. Such demands . . . are wholly inappropriate to the impersonal self-ordering process actually at work. (1988: 73)

Finally, in a definitely polemical tone, he remarks that calls for social justice do 'not belong to the category of error but to that of nonsense, like the term "a moral stone" ' (1976: 78). Thus, from Hayek's viewpoint, the advocates of social justice 'chase a mirage' (1967: 171). The simple insight that the market is a natural process exposes, he thinks, the vacuity of their demands. And, apparently, he believes that this insight ends the debate about social justice once and for all (e.g. 1976: 96–7).

However, this debate is far from closed because spontaneous order in the market and the type of distribution it entails are *not* natural facts. To begin with, the market and its distributions are not naturally given in the sense that there is no alternative to them. Market institutions are artefacts, they do not form part of the natural world. After all, by polemicizing against socialism Hayek himself acknowledges the possibility of at least one basic alternative. A planned economy would have distributive consequences different from those of a market economy. The distribution in the market loses its natural appearance.

Thus choice opens up among at least two different types of economic system, and argument is required as to why a society should adopt and maintain one type of system rather than the other. There is, to my knowledge, only one passage where Hayek shows an awareness that, not being a natural fact, the market system may be in need of moral justification. 'We might . . . question', Hayek writes,

whether a deliberate choice of the market order as the method for guiding economic activities . . . is a just decision, but certainly not whether, once we have decided to avail ourselves of the catallaxy . . . , the particular results it produces . . . are just or unjust. (1967: 171)

Secondly, the market is not naturally given in the sense that together with the planned economy it exhausts the possibilities available of structuring economic co-operation and influencing distribution. There is no such thing as 'the' market or market system. Market systems are malleable. They can make use of markets to a greater and lesser degree, and they can be supplemented in various ways by other co-ordinative and distributive mechanisms. Hayek regularly concedes that distributions resulting from the operation of a market system can be corrected in ways which do not impair the market's unique information-processing capacities. More than once, he proposes the introduction of a 'minimum income assured to all' (1978: 145; likewise 1960: 101; 1976: 87; 1979: 55) and asserts that taxes need not hinder the market process, at least as long as they are 'raised according to uniform principles' (1973: 142). In the light of Hayek's own implicit admission that market systems exhibit great institutional and functional plasticity and, concomitantly, wide variety in their distributive effects, actual distributions lose the air of natural necessity even further.

Hayek, as we remember, advances two main reasons to support his contention that the market can circumvent the moral disagreement about social justice. Distribution in the market, he says, stems from an impersonal process beyond any agent's or agency's responsibility; hence nobody can be accused of distributing incomes unjustly. And, ignorant of what social justice demands, one must abstain from endorsing and applying any distributive principle; this, Hayek thinks, is exactly what the market process does. We can now see more clearly what is wrong with these reasons.

The market, it is true, is an impersonal mechanism, yet its distributions spring *systematically* from the observance of rules and institutions that *are* subject to human control. The role of markets, their institutional shape, the redistributive measures that do or do not supplement them, and the overall distributions eventually generated all depend on deliberate political choice. Such choice requires justification, and considerations of instrumental rationality and viability do not suffice. Even if one accepts Hayek's view that general prosperity and social peace are important and definite political ends, this cannot decide the case in favour of one particular institutional mix, as various alternative arrangements may be considered similarly feasible and similarly conducive to those ends. Moreover prosperity and peace do not exhaust the values deemed essential in social and economic life. Given the obvious impact economic inequalities have on people's lives, distribution has to be among the concerns to which due weight must be assigned. This means that the justification of a particular economic system must include argument explicating why this system ought to accord distributive concerns the importance which they occupy in its actual operation. The argument must show, for example, how distributive aspects are to be balanced against competing values such as considerations of efficiency or the protection of property rights. Such argument is of a moral philosophical nature. Thus, if Hayek wants to pronounce on (the emptiness of) social justice, he must engage too in what is an irreducibly moral discourse. There are no extra-moral considerations available that could definitively resolve the moral controversies about social justice by declaring them irrelevant from the outset.

And what about the suspension of judgement Hayek recommends? Contrary to what he seems to believe, in practical social and economic life the distributive question never remains unanswered. Hayek's suggestion not to champion any specific distributive principle amounts to nothing other than a defence without argument of the status quo (which, for him, is the market) and its distributive implications.

When Hayek presents the market as the only procedure capable of evading the contentious issue of social justice, he is actually putting forward merely his own distributive principle. 'To each according to his market value' is on the same moral footing as any other conception of social justice. It cannot claim natural or instrumental primacy. Its defence, like that of any alternative principle, must rest on moral philosophical argument. To sum up: Hayek's strategy of settling the question of social justice by removing it from the agenda of politics fails. By depicting the distribution in the market as a natural phenomenon Hayek commits the very 'category mistake' (1976: 31) of which he accuses the advocates of social justice. In his refusal 'to concede that there is a genuine question about distributive justice ... he is', as Kukathas notes, 'plainly mistaken'.[8]

MARKET PROCEDURALISM AND THE CONTROVERSIALITY OF INDIVIDUAL ENDS

In modern society, there is, according to Hayek, not only no consensus about distributive justice but also no agreement on the ends and purposes of individual human life. People have different and sometimes incompatible goals over which they are reluctant to compromise. Among the members, Hayek writes, 'who mostly do not know each other, there will exist no agreement on the relative importance of their respective ends' (1976: 3; likewise in 1967: 171; 1976: 14–15; 1988: 95). Again, Hayek thinks that a system of economic and social co-operation must respond suitably to this pluralism of conceptions of the good life to avoid or defuse potential conflict. And again, Hayek sees the market economy and the planned economy as the respective methods of liberalism and socialism to secure internal peace. The planned economy tries to accommodate people's conflicting ends by imposing an order 'in which a single view of the relative importance of the different competing purposes determines the uses to be made of the different resources' (1967: 164). Since reason is unable to arbitrate among conflicting individual ends (1973: 34), any such ranking is rationally and morally equally arbitrary, and equally unable to gain universal acceptance. That is why socialism must, Hayek

[8] Kukathas (1989: 172).

implies, resort to coercion and why it cannot lastingly guarantee peace and stability (1944: 57; 1967: 164–5).

While socialism fails, liberalism succeeds—or so Hayek claims. Liberalism trusts in procedure; it does not succumb to 'the erroneous belief that . . . a common scale of ends is necessary for the integration of the individual activities into an order, and a necessary condition of peace' (1976: 111). The liberal co-ordination method derives from the 'discovery' that people can live 'together in peace and to their mutual advantage without having to agree on common concrete aims, and bound only by abstract rules of conduct' (1976: 136, footnote omitted). It is the spontaneous order of the market, he believes, 'which makes peaceful reconciliation of the divergent purposes possible' (1976: 112).

Hayek's defence of the thesis that the market can harmonize people's divergent strivings rests largely on a rigorous application of the conceptual distinction between individual means and ends. For Hayek, one of the basic features of spontaneous economic order is the fact that it is merely 'means-connected' but not 'ends-connected' (1976: 110, 112). In his view, all ends, projects, and purposes that individuals pursue lie outside the market. 'There are', he says, 'in the last resort . . . no economic ends' (1976: 113). The market process restricts itself to allocating 'means for the competing ultimate purposes which are always non-economic' (1976: 113). Such means do not usually serve just one specific end. Rather, they are generally useful, 'capable of serving a great variety of purposes' (1976: 3). Thus, Hayek's talk of the market's means-connected order is designed to bring out the idea that the economic relations forming such order always serve the production and transaction of means only.

Hayek claims it is this regard for means alone that enables the market to cope with the pluralism of individual goals. All that is required for co-operation and peace to come about is agreement on means (1976: 3, 112–13). As the innumerable exchange transactions in the market demonstrate, such agreement is not difficult to achieve. People need not concur on what, in life, is worth pursuing to be able to coexist harmoniously. It seems, then, that Hayek's idea of a means-connected order provides a model for how modern society can (and does) ensure peace and stability, given the pluralism and controversiality of the ends of human existence.

It has been liberalism's greatest concern that law and the exercise of political power must not be used in the service of any particular conception of the meaning and purposes of life. Rooted in the historical experience of the religious wars in sixteenth- and seventeenth-century Europe, this concern has, for liberalism, lost none of its urgency under the more secular conditions of modern society. Today, the question of what the ends of life should be is no less disputed, and any political regime trying to impose one particular view can do so, liberalism maintains, only at the cost of massive repression. In recent political philosophy, one of the main topics discussed has been whether the liberal demand that with regard to conceptions of the good life the state must be impartial is altogether feasible. Critics have argued that such neutrality is a chimera and, in any case, undesirable because the resulting order lacks social cohesion.[9] It is therefore no surprise that, thus challenged, liberalism's defenders have also turned their attention to Hayek's idea of a spontaneous social order. Charles Larmore[10] and, in more detail, Kukathas[11] have suggested that the notion of a means-connected system without a common hierarchy of ultimate ends may provide a model of society upon which, in Larmore's words, 'political theorists should learn to rely'.

To find out how promising, for liberalism, Hayek's idea of a means-connected order is we must look more closely at the 'peaceful reconciliation of the divergent purposes' (1976: 112) which the market is alleged to bring about. Economic co-ordination serves 'to reconcile the competing ends by deciding for which of them the limited means are to be used' (1976: 113). Now Hayek thinks it is a unique virtue of the market that (unlike socialism) it can reconcile those ends in a way other than by just imposing 'a unitary scale of concrete ends . . . [or] . . . some particular view about what is more and what is less important' (1967: 165). It seems to be this capacity that renders the market attractive as a model for a liberal society. Yet we must be careful to note what is really being reconciled here. Contrary to what Hayek says, the market does not reconcile competing *ends* but competing *demands* people make *on scarce means* in the name of their individual ends. For the ends themselves are, in Hayek's view, always non-economic and outside the market. A price-system, as Allan Gibbard observes

---

[9] For a brief overview and numerous references, see Kukathas (1989: 215–20).
[10] Larmore (1987: 107).   [11] Kukathas (1989: 220).

(in a context unrelated to Hayek), 'can harmonize the conflicting demands people make on limited resources, while leaving each person with a wide latitude of choice'.[12] But we shall see that 'reconciliation' may be a characterization too innocent for what goes on in a market.

Can the accommodation of individual ends brought about by the market secure social peace? In Hayek's view, individuals' ability successfully to pursue their plans depends on their ability to buy the necessary means in the market. Now the distribution of incomes in the market and, hence, the distribution of entitlements to resources can be highly unequal, as Hayek himself admits (1960: 42; 1976: 83). So the market may deny many even the most modest prospects of a life according to their own plans, consigning them to poverty and misery. Such frustration is a seedbed for 'discontent and violent reaction' (1979: 55). Reasons of prudence therefore lead Hayek to argue for a social safety net—as a precautionary measure 'against acts of desperation on the part of the needy' (1960: 285). Thus, he himself pronounces the verdict on the market's alleged capacity for peace and social harmony. On its own, spontaneous order may produce a highly explosive climate which can be defused only if the market is supplemented by comprehensive redistributive arrangements.

The market does achieve some sort of 'reconciliation', but not a 'reconciliation of ends'. The market and its price-system order the rival demands people make on scarce goods. However, 'reconciliation', the term used by Hayek, has a quite misleading connotation. The market is a procedure to *decide* among conflicting claims, admitting some while ruling out others. The goods go to those able and willing to pay for them. This procedure does not harmonize claims as 'reconciliation' falsely implies. The market is not a method allowing people to think that the eventual distribution is the result of a careful and fair weighing of the different claims and needs or the outcome of a negotiating process in which all parties possessed roughly equal bargaining power and had to make similar concessions which they can live with. The market is blind even to the most urgent needs. As Hayek himself concedes, it does not ensure 'that the more important comes before the less important, for the simple reason that there can exist in such a system no single ordering of needs' (1976: 113). This

---

[12] Gibbard (1985: 20).

means those unable to earn a living will end up empty-handed. It would be cynical to say that their demands are in any way 'reconciled' with the claims of the rich.

Where does Hayek's argument go wrong? Contrary to what it suggests, one cannot establish a priori that the market possesses the ability to foster social peace. The legitimacy of the market—the basis of such peace—depends very much on its performance, of which the distribution is an important part. The market will be accepted as a method of allocating means if the resulting distribution gives everybody access at least to the goods required for a tolerable life. How the market distributes incomes and entitlements to goods is an empirical question. As Hayek's own fears indicate, the market on its own is likely to produce a distribution that provokes 'the needy' to 'violent reactions'. His argument about the market's alleged capacity for social peace, however, is an entirely conceptual one, resting on the analytical distinction between all-purpose economic means and specific non-economic ends. Relying on this distinction, Hayek aims to show that an economic system confined to procuring those general means is able to evade possible conflict arising from the pluralism and controversiality of the ends of life. Yet he does not realize that this argument may be valid only if each individual can acquire in the market enough of the means to lead his own life. In a pure market system, this empirical condition will hardly obtain. In other words, the argument assumes that social unrest can be caused only by conflict over ends; it ignores that some people may have to fight for a share in the means.

The distinction between means and ends is troublesome for Hayek in other ways too.[13] We shall only look here at one further problem. As we saw, Hayek criticizes socialism for what he regards as its attempt to accommodate conflicting individual ends by enforcing a single moral conception of their relative importance. By imposing such a conception, Hayek argues, socialism takes sides morally and inevitably becomes embroiled in the controversies about what the ends of life should be. He concludes that, seen by some as morally repressive, it will provoke resentment and unrest rather than ensure peace. But there is a difficulty here for Hayek. If, as he believes, a distinction can be drawn between

[13] For Crowley (1987, esp. chs. 6 and 7) the means/ends distinction and the attendant conception of calculative rationality entail a seriously impoverished notion of the self.

general-purpose economic means and specific moral ends, why should its validity be restricted to a market system? Hayek says nothing that would rule out its also being applied to a planned economy. If economic activity is about the production and allocation of widely useful means, the planned economy, like the market economy, does not endorse certain specific moral ends and remains impartial. Socialism cannot then be accused any more than liberalism of imposing a particular moral view.

So what should we think of the suggestion set forth by Hayek and taken up by Larmore and Kukathas that the idea of a 'means-connected' order offers a promising model for a liberal society neutral among people's ends and plans? Notwithstanding Hayek's claim to the contrary, the market does nothing, as I have said, to harmonize conflict among individuals pursuing incompatible conceptions of the good life. It only decides among rival demands on scarce means. But, then, how in a Hayekian market society are the potential conflicts arising from mutually antagonistic ends avoided or settled? The 'reconciliation of ends' is brought about by the universal observance of rules of just conduct. They define what is and what is not permissible, assigning to everybody a 'protected domain' or 'sphere' (1967: 167) of autonomous choice. An individual is free to pursue whatever ends he wishes to as long as their realization does not involve an encroachment on other people's protected domain. *This* is how, in Hayek's framework, ends are reconciled. Yet, in fact, they are not 'reconciled' altogether. Ends entailing infringements on other people's spheres of autonomy are simply prohibited. Thus, if in a Hayekian market society the members are allowed to pursue a plurality of divergent ends, they can do so not because that society represents a 'means-connected' order but because it rests on *liberal rules and institutions*. This is to say that the type or degree of neutrality among conceptions of the good life a society offers does not depend on the 'means-connectedness' of its economic system but on the kind of rules and laws it enforces.

What liberal laws should be cannot be derived from Hayekian social theory. Even if one accepts that private property, contract, and tort are among the institutions indispensable for a spontaneous economic order to form, their shape remains largely indeterminate. This the early Hayek acknowledges himself when he warns of 'the error that the formulas "private property" and "freedom

of contract" solve our problems' (1949: 113). 'It is only after we
have agreed on these principles', he says, 'that the real problems
begin' (1949: 111). One must decide, to take just one obvious
example, whether the rules instituting freedom of contract should
be defined with libertarian latitude or paternalistic rigour. How
they are defined affects their neutrality among people's conceptions
of the ends of life. Apart from the problem of specifying these
more narrowly economic institutions, there is the question of what
weight and scope to accord to important further liberties such as
freedom of political, artistic, and religious expression. Again,
Hayekian social theory is unable to offer any guidance. It even
seems that Hayek's thought does not really have the structure
required to accommodate these freedoms, which are after all central
liberal concerns. For, the distinction he draws between economic
means and non-economic ends makes him completely overlook
the fact that certain ends and projects depend for their successful
realization not primarily on marketable means but on institutional
preconditions such as rights.[14]

To sum up: it is not the 'means-connectedness' of a market
society, but its system of rules and institutions, which determine
the character and degree of its liberal neutrality. What neutrality
requires and how it must find expression in liberal rules is largely
a moral philosophical problem. The conclusion seems inevitable
that the idea of a 'means-connected' order is unable to make any
significant new contribution to the debate about liberal neutrality
and about how it could be grounded; that it fails to document the

---

[14] This does not mean that in Hayek's account of liberalism rights such as
freedom of expression or due process would not feature. Whenever he expounds
his conception of liberalism (see e.g. 1960; 1978: 119–51), Hayek does make
mention of such rights as part of the liberal creed. My claim, however, is that the
theoretical framework built around the idea of a spontaneous order is unable to
give liberal rights and freedoms a systematic foundation. In Hayek's liberalism (in
so far as it springs from his social theory), all rights and liberties other than those
functionally indispensable for spontaneous economic order appear as accidental
accessories rather than core liberal demands. Equally insufficient is the second
rationale Hayek offers for liberal rights and freedoms when he attempts to ground
them in '[t]he basic liberal principle of limiting coercion to the enforcement of
general rules of just conduct' (1978: 137). The shortcomings of the theory of the
rule of law lead Hayek, as Kukathas (1989: 162) observes, to condone 'many kinds
of laws which most liberals would reject' and drive him 'on many occasions . . . to
present "ad hoc" justifications for certain rules or institutions'. We need not pursue
these problems further as Kukathas (1989: ch. 4) has an excellent discussion of
Hayek's theory of liberty.

need, within that debate, for a shift of emphasis from moral to social theoretic considerations; and that therefore the scientific defence he seeks of liberalism collapses. This is not, of course, to say that in a society aspiring to be a liberal one markets do not play an important role—but for reasons other than their 'means-connectedness'.

This ends our discussion of Hayek's proceduralist argument, in which he tries to demonstrate that only liberalism, and the liberal method of social and economic co-ordination, can cope with the circumstances of modern society and guarantee peace and welfare. In the case of all three circumstances singled out, his instrumental justification of liberal institutions is inconclusive or fails—largely because he equates such institutions all too readily with those of the market. While it is true that only markets can deal successfully with the dispersion, latency, and fugacity of economic information, Hayek's argument is unable to spell out what scope markets should be given, and he cannot identify and justify specifically liberal rights, laws, and institutions. While he presents the market as standing above, and capable of overcoming, the disagreement on social justice, he is in fact merely advancing his own contentious conception of distributive justice. And when he recommends the market as a method able to reconcile people's conflicting ends and plans, he fails to recognize, among other things, that social strife may stem not only from clashes over ends but also from a grossly unequal distribution of means, and that in a pluralistic society peaceful coexistence is secured not by the market but by the liberal legal framework, of which the market institutions form only part.

THE INSTRUMENTAL PERSPECTIVE AND THE MORAL FOUNDATIONS OF HAYEK'S LIBERALISM

In this book I have been arguing that the defence Hayek seeks for liberalism largely takes the shape of an instrumental justification. As I understand him, it is ultimately his view that the institutions together forming the basis of the liberal market society can be shown to be morally legitimate by demonstrating that they alone are capable of co-ordinating social and economic life in a way that prevents mass hunger, produces general prosperity, and ensures social peace. Only if we read Hayek as attempting an instrumental

justification, I believe, are we able to make sense of his repeated
assertion that liberalism and liberal institutions can be defended
'scientifically', that is, on a purely social theoretic basis, without
resort to moral reflection about political values. Only such a reading, I think, gives Hayek's political thought at least a measure of
unity and coherence.

To make good my reading of Hayek I have reconstructed and
discussed two arguments which in various versions and guises
pervade his writings and carry out his programme of instrumental
justification. In what I called his traditionalist argument Hayek
aims to prove that only the continued adherence to the inherited
institutions of the market will enable mankind to survive in its
present size. Hayek's second, proceduralist, argument purports to
show that only market co-ordination answers appropriately to
certain circumstances characteristic of modern society, thus securing
prosperity and peace.

The two arguments do not exhaust all Hayek says about liberalism and its justification. Not infrequently he appears to take
not an instrumental but a genuinely moral philosophical stance
and to argue from partly utilitarian, partly Kantian positions. Before
giving a final assessment of Hayek's enterprise I must therefore
explain why the instrumental perspective still overrides those
seemingly moral foundations.

Chandran Kukathas, to whom we owe the most detailed analysis
of the moral philosophy grounding Hayek's liberalism, identifies
three different strands of argument. Depending on the angle taken,
Hayek's liberalism, he maintains, appears to us as resting either on
a *Kantian*, a *conservative*, or a *utilitarian* moral theory.[15] Now these
three types of moral argument are not only in irresolvable conflict
with one another. Due to their foundationalist nature each of
them, it seems, is also systematically prior to the merely instrumental justification I have been attributing to Hayek. So my interpretation is in need of further elaboration if it is to stand. In what
follows the aim is to make clear that the various foundations of
Hayek's liberalism are not as disconnected as they appear at first
sight. I do not wish to dispute the results of Kukathas's analysis.
All that is intended here is a demonstration that, at bottom, those
three kinds of moral argument have much in common, as there is

[15] Kukathas (1989: 166–204).

an unmistakably instrumental perspective running through them all, giving Hayek's justification of liberalism at least some coherence of outlook. However, what I shall say does nothing to remove all the inconsistencies plaguing that justification.

Let us begin with Hayek's moral *conservatism*. The conservative moral argument, Kukathas[16] explains, is designed to elucidate the value of established traditions and to deflate excessive demands advanced in the name of reason for a full justification of a society's institutions. In what sense does this argument betray an instrumental attitude? For an answer we must go back to Hayek's theory of cultural evolution.

Hayek regards traditional institutions and rules as uniquely valuable because he believes mankind has no other similarly powerful resource in hand to grapple with the human predicament. He thinks reason, to which one might wish to look for guidance, is too feeble to tell us how we would have to shape our institutions to make them as effective as they are. In his view, reason is not even potent enough to grasp how traditional institutions actually adapt us to the natural and social world. The crucial notion here is that of adaptation. Hayek sees institutions and rules as 'tools' (e.g. 1960: 27; 1976: 21) whose significance consists in their 'adapting' us to our 'environment'. He is not a conservative treasuring traditional institutions and practices because they foster or constitute a singularly precious type of self or community. For Hayek, their value is of an entirely instrumental nature. The fact that they are not tools in the sense of artefacts springing from individual ingenuity does not nullify their instrumental character. According to Hayek, a largely incomprehensible process of 'cultural evolution' developed those institutional tools on our behalf, for we ourselves 'were not intelligent enough for that' (1979: 164). The limits of reason and the opacity of that process, he concludes, render it impossible not only fully to understand but also completely to justify the traditional institutions. Hayek's conservatism follows from his scepticism and his concern for maximum institutional effectiveness. The legitimacy of the established system roots in its unknowable yet unique adaptive value. To put it differently: Hayek's argument is conservative in its practical implications but instrumental in spirit.

[16] Ibid. 174–91.

Hayek's liberalism appears also to evince a *Kantian* side. More than anything else it is Hayek's recourse to the test of universalizability (e.g. 1967: 168; 1976: 27–9, 42–3) that has led Gray[17] and Kukathas[18] to claim that his liberalism is at least partly grounded in Kantian moral considerations. A Kantian foundation would be difficult to reconcile with the merely instrumental justification I see in Hayek's liberalism.

Kant intended the idea of universalizability to capture and express the substance of morality. The universalization test would reveal, Kant believed, whether or not a particular maxim or principle of action was a rule of morality. Sometimes calling it also 'the test of internal consistency' (e.g. 1976: 27–8), Hayek characterizes it as follows:

The test of the justice of a rule is usually (since Kant) described as that of its 'universalizability', i.e. of the possibility of willing that the rules should be applied to all instances that correspond to the conditions stated in it (the 'categorical imperative'). (1967: 168)

Now it is notoriously obscure exactly what Kant's test demands us to do when requiring us to 'universalize' a maxim.[19] Yet one thing is clear. We must conduct the test in our capacity as *rational beings* or, as Kant also says, as *members of the 'intelligible world'*.[20] '[I]f a rule or maxim is to be acceptable as just', Gray writes, 'its application must be endorsed by rational agents across all relevantly similar cases.'[21]

A close examination of Hayek's writings shows, however, that his conception is altogether different from the universalization test Kant and moral philosophers generally have in mind. While the Kantian version requires us to deliberate as rational beings and members of the world of reason, Hayek wants us to do so as members of an already existing market society. The criterion by which we must decide whether or not a particular rule is to be accepted as just lies, for Hayek, in the *functional contribution* it makes to the *generation of spontaneous economic order*. In this way, the Hayekian universalization test comes down to an

'immanent criticism' . . . that moves within a given system of rules and judges particular rules in terms of their consistency or compatibility with

---

[17] Gray (1986: 61–9, 96–8).   [18] Kukathas (1989: 167–74).

[19] For a discussion I have found particularly helpful, see Wiggins (1987: 59–86).

[20] For a brief account of Kant's position, with the relevant references, see Kukathas (1989: 31–42).   [21] Gray (1986: 7).

all other recognized rules in inducing the formation of a certain kind of order of actions. (1976: 24)

The great body of rules which in this sense is tacitly accepted determines the aim which the rules being questioned must also support; and this aim . . . is . . . the maintenance or restoration of an order of actions which the rules tend to bring about more or less successfully. (1976: 25)

[A]ny doubt about the justice of a particular rule must be resolved within the context of this body of generally accepted rules, in such a manner that the rule to be accepted will be compatible with the rest: that is, it must serve the formation of the same kind of abstract order of actions which all the other rules of just conduct serve . . . (1978: 139; similarly in 1979: 167)

When he insists that this 'ultimate test' (1976: 25) can be carried out only against the background of an accepted system of rules, he presupposes (but fails to say) that more or less that system must already be one of *market* rules. This is an all too narrow ambit for a test aiming to examine the morality or justice of rules. The passages quoted leave hardly a doubt that for Hayek's 'universalization test' the question of whether or not the market system is morally legitimate is a foregone conclusion. Indeed, one is tempted to say that Hayek's own categorical imperative (if such there is) consists in the peremptory demand to establish and uphold a market system. The practical thrust of his test amounts to the instruction tirelessly to refine the market's institutional framework in order to further improve the smoothness of its co-ordination. For Hayek, rules of conduct are in the first place causal antecedents to co-ordination and efficient co-operation. They are moral or just to the extent to which their observance contributes to the generation or continuation of spontaneous economic order. As Hayek himself writes, 'justice is an attribute of human conduct which we have learnt to exact because a certain kind of conduct is required to secure the formation and maintenance of a beneficial order of actions' (1976: 70). Crowley is therefore quite correct to say that for Hayek '[j]ustice, morality, and duty are simply descriptive terms for those ways of acting that are conducive to the maintenance of such an order of liberty'.[22]

Hayek's allegedly Kantian argument turns out to be altogether unable to ground a liberal market system: it takes its moral

---

[22] Crowley (1987: 83).

legitimacy for granted. There is no need here to illustrate in greater detail that Hayek's views on universalization could not be further from the Kantian endeavour to explain why, if the essence of morality is to be expressed in a single master idea, it must be the notion of universalizability. Hayekian universalization betrays, and is subordinate to, a consequentialist outlook. For Hayek, the market rules are rules of justice because their observance is seen as producing a generally desired and morally desirable result: 'a beneficial order of actions'.[23] Now this gives him the appearance of a utilitarian. So finally let us see whether he offers, for his market liberalism, a utilitarian moral foundation, and how such a justification relates to his instrumental perpective.

There exists some consensus that Hayek is a *utilitarian* of sorts or, at least, that his justification of a market system includes utilitarian arguments. Gray interprets him as an indirect or system utilitarian for whom 'the test of any system of rules is whether it maximizes an anonymous individual's chance of achieving his unknown purposes'.[24] Leland B. Yeager sees Hayek as subscribing to a 'rules-utilitarianism',[25] while for Russell Hardin he is a 'conservative utilitarian'.[26] Kukathas presents a number of reasons for considering him, as Gray does, an indirect utilitarian.[27] Still, in the end he thinks that important aspects militate against a utilitarian interpretation. We shall now look at Kukathas's reasons for rejecting such an interpretation, and I shall argue that they further strengthen the case for an instrumental reading of Hayek.

---

[23] I therefore find it difficult to accept Crowley's (1987: 17 *passim*) characterization of Hayek as a 'deontological liberal'. As I mentioned in my Introduction, it is true that occasionally Hayek does refer to a vaguely Kantian notion of individual autonomy. And it is also the case that he sometimes suggests a deontological perspective, saying, for example, that liberty (as defined by the rules of just conduct) 'demands that it be accepted as a value in itself, as a principle that must be respected without our asking whether the consequences in the particular instance will be beneficial' (1960: 68). Yet instrumental or consequentialist considerations are always close at hand; the passage just quoted illustrates this. In it, Hayek seems to express his endorsement of the deontological priority of the right over the good. Already in the next sentence, however, he reveals his consequentialist outlook when he writes that '*[w]e shall not achieve the results we want* if we do not accept it as a creed or presumption so strong that no consideration of expendiency can be allowed to limit it' (1960: 68, emphasis added; likewise in 1973: 55–62). The quasi-deontological nature of the Hayekian rules of just conduct depends on certain contingent *empirical* circumstances. If they happen to be such that a principled intervention (i.e. a change of the rules) is believed to produce superior outcomes, it is entirely legitimate.   [24] Gray (1986: 60, footnote omitted).
[25] Yeager (1984: 73).   [26] Hardin (1988: 133, 190).
[27] Kukathas (1989: 62–5, 135–6, 191–201).

As I understand him, Kukathas gives essentially two arguments for not regarding Hayek as a utilitarian. Hayek, he says, takes a sceptical stance, declaring rationality incapable of furnishing a valid criterion by which to evaluate the different states of affairs that alternative systems of rules might bring about.[28] And Hayek, he says, rejects the notion of 'utility' commonly employed by utilitarians.[29]

I agree with Kukathas that Hayek denies practical reason the power to decide rationally among conflicting values. Kukathas and I differ in the conclusions to be drawn. He thinks that reason thus conceived is unable to justify utilitarianism's basic criteria and that Hayek cannot therefore give his liberalism a utilitarian foundation. In my view, Hayek's narrow conception of practical reason strongly points to, and even leaves him with no option other than, an instrumental justification. For, by presenting reason as instrumental rationality, he does deem it capable of judging the aptness of alternative means to given ends. So, even if his ethical scepticism may disqualify him as a utilitarian, it does not impair the consistency of my instrumental interpretation.

The second argument Kukathas advances against a utilitarian interpretation of Hayek turns on the alleged absence of a definite criterion of 'utility'. It is true that Hayek claims that '[t]he only "utility" which can be said to have determined the rules of conduct is ... not a utility known to the acting persons, or to any one person, but only a hypostatized "utility" to society as a whole' (1976: 22). He appears again to reject any simple notion of 'utility' when he insists that the usefulness of the market rules does not derive 'from the importance of particular foreseen future uses' and does not 'constitute a reflection of the importance of particular ends' (1976: 18). And he explicitly criticizes utilitarianism for its demand

that every action should be judged in full awareness of all its foreseeable results—a view which in the last resort tends to dispense with all abstract rules and leads to the claim that man can achieve a desirable order of society by concretely arranging all its parts in full knowledge of all the relevant facts. (1967: 88)[30]

---

[28] Ibid. 196–7.   [29] Ibid. 64–5, 195, 200.

[30] Hayek gives the impression he is rejecting utilitarianism for the (in his view) exaggerated demands it makes on knowledge and foresight. So he writes: 'The trouble with the whole utilitarian approach is that, as a theory professing to account for a phenomenon which consists of a body of rules, it completely eliminates

A system of rules, Hayek seems to say, is uniquely beneficial but we cannot know in advance and detail the ways in which such usefulness manifests itself. This has led Barry to characterize Hayek as a consequentialist who, unlike 'orthodox' utilitarians, avoids any 'crude empirical or quantitative' notion of 'utility' and sees the value of liberty and of the rules embodying it in certain 'long-term, inherently unquantifiable advantages'.[31] Gray thinks the openness of Hayek's criterion of 'utility' and his anti-hedonistic stance (as found, for example, in 1960: 41) are combined and expressed best in the indirect utilitarian formulation that 'the test of any system of rules is whether it maximizes an anonymous individual's chance of achieving his unknown purposes'.[32] Kukathas, examining Hayek's attitude towards utilitarianism and reviewing various characterizations of Hayek offered in the secondary literature, concludes that his moral perspective is consequentialist but not utilitarian. He argues that while the Hayekian defence of the liberal order relies heavily on consequentialist considerations, Hayek rejects any welfarist end-state principle demanding the maximization of happiness or pleasure or well-being.[33]

Now the problem with such an interpretation of Hayek is, as Kukathas recognizes,[34] that it leaves his non-utilitarian consequentialism dangling. Hayek's claim that the market rules are useful in ways which we do not really know and cannot specify has an air of paradox. A consequentialist outlook requires a clear-cut criterion by which the performances of alternative socio-economic systems can be compared. To deny the availability or applicability of such a criterion is to rule out a consequentialist defence of such a system. Hayek cannot declare the market rules superior to any alternative system of rules and at the same time

the factor which makes rules necessary, namely our ignorance' (1976: 20). Yet it is difficult to see how this *epistemological* problem could lead to the abandonment of the utilitarian *moral* outlook. As Hardin (1988: 4) comments: 'He [Hayek] is right that ignorance often makes rules necessary, but neither recognition nor failure of recognition of our ignorance is inherently a part of utilitarianism. . . . If we develop a better system for determining relevant causal relations so that we are able to choose actions that better produce our intended ends, it does not follow that we then must change our ethics. The moral impulse of utilitarianism is constant, but our decisions under it are contingent on our knowledge and scientific understanding.' In practice, Hayek does repudiate the conventional welfarist criterion of 'utility' but otherwise treads a consequentialist path, as we shall see.

[31] Barry (1984: 278–9).   [32] Gray (1986: 60).
[33] Kukathas (1989: 64, 136, 196, 200).   [34] Ibid. 197–8.

maintain that their usefulness is unknown and unknowable. So what should we make of his aimless consequentialism?

I think we must not take Hayek's critique of utilitarianism for a complete repudiation of any end-state principle. He considers 'utility' an impracticable criterion because it presupposes a transparency and predictability which the social world does not possess. Yet his criticism does not prevent him from employing for himself an end-state standard, 'income', whose application does not appear to rest on such a far-reaching assumption. In my analysis, in Chapter 4, of Hayek's claim about the beneficial nature of spontaneous economic order I have worked out how his seemingly probabilistic and preference-oriented principle, put forward in the demand that the best economic system maximizes the chances of any member of society selected at random, eventually comes down to average income maximization. For Hayek, the market system is to be preferred over other economic systems because it generates a higher income, a higher output, per head. To be sure, 'income' is a very simple one-dimensional criterion which, unlike the comprehensive welfarist notion of 'utility', is not meant to reflect the members' well-being.[35] So Hayek's income-based consequentialism is not, in any strict sense, of a utilitarian nature. However, what he shares with standard utilitarianism is an indifference to the problem of how advantages are distributed. Hayek's talk about the indeterminacy of the benefits flowing from the observance of the market rules merely mirrors, I believe, his view that in the market the distribution of incomes, governed by chance, does not conform to any predictable pattern and may be highly unequal, and that therefore the market system cannot be demonstrated to be maximally (or even reasonably) advantageous to *every* individual.

Now one may, like Kukathas, wish to accentuate Hayek's opposition to welfarist standards of evaluation, thus stressing his distance from utilitarianism. In view of Hayek's undeniable consequentialism and of his own income-oriented criterion, such emphasis only strengthens the plausibility of the instrumental

---

[35] To reiterate: though he rejects welfarist criteria, which presuppose the measurability of happiness and well-being, Hayek does talk of 'general welfare' (e.g. 1976: 2, 5, 6) as one of the things an acceptable socio-economic system must achieve, and equates it, as I have tried to explain, with income and the entitlement to economic goods that income represents.

interpretation I am advocating. Avoiding the problems of measuring happiness, 'income maximization' is of a simplicity and distinctness that make it an aim fitting for an instrumental justification. It is not difficult to think of alternative economic systems as means to the end of maximum overall income or output. And, as I showed earlier, it is such a perspective that actually informs Hayek's defence of the market society. Thus, behind his critique of utilitarianism's welfarist or hedonistic standards of evaluation, we can discern again, I think, his basically instrumental approach to the justification of liberal social and economic institutions.

In this section, I have sought to explain how an instrumental reading of Hayek can take account of the various moral philosophical arguments he seems to advance in defence of liberal institutions. It is true that those conservative, Kantian, and utilitarian considerations, if they are genuinely such, cannot possibly be seen as springing from a single unified moral theory, and that therefore his liberalism appears to rest on hopelessly inconsistent moral foundations. However, I think such a diagnosis, though correct, has already missed Hayek's basic intentions, which are *not moral philosophical*. In view of his ethical scepticism, and considering his conception of practical reason as means–ends rationality, he cannot plausibly be interpreted as seeking a genuine moral philosophical justification for his liberalism. On close inspection his Kantian and other moral arguments invariably reveal a palpably instrumental perspective. Only an instrumental reading, I believe, captures the spirit of Hayek's enterprise and gives his political thought at least some unity.

Conclusion
The Prospects for Comprehensive Instrumental Justification

It is the unequivocal conclusion of this book that Hayek's instrumental approach to the justification of the institutions of liberal market society, his defence of its system of rules on grounds of their conduciveness to human survival, general prosperity, and social peace, fails. Yet one question remains: could such an approach ever have succeeded? That instrumental considerations form an indispensable part of the defence of liberalism and liberty is not to be disputed. 'The arguments for the instrumental value of liberty', Joseph Raz writes, 'are crucially important. Without them no political morality is complete.'[1] The question must therefore be: could an instrumental approach *alone* ever suffice to establish the legitimacy of a liberal market regime?

A discussion of certain premisses underlying Hayek's instrumental project may shed some light on the limits to instrumental reasoning in political philosophy. To locate these limits is at the same time to say something about the contribution social theory can make to legitimizing a particular type of institutional system. For in an instrumental justification social theoretic considerations are decisive, telling us which among alternative institutional arrangements achieve their ends most fully.

An instrumental justification as it is pursued by Hayek rests on at least four crucial assumptions. It presupposes, first, that the social and political ends are given and, secondly, that they are uncontested; it postulates, thirdly, that the means—the various institutional systems available—are morally neutral and, fourthly, that they represent a class of distinct and specific options. Each of these assumptions is problematic in its own way.

1. The least questionable assumption is probably the first, which is that the ends the basic system of social and economic

---

[1] Raz (1986: 7).

institutions should serve are *given*. It does not require much argument to realize that survival is preferable to starvation, general welfare better than economic misery, and social peace nicer than civil strife. Indeed, survival, prosperity, and peace presumably represent what almost everybody hopes for. But does not the move from what is actually desired to what is genuinely desirable involve an is–ought fallacy? I think not. The ends a society's institutions are to advance must certainly mirror the factual circumstances under which people live. They must take account of people's wants and aspirations, and of the potential for conflict inhering in social life. To be sure, they need not (and cannot) consider every whim some member of society may entertain; what ends the institutional system should promote requires reflection and critical scrutiny.[2] Still, whatever their specific contents finally are, these ends are rooted in the human condition and are, thus, not freely chosen. So there is a sense in which they are given.

2. Yet for an instrumental justification to work the ends must also be sufficiently determinate (and reasonably harmonious among themselves). Only if they are given *and* specific enough do they provide the *undisputed* starting-point indispensable for instrumental reasoning in general and for Hayek's defence of liberal institutions in particular. 'Ultimately', as Norman Barry quite rightly observes, 'the whole of Hayek's system does depend upon agreement about fundamental values.'[3]

Now, for modern Western society this assumption seems highly unrealistic. Even if people recognize that somehow the ends of society reflect the human predicament, they need not concur in their views about what more specifically these ends or 'fundamental values' (as Barry calls them) demand. To take just one example: is it really 'welfare' that should count when one attempts to measure the quality of the lives the members of society are able to lead? And which distributive principles should '*general* welfare' involve?[4] We have every reason to believe that an easy consensus does not—or, perhaps, does no longer—exist. Disagreement about the ends calls radically into question the appropriateness of an instrumental conception of justification for the purposes of political philosophy. If it is the task of liberal political philosophy to

---

[2] For more on what such reflection involves, see Rescher (1973: 138–43; 1988: 92–118).   [3] Barry (1979: 200).

[4] For wide-ranging discussions of the problem of how to measure the quality of life, see the contributions in Nussbaum and Sen (1993).

show why one should accept as legitimate liberal rather than other social and economic institutions, and if a broad consensus about the ends of a society's socio-economic system does not exist, any comprehensive instrumental approach must fail. For, the conclusion yielded by instrumental reasoning, that such and such institutional arrangement is the rational option since it attains its ends to the largest degree possible, would not be accepted generally because many did not accept the ends in the first place.

It seems that under modern conditions, in the absence of a consensus about ends, a justification of a particular type of institutional system must to some extent be *foundationalist* or *coherentist*, along the lines suggested, for example, by Rawls.[5] A foundationalist justification seeks to uncover, and to issue from, shared points of reference (such as, in Rawls's case, a particular conception of the person) which are seated in the political culture of Western democracy more deeply than the ends from which Hayek's instrumental approach wants to start. A coherentist justification proceeds from various uncontested and seemingly unconnected elements of that culture which it tries to relate to each other so that eventually we can recognize and acknowledge them as forming a systematic basis for an argument in favour of certain institutional arrangements.

3. A further assumption necessary for a Hayekian instrumental justification to succeed is that the various institutional systems regarded as alternative means to the social and political ends given must themselves be *morally neutral*, or at least morally uncontroversial. An instrumental justification can be a matter of value-free, scientific reasoning guided by the precepts of means–ends rationality only if the choice among the alternative systems is not at the same time inevitably also a decision about possibly contentious moral issues. This condition does not hold. A system of social and economic institutions cannot simply be seen as neutral means to certain ends external to it.[6] Any such system has its own distinctive 'side-effects' influencing the members' lives, shaping their

---

[5] See Rawls (1971; 1993). Rawls's method of reflective equilibrium combines, I believe, the foundationalist and coherentist approaches. For a reconstruction and discussion of this method, see Kley (1989: chs. 1 and 7).

[6] In his purely instrumental view of socio-economic systems, Hayek is not alone. In fact, his perspective is just one further instance of the 'engineering approach' to economics, an approach which according to Amartya Sen (1987: 2–10) has a long tradition in economics and is still very influential, though, as Sen argues, often not to the discipline's advantage.

prospects, and moulding their identities in morally significant respects other than merely by securing, or failing to secure, survival,
prosperity, and peace. To realize that in the choice of an institutional system other moral aspects and values, intrinsic and instrumental, are at stake, we need only consider whether we would find
acceptable a system that rigorously subjected all its institutions to
the pursuit of those Hayekian ends. In such a system there would
probably be no room for democratic rule and political contest
among rival parties and no scope for industrial disputes. Political
and economic decisions would be taken by a technocratic élite. On
a strictly instrumental account, the Orwellian Big Brother may in
the end do better than a Western liberal constitutional regime.
Once it is recognized that an institutional system is morally not
neutral, the case for an instrumental justification collapses. What
type of system is to be preferred requires moral philosophical
argument and cannot be decided on social theoretic grounds alone.

4. Hayek's instrumental justification assumes, finally, that the
choice is among alternative types of institutional *systems*. Such a
justification presupposes that the options to be considered represent a class of clearly distinct and sufficiently specific systems of
social and economic institutions so that favouring one particular
type of system largely decides also what particular form its institutions should take. That there are distinct alternatives follows,
for Hayek, from the fact that societies, like all other kinds of
associations and collectives, are either 'spontaneous orders' or
'organizations'. In his view, therefore, to choose a type of socio-
economic system is to opt for one of these two possibilities. Yet
such a social theoretic taxonomy is too abstract to be of much use
in the justification of liberal (or other) social and economic institutions. At best, 'spontaneous order' stands for the principle of
economic self-co-ordination as embodied in markets, and 'organization' for central economic direction. Now, while a decision in
favour of either of these principles has undeniably far-reaching
consequences for how the system should be structured, it still
leaves open many important questions about what the main institutions should look like. The institutional system even of a modern society is not functionally so tight that the basic decision in
favour of, say, the market system would in itself already suffice
also to answer all major questions about what shape its institutions should take. To give them an emphatically liberal character

demands further justification. This suggests that a wholesale approach to the defence of a particular institutional system, as we find it in Hayek, does not work. The justification of a liberal (or other) regime and its institutions requires additional argument, instrumental or moral philosophical, flowing from considerations other than the general instrumental reasons that may advise the reliance on markets or on elements of central direction.

Though an exclusively instrumental justification must founder, does not Hayek's project still point to theoretical resources, important yet neglected, upon which liberal political philosophy could draw when it seeks to provide orientation in public affairs? In their taxonomy of normative theories of the state Alan Hamlin and Philip Pettit aptly classify Hayek's approach as dominated by considerations of 'feasibility'.[7] Kukathas believes this feasibility approach, with its emphasis on social theoretic reflection, deserves further examination. By 'draw[ing] attention to the need to consider the nature of society and the way in which this constrains our choice of political principles', Hayek pushes, he writes, 'contemporary liberal theory in a promising direction'.[8]

That political philosophy should be sensitive to the empirical facts of social and economic life is an obvious general postulate. Yet Hayek and Kukathas have something more specific in mind. They think social theory can determine (Hayek) the institutional contours of a liberal society or at least significantly constrain (Kukathas) the range of feasible institutional alternatives, ruling out certain clearly illiberal blueprints. Yet it must be doubted whether Hayekian (or any other) social theory can say much about '*the* nature of society', let alone that its insights have special sympathies for liberal solutions to the problems of social and economic order.

To be sure, there is Hayek's argument about the informational role of markets in modern society. Only in a system with extensive markets, where prices are allowed to reflect the relative scarcities of resources and the strengths of people's preferences, are efficient co-ordination and production possible. To have shown this is, I believe, an original and lasting achievement of Hayek. The practical implication of this argument is that modern societies cannot do without markets. To this extent, an economic or social theoretic

[7] Hamlin and Pettit (1989: 10).   [8] Kukathas (1989: 228).

consideration can rightly be said to constrain the range of alternative forms a viable society can take. Hayek does have a decisive argument against any socialism opting for a comprehensively
planned economy.

Resting on an insight into the function of a market price-system
the epistemological argument does not depend conceptually on a
particular social theory such as Hayek's own. So what could that
theory, comprising a theory of cultural evolution and the idea of
a spontaneous order, further contribute to specifying a distinctly
liberal system of institutions? The theory of cultural evolution is
altogether unhelpful. Some of its basic features, such as its adaptationism and holist functionalism, render it untenable. Moreover, it offers nothing to warrant the hope that the institutional
systems surviving the natural selection process would be of a more
and more liberal character.

The idea of a spontaneous order is deficient in other respects. In
particular, it has no solution to three problems to which liberals
would wish to get a principled answer.

1. The idea is of no help in what Hayek, borrowing a phrase
from Jeremy Bentham, calls the problem of 'the agenda and nonagenda of government' (1949: 17; 1933b: 134). Being no more
than a generalization of the market model it cannot say anything
about *where* to draw the line between centrally co-ordinated state
activity and market self-co-ordination. Though giving metaphoric
expression to the kind of co-ordination operating in markets, the
idea adds nothing to what we already know: that markets must
play an important part. The lack of a criterion or set of criteria
demarcating the private and public sectors makes Hayek's enu-
meration of legitimate state activities (e.g. 1979: ch. 14) an *ad hoc*
assemblage of trivial and less trivial governmental tasks and leads
him, for example, to endorse anti-cyclical expenditure policies (e.g.
1979: 59), something the idea of a *spontaneous* order would seem
to rule out.

2. The idea of a spontaneous order is, on Hayek's own account,
unable to identify the limits to redistribution and thus cannot say
much about the possibility or impossibility of *social justice*. It does
rule out a distribution according to merit or need—criteria, however, whose impracticability we can recognize anyway, without our
resorting to that idea. But it does not rule out all redistribution

since Hayek himself unreservedly supports the introduction of a minimum income scheme, if only for prudential rather than moral reasons.

3. The idea of a spontaneous order cannot give much orientation as to what the political, legal, and economic institutions of a liberal society should look like. Even if a particular system of rules helps us survive and promotes general prosperity and social peace, this does not entail, nor suffice to justify, a liberal order. In combination with Hayek's holist functionalism—according to which *all* enduring social structures and institutions contribute to a society's economic success—his suggestion that only the rules conducive to spontaneous order should be enforced does not preclude authoritarian or otherwise illiberal regimes, which espouse a free market ideology while simultaneously pursuing strategies of political, cultural, or religious repression.

I believe it is because the idea of a spontaneous order lacks distinctness and internal structure that the moral philosophical foundations of Hayek's liberalism are so incoherent. The inability of that *social theoretic* but not value-free idea to furnish a single comprehensive, and at the same time sufficiently specific, *moral* perspective forces Hayek to take recourse to various *ad hoc* arguments when he attempts to justify his preferred version of liberal order. This, together with his unawareness of the unity and consistency required by a moral theory, explains the hotchpotch of conservative, Kantian, and utilitarian arguments which he ends up with.

At the heart of Hayek's instrumental approach lies a social theory that combines a naturalistic outlook with an almost complete blindness to the institutional diversity of markets and market elements in actual societies. He suggests that there is in the social world a potential of spontaneously ordering 'forces' of which we can avail ourselves if only we implement the right institutions. These, for Hayek, are above all those of private property, contract, and tort. The functional requirements of spontaneous orders, his social theory wants us to believe, are such that they permit only minimal institutional variation and no element of central economic co-ordination, should the market mechanism not be impaired and, consequently, the advantages it produces not be smaller than they could be. Having acquired a correct understanding of the nature of social and economic processes, social theory can, Hayek believes, tell us which type of institutional system will work at all and which demands of political morality are in the long run altogether compatible with the causal regularities governing the social world. In other words, Hayekian social theory is meant to set the boundaries within which normative political philosophy is free to roam. For him, these boundaries turn out to be as narrow as to admit of only one political solution: classical liberalism.[9] To put Hayek's position as pointedly as possible: social reality constrains the range of acceptable and viable alternative systems in a way that leaves no option other than a classical liberal regime.

However, the institutional diversity of successful economies demonstrates that there is more plasticity to social and economic systems than Hayekian social theory has it. To be sure, not everything goes.[10] Markets must, as he rightly insists, play an impor-

---

[9] A similar conception of the relationship between positive (economic) theory and normative ethics, and a comparable overestimation of the power of the former, also underlies, I believe, Kirzner's (1988; 1989) defence of 'capitalist morality', in essence the claim that the distribution of incomes in the market is just. Kirzner argues that the socialist calculation debate of the 1920s and 1930s between the Austrian (L. Mises, F. A. Hayek) and the socialist economists about the possibility or impossibility of rational economic calculation in planned economies did not only bring about revolutionary scientific progress in positive economics but has also 'correspondingly revolutionary implications for the moral appraisal' of capitalism (Kirzner 1988: 166). He thinks the Austrians' view of the market as a discovery procedure, which includes the view that market incomes and profits are gained as a result of entrepreneurial discovery, implies a 'finders-keepers ethic' declaring 'discovered incomes won by resource owners in the market to be rightfully theirs' and exposes the lack of realism in 'the standard perspectives on the ethics of distribution' (Kirzner 1988: 182). What Kirzner overlooks, it seems, is that to present the market as a discovery procedure is not to capture a hard empirical fact about it but to *interpret* it in a particular fashion. Now it is certainly the case that our views of how society works contribute to shaping what we consider morally relevant and that they play a role when we assess the plausibility of a particular conception of justice (for an exploration and illustration of this theme, see David Miller (1976: esp. pt. II)). Yet to acknowledge that moral and normative political conceptions make full sense only against the background of a (largely interpretive) theoretic account of social and economic life is far from suggesting that social and economic theory can *determine* what is just or unjust.

[10] For an example of a political programme in which social imagination seems to have gone wild and apparently 'anything goes' indeed, see Unger's (1987) *Constructive Social Theory*. Unger seeks an alternative to both Marxism and Western liberalism, claiming that even the latter's institutions of decentralized economy and pluralistic democracy thwart rather than promote the ideals of liberty and equality for whose sake they were set up. And he wants his project of radical institutional reconstruction to be complemented by an attendant 'cultural revolution' that also fundamentally transforms people's personal relations and self-understanding. Unger's

tant role. Yet how far they should extend, how far they should be constrained and in what ways supplemented, and in what kind of political framework they should be embedded, cannot be decided on grounds of feasibility alone. Answering these questions requires genuine moral reflection and falls in the province of normative political philosophy.

programme raises many problems. One of them is the difficulty of seeing why we should ever consider opting for a political and social alternative if under it we would be persons with attachments, identities, and projects which now we not only do not know but also could not recognize as at least similar to those we actually have. Unger's radicalism seems to be such that it deprives him, and us, of any safe ground from which to compare the present with his Utopian future and to make a reasonable choice. For more on Unger's project, see e.g. Lovin and Perry (1990).

BIBLIOGRAPHY

AKERLOF, GEORGE A. (1970), 'The Market for "Lemons": Qualitative Uncertainty and the Market Mechanism', *The Quarterly Journal of Economics*, 84: 488–500, repr. in George Akerlof, *An Economic Theorist's Book of Tales*, Cambridge: Cambridge University Press, 1984.

ASHWORTH, TONY (1980), *Trench Warfare: The Live and Let Live System*, New York: Holmes & Meier.

ATIYAH, P. S. (1979), *The Rise and Fall of Freedom of Contract*, Oxford: Clarendon Press.

AXELROD, ROBERT (1984), *The Evolution of Cooperation*, New York: Basic Books.

BARRY, NORMAN P. (1979), *Hayek's Social and Economic Philosophy*, London: Macmillan.

—— (1982), 'The Tradition of Spontaneous Order', *Literature of Liberty*, 5/2: 7–58.

—— (1984), 'Hayek on Liberty', in Zbigniew Pelczynski and John Gray (eds.), *Conceptions of Liberty*, London: Athlone Press, 263–88.

—— (1986), *On Classical Liberalism and Libertarianism*, London: Macmillan.

BATESON, PATRICK (1988), 'The Biological Evolution of Cooperation and Trust', in Diego Gambetta (ed.), *Trust: Making and Breaking Cooperative Relations*, Oxford: Blackwell, 14–30.

BECKER, GARY S. (1976), *The Economic Approach to Human Behavior*, Chicago: University of Chicago Press.

BEINER, RONALD (1983), *Political Judgment*, London: Methuen.

BÖHM, STEPHAN (1989), 'Hayek on Knowledge, Equilibrium, and Prices: Context and Impact', *Wirtschaftspolitische Blätter*, 36: 201–13.

BOUILLON, HARDY (1991), *Ordnung, Evolution und Erkenntnis: Hayeks Sozialphilosophie und ihre erkenntnistheoretische Grundlage*, Tübingen: J. C. B. Mohr.

BUCHANAN, JAMES M. (1977), 'Law and the Invisible Hand', in id., *Freedom in Constitutional Contract: Perspectives of a Political Economist*, London: Texas A & M University Press, 25–39.

BUTOS, WILLIAM N. (1985/86), 'Hayek and General Equilibrium Analysis', *Southern Economic Journal*, 52: 332–43.

CALDWELL, BRUCE J. (1987), 'Hayek's "The Trend of Economic Thinking" ', *The Review of Austrian Economics*, 2: 175–8.

—— (1988), 'Hayek's transformation', *History of Political Economy*, 20: 513–41.

—— (1992*a*), 'Hayek the Falsificationist? A Refutation', *Research in the History of Economic Thought and Methodology*, 10: 1–15.

—— (1992*b*), 'Reply to Hutchison', *Research in the History of Economic Thought and Methodology*, 10: 33–42.

CAMPBELL, ANNE (1984), *The Girls in the Gang: A Report from New York City*, Oxford: Blackwell.

CAMPBELL, JEREMY (1984), *Grammatical Man: Information, Entropy, Language and Life*, Harmondsworth: Penguin.

CATANZARO, RAIMONDO (1985), 'Enforcers, Entrepreneurs, and Survivors: How the *mafia* has Adapted to Change', *The British Journal of Sociology*, 36: 34–57.

CHOMSKY, NOAM (1980), *Rules and Representations*, Oxford: Blackwell.

CLITEUR, PAUL B. (1990), 'Why Hayek is a Conservative', *Archiv für Rechts- und Sozialphilosophie*, 76: 467–78.

COLEMAN, JAMES S. (1990), *Foundations of Social Theory*, Cambridge, Mass.: Belknap Press of Harvard University Press.

COLEMAN, SAMUEL (1968), 'Is There Reason in Tradition?', in Preston King and B. C. Parekh (eds.), *Politics and Experience*, Cambridge: Cambridge University Press, 239–82.

CROWLEY, BRIAN LEE (1987), *The Self, the Individual, and the Community: Liberalism in the Political Thought of F. A. Hayek and Sidney and Beatrice Webb*, Oxford: Clarendon Press.

DE JASAY, ANTHONY (1989), *Social Contract, Free Ride: A Study of the Public Goods Problem*, Oxford: Clarendon Press.

DEMSETZ, HAROLD (1988), *Ownership, Control, and the Firm*, The Organization of Economic Activity, i, Oxford: Blackwell.

DIZEREGA, GUS (1989), 'Liberalism and Democracy: Spontaneous Order, Information, and Values', *Wirtschaftspolitische Blätter*, 36: 159–69.

DOSTALER, GILLES (1991), 'The Debate between Hayek and Keynes', in William J. Barber (ed.), *Perspectives on the History of Economic Thought*, vi: *Themes in Keynesian Criticism and Supplementary Modern Topics*, Aldershot: Elgar, 77–101.

DWORKIN, RONALD (1978), 'Liberalism', in Stuart Hampshire (ed.), *Public and Private Morality*, Cambridge: Cambridge University Press, 113–43.

ELSTER, JON (1979), *Ulysses and the Sirens*, Cambridge: Cambridge University Press.

—— (1985*a*), *Making Sense of Marx*, Cambridge: Cambridge University Press.

—— (1985*b*), 'The Nature and Scope of Rational-Choice Explanation', in Ernest LePore and Brian P. McLaughlin (eds.), *Actions and Events: Perspectives on the Philosophy of Donald Davidson*, Oxford: Blackwell, 60–72.

—— (1986), 'Introduction', in id. (ed.), *Rational Choice*, Oxford: Blackwell, 1–33.

ELSTER, JON (1987), 'The Possibility of Rational Politics', *European Journal of Sociology*, 28: 67–103.

—— (1989*a*), *The Cement of Society: A Study of Social Order*, Cambridge: Cambridge University Press.

—— (1989*b*), *Nuts and Bolts for the Social Sciences*, Cambridge: Cambridge University Press.

FORSYTH, MURRAY (1988), 'Hayek's Bizarre Liberalism: A Critique', *Political Studies*, 36: 235–50.

FOX, ROBIN (1977), 'The Inherent Rules of Violence', in Peter Collett (ed.), *Social Rules and Social Behaviour*, Oxford: Blackwell, 132–49.

FRANCIS, MARK (1985), 'The Austrian Mind in Exile: Kelsen, Schumpeter and Hayek', in Mark Francis (ed.), *The Viennese Enlightenment*, London: Croom Helm, 63–87.

FURTH, J. HERBERT (1989), 'Erinnerungen an Wiener Tage', *Wirtschaftspolitische Blätter*, 36: 247–53.

GALEOTTI, ANNA ELISABETTA (1987), 'Individualism, Social Rules, Tradition: The Case of Friedrich A. Hayek', *Political Theory*, 15: 163–81.

GAMBETTA, DIEGO (1988), 'Mafia: the Price of Distrust', in id. (ed.), *Trust: Making and Breaking Cooperative Relations*, Oxford: Blackwell, 158–75.

GAUTHIER, DAVID (1986), *Morals by Agreement*, Oxford: Clarendon Press.

GIBBARD, ALLAN (1985), 'What's Morally Special About Free Exchange', *Social Philosophy and Policy*, 2/2: 20–8.

GRAF, HANS-GEORG (1978), *'Muster-Voraussagen' und 'Erklärungen des Prinzips' bei F. A. von Hayek*, Tübingen: J. C. B. Mohr.

GRAY, JOHN (1980), 'F. A. Hayek on Liberty and Tradition', *Journal of Libertarian Studies*, 4: 119–37.

—— (1986), *Hayek on Liberty*, Oxford: Blackwell (2nd rev. edn., first pub. 1984).

—— (1987), 'The Idea of a Spontaneous Order and the Unity of the Sciences', in Gerard Radnitzky (ed.), *Centripetal Forces in the Sciences*, New York: Paragon, i. 237–49.

—— (1988*a*), 'F. A. von Hayek', in Roger Scruton (ed.), *Conservative Thinkers: Essays from The Salisbury Review*, London: Claridge Press, 249–59.

—— (1988*b*), 'Hayek, the Scottish School, and Contemporary Economics', in Gordon C. Winston and Richard F. Teichgraeber III (eds.), *The Boundaries of Economics*, Cambridge: Cambridge University Press, 53–70.

—— (1989), 'Hayek on the Market Economy and the Limits of State Action', in Dieter Helm (ed.), *The Economic Borders of the State*, Oxford: Oxford University Press, 127–43.

GRIFFIN, JAMES (1986), *Well-Being: Its Meaning, Measurement, and Moral Importance*, Oxford: Clarendon Press.

HAAKONSSEN, KNUD (1988), 'The Philosophy of Law in Hayek's New Constitutionalism', *Rechtstheorie*, 19: 289–303.

HABERLER, GOTTFRIED (1989), 'Reflections on Hayek's Business Cycle Theory', *Wirtschaftspolitische Blätter*, 36: 220–30.

HALL, JOHN A. (1985), *Powers and Liberties: The Causes and Consequences of the Rise of the West*, Oxford: Blackwell.

—— (1986), 'States and Economic Development: Reflections on Adam Smith', in John A. Hall (ed.), *States in History*, Oxford: Blackwell, 154–76.

—— (1988), 'States and Societies: the Miracle in Comparative Perspective', in John A. Hall and Michael Mann (eds.), *Europe and the Rise of Capitalism*, Oxford: Blackwell, 20–38.

HALLPIKE, CHRISTOPHER R. (1986), *The Principles of Social Evolution*, Oxford: Clarendon Press.

HAMLIN, ALAN, and PETTIT, PHILIP (1989), 'The Normative Analysis of the State: Some Preliminaries', in id. (eds.), *The Good Polity: Normative Analysis of the State*, Oxford: Blackwell, 1–13.

HAMOWY, RONALD (1961), 'Hayek's Concept of Freedom: A Critique', *New Individualist Review*, 1: 28–31.

HARDIN, RUSSELL (1988), *Morality within the Limits of Reason*, Chicago: University of Chicago Press.

HAYEK, FRIEDRICH A. (1931), *Prices and Production*, London: Routledge (rev. edn. 1935).

—— (1933a), *Monetary Theory and the Trade Cycle*, London: Cape.

—— (1933b), 'The Trend of Economic Thinking', *Economica*, 13: 121–37.

—— (1939), *Profits, Interest and Investment*, London: Routledge.

—— (1944), *The Road to Serfdom*, London: Routledge (ARK pbk. edn., Routledge & Kegan Paul, 1986).

—— (1949), *Individualism and Economic Order*, London: Routledge (repr. Routledge & Kegan Paul, 1976).

—— (1952a), *The Counter-Revolution of Science: Studies on the Abuse of Reason*, Glencoe, Ill.: Free Press.

—— (1952b), *The Sensory Order: An Inquiry into the Foundations of Theoretical Psychology*, London: Routledge & Kegan Paul (repr. 1987).

—— (1960), *The Constitution of Liberty*, London: Routledge & Kegan Paul (repr. 1963).

—— (1967), *Studies in Philosophy, Politics and Economics*, London: Routledge & Kegan Paul.

—— (1973), *Law, Legislation and Liberty*, i: *Rules and Order*, London: Routledge & Kegan Paul; repr. with vols. ii and iii in 1982.

—— (1976), *Law, Legislation and Liberty*, ii: *The Mirage of Social Justice*, London: Routledge & Kegan Paul; repr. with vols. i and iii 1982.

HAYEK, FRIEDRICH A. (1978), *New Studies in Philosophy, Politics, Economics and the History of Ideas*, London: Routledge & Kegan Paul.

—— (1979), *Law, Legislation and Liberty*, iii: *The Political Order of a Free People*, London: Routledge & Kegan Paul; repr. with vols. i and ii 1982.

—— (1983), *Knowledge, Evolution, and Society*, London: Adam Smith Institute.

—— (1987a), 'Individual and Collective Aims', in Susan Mendus and David Edwards (eds.), *On Toleration*, Oxford: Clarendon Press, 35–47.

—— (1987b), 'The Rules of Morality are not the Conclusions of Our Reason', in Gerard Radnitzky (ed.), *Centripetal Forces in the Sciences*, New York: Paragon, i. 227–35.

—— (1988), *The Fatal Conceit: The Errors of Socialism*, London: Routledge.

HEATH, EUGENE (1989), 'How to Understand Liberalism as Gardening: Galeotti on Hayek', *Political Theory*, 17: 107–13.

HICKS, JOHN (1967), 'The Hayek Story', in id., *Critical Essays in Monetary Theory*, Oxford: Clarendon Press, 203–15.

HIRSHLEIFER, JACK (1987), *Economic Behaviour in Adversity*, Brighton: Wheatsheaf.

HOBSBAWM, ERIC, and RANGER, TERENCE (eds.) (1983), *The Invention of Tradition*, Cambridge: Cambridge University Press.

HODGSON, GEOFFREY M. (1988), *Economics and Institutions: A Manifesto for a Modern Institutional Economics*, Cambridge: Polity Press.

—— (1991), 'Hayek's Theory of Cultural Evolution: An Evaluation in the Light of Vanberg's Critique', *Economics and Philosophy*, 7: 67–82.

HOLLIS, MARTIN (1987), *The Cunning of Reason*, Cambridge: Cambridge University Press.

HONT, ISTVAN, and IGNATIEFF, MICHAEL (1983), 'Needs and Justice in the *Wealth of Nations*: An Introductory Essay', in id. (eds.), *Wealth and Virtue: The Shaping of Political Economy in the Scottish Enlightenment*, Cambridge: Cambridge University Press, 1–44.

HUTCHISON, TERENCE W. (1981), *The Politics and Philosophy of Economics: Marxians, Keynesians and Austrians*, Oxford: Blackwell.

—— (1992), 'Hayek and "Modern Austrian" Methodology: Comment on a Non-Refuting Refutation', *Research in the History of Economic Thought and Methodology*, 10: 17–32.

IOANNIDES, STAVROS (1992), *The Market, Competition, and Democracy: A Critique of Neo-Austrian Economics*, Aldershot: Elgar.

KEIZER, W. (1989), 'Recent Reinterpretations of the Socialist Calculation Debate', *Journal of Economic Studies*, 16/2: 63–83.

KENNEDY, PAUL M. (1988), *The Rise and Fall of the Great Powers: Economic Change and Military Conflict from 1500 to 2000*, London: Unwin Hyman.

KIRZNER, ISRAEL M. (1973), *Competition and Entrepreneurship*, Chicago: University of Chicago Press.

—— (1984), 'Prices, the Communication of Knowledge, and the Discovery Process', in Kurt R. Leube and Albert H. Zlabinger (eds.), *The Political Economy of Freedom: Essays in Honor of F. A. Hayek*, Munich: Philosophia Verlag, 193–206.

—— (1987), 'The Economic Calculation Debate: Lessons for Austrians', *The Review of Austrian Economics*, 2: 1–18.

—— (1988), 'Some Ethical Implications for Capitalism of the Socialist Calculation Debate', *Social Philosophy and Policy*, 6/1: 165–82.

—— (1989), *Discovery, Capitalism and Distributive Justice*, Oxford: Blackwell.

KLEY, ROLAND (1989), *Vertragstheorien der Gerechtigkeit: Eine philosophische Kritik der Theorien von John Rawls, Robert Nozick und James Buchanan*, Berne/Stuttgart: Paul Haupt.

KRIPKE, SAUL (1982), *Wittgenstein on Rules and Private Language*, Oxford: Blackwell.

KUKATHAS, CHANDRAN (1989), *Hayek and Modern Liberalism*, Oxford: Clarendon Press.

LARMORE, CHARLES E. (1987), *Patterns of Moral Complexity*, Cambridge: Cambridge University Press.

LAVOIE, DON (1985), *Rivalry and Central Planning: The Socialist Calculation Debate Reconsidered*, Cambridge: Cambridge University Press.

LEONI, BRUNO (1972), *Freedom and the Law*, Los Angeles: Nash.

LEVY, DAVID J. (1987), *Political Order: Philosophical Anthropology, Modernity, and the Challenge of Ideology*, Baton Rouge and London: Louisiana State University Press.

LEWIS, DAVID K. (1969), *Convention: A Philosophical Study*, Cambridge, Mass.: Harvard University Press.

LINDBLOM, CHARLES E. (1965), *The Intelligence of Democracy: Decision Making Through Mutual Adjustment*, New York: Free Press.

LIVINGSTON, DONALD W. (1984), *Hume's Philosophy of Common Life*, Chicago: University of Chicago Press.

LOVIN, ROBIN W., and PERRY, MICHAEL J. (eds.) (1990), *Critique and Construction: A Symposium on Roberto Unger's 'Politics'*, Cambridge: Cambridge University Press.

LUKES, STEVEN (1991), 'The Principles of 1989: Reflections on the Political Morality of the Recent Revolutions', in id., *Moral Conflict and Politics*, Oxford: Clarendon Press, 305–17.

MACBEATH, ALEXANDER (1952), *Experiments in Living: A Study of the Nature and Foundation of Ethics or Morals in the Light of Recent Work in Social Anthropology*, London: Macmillan.

McGINN, COLIN (1984), *Wittgenstein on Meaning*, Oxford: Blackwell.

MANN, MICHAEL (1986), *The Sources of Social Power*, i: *A History of Power From the Beginning to* AD *1760*, Cambridge: Cambridge University Press.

MARSHALL, GEOFFREY (1983), 'The Roles of Rules', in David Miller and Larry Siedentop (eds.), *The Nature of Political Theory*, Oxford: Clarendon Press, 183–95.

MESTMÄCKER, ERNST-JOACHIM (1985), *Regelbildung und Rechtsschutz in marktwirtschaftlichen Ordnungen*, Tübingen: J. C. B. Mohr.

MILLER, DAVID (1976), *Social Justice*, Oxford: Clarendon Press.

—— (1989), *Market, State, and Community: Theoretical Foundations of Market Socialism*, Oxford: Clarendon Press.

NENTJES, A. (1988), 'Hayek and Keynes: A Comparative Analysis of Their Monetary Views', *Journal of Economic Studies*, 15/3–4: 136–151.

NUSSBAUM, MARTHA C., and SEN, AMARTYA K. (eds.) (1993), *The Quality of Life*, Oxford: Clarendon Press.

NYIRI, J. C. (1988), 'Tradition and Practical Knowledge', in J. C. Nyiri and Barry Smith (eds.), *Practical Knowledge: Outlines of a Theory of Traditions and Skills*, London: Croom Helm, 17–52.

OAKESHOTT, MICHAEL (1975), *On Human Conduct*, Oxford: Clarendon Press.

O'DRISCOLL, GERALD P., jun. (1977), *Economics as a Coordination Problem: The Contributions of Friedrich A. Hayek*, Kansas City: Sheed Andrews and McMeel.

—— (1978), 'Spontaneous Order and the Coordination of Economic Activities', in Louis M. Spadaro (ed.), *New Directions in Austrian Economics*, Kansas City: Sheed Andrews and McMeel, 111–42.

—— and RIZZO, MARIO J. (1985), *The Economics of Time and Ignorance*, Oxford: Blackwell.

OYE, KENNETH A. (ed.) (1986), *Cooperation Under Anarchy*, Princeton, NJ: Princeton University Press.

PAGDEN, ANTHONY (1988), 'The Destruction of Trust and its Economic Consequences in the Case of Eighteenth-Century Naples', in Diego Gambetta (ed.), *Trust: Making and Breaking Cooperative Relations*, Oxford: Blackwell, 127–41.

PAQUÉ, KARL-HEINZ (1990), 'Pattern Predictions in Economics: Hayek's Methodology of the Social Sciences Revisited', *History of Political Economy*, 22: 281–94.

PARFIT, DEREK (1984), *Reasons and Persons*, Oxford: Clarendon Press (repr. with corrections 1987).

PAUL, ELLEN FRANKEL (1988), 'Liberalism, Unintended Orders and Evolutionism', *Political Studies*, 36: 251–72.

PHEBY, JOHN (1988), *Methodology and Economics: A Critical Introduction*, Basingstoke: Macmillan.

POLANYI, MICHAEL (1958), *Personal Knowledge: Towards a Post-Critical Philosophy*, London: Routledge & Kegan Paul.

—— (1967), *The Tacit Dimension*, London: Routledge & Kegan Paul.

POPPER, KARL (1945), *The Open Society and Its Enemies*, 2 vols., London: Routledge.

—— (1957), *The Poverty of Historicism*, London: Routledge & Kegan Paul.

—— (1963), *Conjectures and Refutations: The Growth of Scientific Knowledge*, London: Routledge & Kegan Paul.

PULLEN, GLENDON R. (1989), 'Liberty and Spontaneous Order in the Thought of Friedrich A. von Hayek', *Wirtschaftspolitische Blätter*, 36: 149–57.

RAVALLION, MARTIN (1987), *Markets and Famines*, Oxford: Clarendon Press.

RAWLS, JOHN (1971), *A Theory of Justice*, Cambridge, Mass.: Belknap Press of Harvard University Press.

—— (1982), 'Social Unity and Primary Goods', in Amartya K. Sen and Bernard Williams (eds.), *Utilitarianism and Beyond*, Cambridge: Cambridge University Press, 159–85.

—— (1993), *Political Liberalism*, New York: Columbia University Press.

RAZ, JOSEPH (1979), 'The Rule of Law and Its Virtue', in id., *The Authority of Law*, Oxford: Clarendon Press, 210–29.

—— (1986), *The Morality of Freedom*, Oxford: Clarendon Press.

RESCHER, NICOLAS (1973), *The Primacy of Practice*, Oxford: Blackwell.

—— (1988), *Rationality: A Philosophical Inquiry into the Nature and the Rationale of Reason*, Oxford: Clarendon Press.

ROTHBARD, MURRAY N. (1982), 'F. A. Hayek and the Concept of Coercion', in id., *The Ethics of Liberty*, Atlantic Highlands, NJ: Humanities Press, 219–28.

ROWLAND, BARBARA M. (1988), 'Beyond Hayek's Pessimism: Reason, Tradition and Bounded Constructivist Rationalism', *British Journal of Political Science*, 18: 221–41.

RUNCIMAN, WALTER G. (1986), 'On the Tendency of Human Societies to Form Varieties', *Proceedings of the British Academy*, 72: 149–65.

—— (1989), *A Treatise on Social Theory*, ii: *Substantive Social Theory*, Cambridge: Cambridge University Press.

RYLE, GILBERT (1945/46), 'Knowing How and Knowing That', *Proceedings of the Aristotelian Society*, 46: 1–16.

—— (1949), *The Concept of Mind*, London: Hutchinson.

SCANLON, T. M. (1988), 'Down With Liberalism', *New York Review of Books*, 35/7: 28, 36–40.

SCHELLING, THOMAS (1978), *Micromotives and Macrobehavior*, New York: Norton.

SCHMIDTCHEN, DIETER, and UTZIG, SIEGFRIED (1989), 'Die Konjunkturtheorie Hayeks: Episode in einem Forscherleben oder Ausdruck eines lebenslangen Forschungsprogramms?' *Wirtschaftspolitische Blätter*, 36: 231–43.

SEN, AMARTYA K. (1981), *Poverty and Famines: An Essay on Entitlement and Deprivation*, Oxford: Clarendon Press.

—— (1987), *On Ethics and Economics*, Oxford: Blackwell.

SHACKLE, G. L. S. (1972), *Epistemics and Economics: A Critique of Economic Doctrines*, Cambridge: Cambridge University Press.

—— (1981), 'F. A. Hayek, 1899– ', in D. P. O'Brien and John R. Presley (eds.), *Pioneers of Modern Economics in Britain*, London: Macmillan, 234–61.

SHAPIRO, DANIEL (1989), 'Reviving the Socialist Calculation Debate: A Defense of Hayek against Lange', *Social Philosophy and Policy*, 6/2: 139–59.

SHEARMUR, JEREMY (1986), 'The Austrian Connection: Hayek's Liberalism and the Thought of Carl Menger', in B. Smith and W. Grassl (eds.), *Austrian Economics: Philosophical and Historical Background*, London: Croom Helm, 210–24.

SICARD, FRANÇOIS (1989), 'La Justification du Libéralisme selon F. von Hayek', *Revue Française de Science Politique*, 39: 178–99.

SOWELL, THOMAS (1987), *A Conflict of Visions*, New York: Morrow.

SULLIVAN, ROGER J. (1989), *Immanuel Kant's Moral Theory*, Cambridge: Cambridge University Press.

TAYLOR, CHARLES (1985), *Philosophy and the Human Sciences* (Philosophical Papers 2), Cambridge: Cambridge University Press.

TAYLOR, MICHAEL (1987), *The Possibility of Cooperation*, Cambridge: Cambridge University Press.

TOMLINSON, JIM (1990), *Hayek and the Market*, London: Pluto Press.

ULRICH, HANS, and PROBST, GILBERT J. B. (eds.) (1984), *Self-Organization and Management of Social Systems: Insights, Promises, Doubts, and Questions*, Berlin: Springer.

UNGER, ROBERTO MANGABEIRA (1987), *Politics, a Work in Constructive Social Theory*, i: *False Necessity: Anti-Necessitarian Social Theory in the Service of Radical Democracy*, Cambridge: Cambridge University Press.

VANBERG, VIKTOR (1986), 'Spontaneous Market Order and Social Rules: A Critical Examination of F. A. Hayek's Theory of Cultural Evolution', *Economics and Philosophy*, 2: 75–100.

VAN LOON, J. F. G. (1958), 'Rules and Commands', *Mind*, NS 67: 514–21.

VERNON, RICHARD (1979), 'Unintended Consequences', *Political Theory*, 7: 57–73.

WALDRON, JEREMY (1989), 'The Rule of Law in Contemporary Liberal Theory', *Ratio Juris*, 2: 79–96.

WEIMER, WALTER B. (1987), 'Spontaneously Ordered Complex Phenomena and the Unity of the Moral Sciences', in Gerard Radnitzky (ed.), *Centripetal Forces in the Sciences*, New York: Paragon, i. 257–95.

WIGGINS, DAVID (1987), *Needs, Values, Truth*, Oxford: Blackwell.

WILLIAMS, BERNARD (1978), *Descartes: The Project of Pure Enquiry*, Harmondsworth: Penguin.

YEAGER, LELAND B. (1984), 'Utility, Rights, and Contract: Some Reflections on Hayek's Work', in Kurt R. Leube and Albert H. Zlabinger (eds.), *The Political Economy of Freedom: Essays in Honor of F. A. Hayek*, Munich: Philosophia Verlag, 61–80.

INDEX